THE FINAL BATTLE

THE SPIRITUAL ATTACK ON MARRIAGE AND THE FAMILY

ANNA M. HUGHES

The opinions expressed in this book are strictly the thoughts of the principle author, Anna M. Hughes, and in no way are these thoughts officially endorsed by any person(s), entity, company, or organization used as a reference (source) in this publication. Following any advice, opinions, or suggestions by the author, Anna M. Hughes, will be completely at your own discretion.

Warning - Some Internet sites may contain viruses or other harmful content that may cause harm to your computer or other electronic devices. Therefore, opening any suggested Internet sites recommended or listed as a source in this book will be completely at your own risk. The author, Anna M. Hughes, or any other party participating or referred to in this book, including the owner(s) of the Internet site(s) from where the potential harm may come from, will not be liable for any damages that may result.

Front and back cover artwork is from ChatGPT

ISBN: 979-8-9949022-0-2 (Paperback)
ISBN: 979-8-9949022-1-9 (Hardcover)
ISBN: 979-8-9949022-2-6 (eBook)

Library of Congress Control Number: 2026907449

PRINTED IN THE UNITED STATES OF AMERICA

Dedication

I dedicate this book to my Lord and Savior, Jesus Christ,
for without Him nothing is possible.

To Our Lady of Fatima,
who will crush the serpent's head.

To my children and grandchildren—
my reason for writing this book.

And to every family fighting to stay together,
every struggling marriage,
all who long for healing and restoration,
and everyone seeking the Truth about the covenant of marriage—

What is sacred is worth defending.

"As for me and my house, we will serve the Lord."
— Joshua 24:15

‘The final battle between the Lord and the kingdom of Satan will be about marriage and the family.’ Don’t be afraid, she added, because whoever works for the sanctity of marriage and the family will always be fought against and opposed in every way, because this is the decisive issue. Then she concluded: ‘Nevertheless, Our Lady has already crushed his head” (1).

Contents

Acknowledgements

Writing this book has been an incredible journey, filled with great oppositions, trials, healing, and tremendous personal growth. Yet, none of this would have been even remotely possible without the guidance, grace, wisdom, strength, and insight provided by Jesus, my Lord, my Savior, my Healer, and my All, and our beautiful Blessed Mother Mary, who has provided me also with endless insight and love to carry on when I didn't think I could. I am merely an instrument in Jesus' hands, and I pray that His words will reach all who read these pages.

I am also eternally thankful to my amazing family, who, without their endless love, support, and prayers, I would not have made it through life, let alone writing this book. Immeasurable thanks to my mom for instilling faith in all of us kids, for her and my step-dad's endless love and support, and for always being my biggest cheerleader with writing this book, and all I undertake in life. Limitless thanks to my brothers and sisters-in-law for loving, supporting, and helping me throughout my life, and for always knowing you would literally do anything for my children and me, and have! I can never begin to thank you all enough. Jesus blessed me unfathomably with my family, and it is your love and support that gave me the encouragement to write this.

To my beautiful children, daughters-in-love, and grandchildren, I give eternal thanks. You are my heart, my joy, and my inspiration for writing this book. I pray that Jesus will use it to draw you closer and closer to Him, and to help make marriage, the world, and the future a better and holier place for all of you. Endless gratitude and love to each of you for your unconditional love and support, despite how incredibly flawed I am. You are the greatest gifts and blessings Jesus could have ever given me!

I am also eternally grateful to my beautiful friends who are always there for me with your unconditional prayers, love, and support, not just for me, but for my children as well! I know Jesus handpicked each of you to be my forever friends, and I am eternally grateful for each of you. Your encouragement has made it possible for me to write this.

For my dear friend, Katherine Allen, for rescuing me from the narcissist's web, encouraging me to continue writing this book when I wanted to give up, for sharing your infinite knowledge and expertise, and for keeping me on track by starting our Dream Nights! I'm forever grateful for your prayers, friendship, love, and support! You are such a blessing from Jesus.

To my family pastor, I give eternal thanks as well. The limitless time, effort, and prayers you have poured into my children and me are immeasurable, making it possible for us to heal. I can also never thank you enough for the insight and wisdom you shared with me regarding marriage, which I was able to use in the pages of this book.

Finally, my sincere thanks to my college professor who provided me with feedback, support, and encouragement in writing the first draft of this book 16 years ago! Your initial help is forever appreciated! I will always appreciate you sharing that, unbeknownst to me, you had been going through a divorce the whole time you were reading and providing me with feedback. Thank you for encouraging me by letting me know how much it helped you through your own divorce. Jesus works in the most amazing ways!

FOREWORD

As a certified marriage preparation and marriage enrichment minister, I have witnessed this battle firsthand. Over 90% of our couples planning to get married today are cohabitating prior to marriage. My wife and I, during our meetings with our couples, always tell them both to seriously consider remaining celibate until they are married. Most of the couples seem open to this, but there is no way to verify that they will actually listen. We have had several couples tell us later, after they stopped living in sin, that this was one of the best things they ever did for their relationship, as they stopped fighting and finally found peace. Removing mortal sin from your life has a way of doing this.

But unfortunately, today, it is just the norm to live together before getting married, and those who belong to the Catholic faith are no exception. The teaching of the Catholic Church has not changed, which is clearly against premarital sex, but unfortunately, this important teaching has been put in the backseat and is not being preached from the pulpit as it should be. Living together before marriage has had devastating consequences.

Even well-respected secular research groups have concluded in their studies that those who live together before marriage have a higher chance of divorce and an unsatisfactory marriage.

You would think this would be just the opposite, using worldly common sense. After all, trying out the used car before you buy it sounds like a good idea. But the couple cohabitating prior to marriage causes scandal by leading others to evil, setting the example that living together is acceptable before marriage. The mortal sin of premarital sex along with scandal, completely offsets any gains that may come from cohabitation. Most concerning, these serious sins place the couple in spiritual jeopardy.

Properly preparing for marriage is one of the most important things you can do for yourself, your future spouse, and your family.

Marriage has become increasingly more difficult. The attack against marriage and the family from the evil one is out in the open, infiltrating every aspect of our culture, with very few immune to its poison and deadly grip.

Premarital sex, coveting those around us, materialism, obsession with self, engaging in lustful activities, through movies, the Internet, social media, it's all around us, and almost impossible to get rid of unless we lock ourselves into complete isolation.

Being steadfast in your Catholic faith and actively participating in it is the only true remedy to avoid being sucked into this vacuum of evil.

And just because you are steadfast in your faith doesn't mean you won't be attacked; in fact, you will be attacked even more because the evil one will want to destroy you and everyone around you.

This is where you need to be well prepared, to put on the armor of God, and have our Lord's wisdom to strengthen, guide, and lead you through this minefield of evil upon us.

There will be success if we remain faithful, but along the way, there will be casualties as well.

The author will go into detail, covering all of this, and will provide a practical roadmap to help navigate the difficult road we face.

Her story here is a gut-wrenching account of what it feels like to be attacked when you are doing the right things, but she will also testify how God got her through it all, even when it seemed impossible, because with God, all things are possible.

The author teaches us how to never give up, no matter how dire the situation. Her story will be a lifesaver for so many struggling right now, because she really understands that this battle does not belong to us, but rather to God.

After an unexpected and heartbreaking divorce, she was left with very few options, and at times, felt like giving up. She went through the most difficult time of her life, all while quickly having to learn how to financially support herself and her four young children.

There was no time to feel sorry for herself, she had to act quickly. She plastered Holy Scripture all over her house as a constant reminder of who was really in control, and with little baby steps, she gradually began to climb out of the great abyss she had been so forcibly sucked into.

Instead of letting it destroy her and her children, she put all her efforts and emotions into complete trust in Jesus.

Today, after many years of struggling just to get by, she has become a successful college-level educator, author, actor, speaker, and, most importantly, a dedicated mom and beloved daughter of the Most High God.

She has painstakingly put together a brilliant survival manual full of interesting stories, facts, illustrations, and most importantly, a practical spiritual guide to help overcome these hardships.

Her story is wonderfully written, and a must-read for anyone old enough to be in a relationship, be married, or have been divorced. This is an excellent resource on how to go about planning for marriage the right way, as God intended it.

It would be my wish if every youth group, every parish, every marriage prep program, every marriage enrichment program, every married couple who are struggling, every divorced person, could get a copy of this book in their hands.

It truly is transforming, and it will help bring you closer to Jesus and to the loved ones in your life.

~ Paul Francis
BSE, BCEWS, CFF
(Certified FOCCUS® Facilitator)

PROLOGUE

"PROPHECY FULFILLED"

On May 13th, 1917, on the feast of our Lady of the Blessed Sacrament, the Blessed Mother first appeared to three shepherd children at a place called the Cova da Iria, near Fatima, Portugal. On this first apparition, her main message to the children was to pray the rosary daily for an end to World War I, warning that if people didn't stop offending God, a worse war would follow.

She continued to appear to them for six more consecutive months, with the final apparition being on October 13th, 1917, where she revealed herself to the children as Our Lady of the Rosary. It was during this apparition that the miracle of the sun took place, as Our Lady had promised the children that a miracle would happen for all to see during this last apparition.

Besides this incredible miracle where all spectators saw the sun spinning close to the earth bearing a kaleidoscope of colors, the entire Holy Family also appeared, with Mary dressed in white with a blue mantle and St. Joseph dressed in white holding the infant Jesus who was donning a red tunic. In this apparition, both St. Joseph and the Infant Jesus were blessing the whole world by making the Sign of the Cross three times (1). Knowing the prophecy that would later be revealed through the oldest visionary, Sr. Lucia, given to her by Our Lady of Fatima, I see the vision of the Holy Family as a foreshadowing of the final battle yet to come, a war worse and more devastating to the world than all others.

To understand what I am referring to, fast-forward to 1981, when St. Pope John Paul II appointed, then Monsignor Caffara, to be head of the John Paul II Institute for Studies on Marriage and the Family in Rome. In a February 16, 2008, radio interview with the Italian radio station Tele Radio Padre Pio, Caffara revealed that when he first began this assignment in 1981, he faced significant opposition and trials. Knowing that St. Pope John Paull II had, from the very beginning, placed the institute under the patronage of Our Lady of Fatima, he decided to write a letter to Sr. Lucia, the only one of the living visionaries of Fatima, to ask for her prayers for the institute, not expecting a response, as the only way to contact her was through the bishop (2).

Much to Cardinal Caffara's great surprise, she not only responded personally, but with a lengthy letter at that, with the letter ending by revealing a profound prophecy that came from Fatima, telling him:

> Father, a time will come when the decisive battle between the kingdom of Christ and Satan will be over marriage and the family. And those who will work for the good of the family will experience persecution and tribulation. But do not be afraid, because Our Lady has already crushed his head (2).

The chapters of this book will illustrate how and why this prophecy is playing out in our world today, including in my own life. It is indisputable that we are in a war, greater than any other, just as Sr. Lucia said, between God and satan over family and marriage. Yet, I pray that as you read the pages of this book, you will find insight, renewed hope, wisdom, and encouragement that in the end, satan will not win this war. As Our Lady said, we do not need to be afraid because she has already crushed his ugly head. And, Jesus promises us victory, too, when He says, "Little children, you are of God [you belong to Him] and have [already] defeated *and* overcome them [the agents of the antichrist], because He Who lives in you is greater (mightier) than he who is in the world" (3).

Chapter One

"Till Divorce Do Us Part"

Just as the prophecy from Sr. Lucia stated, everywhere around us, at every turn, another marriage in America is disintegrating. America's divorce rate continues to accelerate, threatening the sacred institution of marriage and redefining it to such a degree that former generations may not recognize it or acknowledge its validity. Divorce knows no boundaries, affecting the rich and poor, those with faith and those without, the young, the old, new marriages and thirty-year marriages, those with children, and marriages with no children. The vow "till death do us part" has become more of a wedding cliché than a sacred contract, leaving few to argue that if the current tide continues, America is quickly on its way to transforming from a culture of marriage to a culture of divorce.

Despite this growing crisis in our country, I was amazingly fortunate for most of my life to view divorce as something that "only happened to other people." Although my immediate family is filled with many other idiosyncrasies and dysfunctions of all different flavors, divorce is not one of them. Both my maternal and paternal great-grandparents', grandparents', and parents' marriages had miraculously survived the going trend of divorce and the inevitable fate of marriage.

As far back as I can trace, the only divorce in my immediate family history is from a somewhat distant relative that we never count as an "official" family member. He has always accomplished being the black sheep of the family. So, when I blindly and very naively said, "I do," at the precious young age of 19, the only concept in my mind was "till death do us part," never questioning that my groom might view marriage from a different perspective.

Divorce was simply not part of my vocabulary, and especially not my Catholic Christian faith. I readily, and even consciously, ignored the truckload of signs and red flags that God, in his loving mercy, placed before me. He was trying to warn me that I was not making the right decision. Yet, I continued to assure myself that if my grandparents' and parents' marriages could survive being as dysfunctional as they were, any marriage could make it. Divorce would certainly never happen to me.

Despite weathering 18 years of what I have now recognized to be relatively complete dysfunction (neglect, abuse, deception, delusion, and adultery), I held true to my firm convictions that I was somehow untouchable by divorce. Not only did I fail to see just how vulnerable my marriage was, but my attitude had also transferred from being one of naïve yet admirable conviction, to one polluted by arrogance, and may I say it, "Christian" pride. I remember looking my nose down on "those people" who "chose" divorce. I categorized them in my mind as "quitters," "selfish," and "lazy." I couldn't imagine letting something like that happen to my four beautiful children, and honestly wondered what was wrong with "those people" that they refused to work it out.

As God promises in His Word, however, "Pride goes before destruction and a haughty spirit before a fall" (1), and fall I did, with such force that I wonder to this day how I survived the impact. My perfect marriage, that sadly existed only in my deluded imagination, came to an end overnight. I had become so good at "seeing things as I wanted them to be" rather than how they truly were, my ex-husband's seemingly "overnight" decision to divorce me came as a complete shock, turning my life upside down and shattering my dream of ever after.

There was no working it out for the "kid's sake," or for our sake, for that matter, and because we did not share a faith, the "God" factor did not have any influence either. I realized very quickly there was nothing I could do or say that would change his mind. He was convinced he never loved me, that it was his turn to be happy and was going to take it, and if I tried to stand in his way, he would sue me for a divorce.

All of my perceptions of "those" people who "chose" a divorce became unveiled in a day. I felt ashamed that I had been so quick to judge and had so little compassion for those I had witnessed around me who had suffered this path.

As I was growing up, my mom would constantly remind us of the old Native American proverb that you should walk a mile in your brother's moccasins before judging him, and this now took on new meaning. Divorce had struck my home, making me the first one in my immediate family to experience its horrors.

Over the last 20 years, I have traveled a journey I never thought I would have to take. Thankfully, I have not traveled this alone but with the Lord, my children, and loving family and friends by my side all along the way. In this book, I take you on a journey with me, sharing my life experiences and those of others who have traveled a similar path, and who, by God's Grace, have not only survived but also thrived, finding hope, restoration, healing, and a new future. In addition to these experiences, you will receive valuable information on the history of the breakdown of the marriage, practical suggestions, and direction for:

- Receiving an increased awareness of this crisis and its root causes
- Becoming informed of laws that aid our divorce culture
- Helping to choose your God-appointed mate
- God's design for marriage and the family
- My journey
- Recognizing and identifying danger signs of different types of abuse while you're dating or in a marriage
- Overcoming
- How to protect yourself, and warning signs to look for if you think your spouse is contemplating divorce

- What to do when it's over
- Understanding that children are not necessarily "resilient"
- Dealing with being "suddenly single!"
- Healing – Forgiveness is key!
- Beginning again!

As you read this book, keep in mind that ". . . with God, all things are possible" (2) and we already have assurance of Who wins in the end! If you let Him, God will direct every step of your life and lead you to your God-given destiny. You're never in too deep, and it's never too late to begin giving Him complete control of your life. He can take all of our mistakes, wrong choices, and presumably lost years and make something beautiful out of them. In fact, God promises He can give us "... a crown of beauty instead of ashes, the oil of joy instead of mourning, and a garment of praise instead of a spirit of despair" (3). Amazingly, He also promises He will ". . . repay you for the years the locusts have eaten. . ." (4).

I pray this book can be a lifeline to help you make the right choices before, during, and even when a marriage ends in divorce. I challenge you to begin this journey with me today, living not as a victim, but with great anticipation and expectancy of the amazing miracles God will create in your life if you let Him. He can also use you and me to help America turn once again to a culture that holds the sanctity of marriage as the holy and sacred covenant God intended it to be. As prophecy foretold, we will face opposition, but it will be worth it all!

As God says in His Word, "13 What would have become of me] had I not believed that I would see the Lord's goodness in the land of the living! **14** Wait *and* hope for *and* expect the Lord; be brave *and* of good courage and let your heart be stout *and* enduring. Yes, wait for *and* hope for *and* expect the Lord" (5).

CHAPTER TWO

"AMERICA'S RISING CRISIS"

Not long ago, I received a phone call from a dear friend of mine. Her 20-year marriage had collapsed seemingly overnight. Her husband had informed her in a formal, cold, and calculated letter that she and their three sons were no longer welcome in the family home, he had changed the locks, and he had filed for divorce. The man she had loved unconditionally for 20 years, shared three beautiful sons with, and had promised to love her until death do them part, had overnight broken their covenant.

Another good friend of mine just recently shared a similar fate. She received a phone call from a friend of hers who works as a property manager and very reluctantly called to let my friend know that her husband had been in her office recently to sign and pay for the down payment on a lease for his girlfriend and him. They were "madly in love," and were counting down the days until they would finally be together . . . another 20-year marriage shattered and ended as another statistic in the growing divorce crisis in America.

Only 70 years ago, stories like these were rarely heard, even in the media. The ideal family in America was the Cleaver's: father, mother, and their two children. Divorce simply wasn't the norm. Stories like these were few and far between. Today, however, similar scenarios happen every day in America, with marriages breaking apart with unprecedented frequency. According to the National Center for Health, the current divorce rate for first marriages is a staggering 42 - 45 percent. The fate for second and third marriages is even bleaker, with 60 percent of all second marriages, and 73 percent of third marriages ending in divorce (1).

Although certain variables influence these statistics slightly, these percentages apply across the board, affecting all sectors of society. Divorce affects the rich and poor, famous and non-famous, educated and non-educated, those with faith and those without, the young, the old, new marriages and thirty-year marriages, marriages with children, and those without children. Marriage in America is suffering from a major identity crisis, and like the continuing depreciation of the dollar bill, its value, respect, and sacredness is threatened daily, just as Sr. Lucia prophesied in her letter to Cardinal Caffara.

A "whole" family is rarely portrayed on television shows or movies anymore. Shows with single-parent homes have replaced *Leave it to Beaver* and *Father Knows Best*, furthering the ideology that the broken family is the societal norm. It provides evidence that America has shifted from being a culture of marriage to a culture of divorce or simply not getting married at all.

Marriage is Overrated, Right?

Over the last ten years, the divorce rate has gone down just a bit, which could seem hopeful, but, unfortunately, it is not because there are fewer divorces; it is because marriage rates have declined and with each passing generation, marriage is not being held to the same esteem and viewed as the sacred covenant from God that it was intended to be.

According to a Pew Research report, 25 percent of millennials are likely never to be married (2). Only 18% of 30- to 18-year-olds are married today versus 31% in 1995. The 30 and over group has gone down too, with 62% married today versus 68% in 1995 (3).

Aside from the younger generations, Pew Research Center has also found that 54% of Americans consider marriage important but not essential, believing that society is just as well off if people have priorities other than marriage and children (4). A drastic change in thinking from past decades.

Cohabitation also plays a significant role in this decline. Over the past five decades, cohabitation has increased by 900% (5). In

1960, an estimated 430,000 were cohabitating; by 2015, that number had grown to an estimated 8.3 million and is even higher today (6). Pew Research Center found that 69% of Americans are okay with it today (5), even though couples cohabiting have a 50 to 80% higher likelihood of divorce than couples not cohabiting (7).

One would think amongst Christians, this percentage would be lower, but that is not the case as 76% of Protestants and 74% (8) of Catholics approve of it, despite the clear teaching in the Bible that it is considered a grave sin. 1 Cor. 6:9 makes this very clear, stating, "Do you not know that the unrighteous will not inherit the kingdom of God? Do not be deceived. Neither fornicators, nor idolaters, nor adulterers, nor homosexuals, nor sodomites" (9).

The Catechism of the Catholic Church also clearly prohibits this. In 2350, it states, "Those who are engaged to marry are called to live chastity in continence (harmony). They should see in this time of testing a discovery of mutual respect, an apprenticeship in fidelity. ... They should reserve for marriage the expressions of affection that belong to married love" (10). The alarmingly high percentages of Christians cohabitating, despite the clear teachings in Scripture and *The Catechism*, are grave examples of how moral relativism is overriding the actual teaching of Christianity. Just as the secular world, Christians are choosing to disregard the clear teachings of the Church.

Spiritual Implications

Sadly, these "modern" choices are having catastrophic effects on souls as well. These effects were clearly illustrated by St. Bridget of Sweden and St. Padre Pio of Pietrelcina. St. Bridget of Sweden was a Catholic mystic born into Swedish nobility who lived from 1303 to 1373. At the age of seven, she experienced her first vision of the crucifixion of Jesus. Given her clear call from God, one would think she would have entered religious life as soon as she was able, but this was surprisingly not the case. Instead, at 13, she married a nobleman and went on to have a happy marriage that produced eight children. So, she clearly understood the beauty and sanctity of a holy marriage and children and had a great devotion to praying for young couples (11).

After the death of her husband, Bridget entered religious life and founded The Order of The Most Holy Savior. It was during this time that her visions began to intensify. In one vision, she was shown what happens when couples cohabit or when there is mortal sin (a sin that can cause damnation if not confessed) within the marriage. In the vision, she saw a house with a man and a woman living inside. Yet, the house had no roof, and demonic creatures were circling over the home, and the demons would enter, whispering ideas into both the man's and woman's minds, planting seeds of discord, lust, despair, and a growing sense of emptiness (11).

St. Bridget said that, little by little, these seeds took root in the man and woman, creating great unhappiness in the relationship and, worst of all, causing the couple to have a great hardness of heart towards God. Jesus showed her that this happened because the couple was not in a sacramental marriage, which protects couples with Divine Grace (11).

St. Padre Pio, a very well-known Catholic priest and saint who had the stigmata, spoke similarly. During his time as a priest, from 1918 to his death in 1962, he heard thousands and thousands of confessions and could read souls. When someone who was cohabitating came to him for confession, he would admonish them, telling them, "Love does not sin. Cohabitating teaches you to leave, not to stay. It causes you to first slide into engagement because you are already living together. You then slide into marriage, and then into divorce" (12). He would admonish the person, telling them that "to live in this state of mortal sin darkens the souls, causes grace to leave, and permits demons to move in" (12).

He would further tell them that if they were cohabitating and still receiving communion, they were committing an even graver sin of sacrilege, which is a violation or blasphemy against something sacred.

"God Is Faithful . . . He Will Always Provide a Way of Escape!" (13).

Just as Jesus always provides a way of escape from temptation, both St. Padre Pio and St. Bridget didn't leave those to whom they spoke without hope. St. Bridget, in her writings, and St. Padre Pio, in the confessional, told people that the ways to escape from this mortal sin were first to admit that what you are doing is a sin, and a grave one at that. Then go to confession and confess the sin. Next, stop fornicating and living together until you can get married in the Church. Finally, receive healing, pray over the wounds caused by sin, and incorporate God into your daily lives and marriage by putting Him first, praying together, and following the teachings of the Church as a couple (12, 14).

As harrowing as it is, couples today have no idea what the spiritual ramifications are. They have never heard of these revelations from St. Padre Pio or St. Bridget of Sweden, and even if they had, our society has done a great job of convincing them otherwise. With all this considered, as a Catholic Christian, I find the outlook on marriage and cohabitation heartbreaking.

Still, one has to acknowledge that the younger generation lived through the pain and suffering of divorce. The younger generations didn't see marriage in a positive light and as a lifetime commitment, so why should they value it? It's easy to understand why they don't. It's also easy to see why so many don't want to get married and consider living together a responsible way to go before committing to marriage. My own children have expressed these very concerns to me, and, although I'm strongly opposed to it, I do understand where they are coming from.

It's easy to understand why a great deal of society believes marriage to be "old-fashioned" and "outdated." So outdated, in fact, a survey taken by millennials shown below shows the growing trend being tossed around about the various ways marriage should be restructured.

According to the survey, the first trend that gained 21% of the millennial vote was that marriage vows should be honored for 8 years, but after that, you can choose a new partner without having to go through a divorce. Another option that garnered 36% approval among millennials stated that marriages should be granted on 5-, 7-, 10-, and 30-year contracts. After each of these terms, the marriage needs to be renegotiated to be extended. 10% of millennials supported allowing multiple partners. The most popular option, garnering 43% of the millennials' vote, stated that after only two years, marriage can either be terminated or formalized. And, sadly, the least popular, with only 10% of the vote, was 'till death do us part with the same partner (15).

These different contract ideas show just how far marriage has strayed from what God intended.

What in the World Is Going On?

I often ask, "How can this have happened?" and "What and who is to blame for this breakdown?" This beautiful covenant created by God to be a mirror of the Holy Trinity has been reduced practically to a mockery, a contract of convenience. Like so many other aspects of morality, human standards have redefined marriage. This holy sacrament's sacredness has been removed and replaced with a man-made secular version, defined by moral relativism instead of the moral absolute that God created it to be.

Rather astonishingly, all that we are seeing was prophesied by many seers throughout the centuries. One of them was a Marian apparition on December 8, 1634, in Quito, Ecuador. During this time, the Venerable Mother Mariana de Jesus Torres was said to be receiving apparitions from Our Lady of Success from 1594 to 1634, which the bishop approved at the time. During her December 8 appearance, she reported that Our Lady of Success appeared along with the Archangels Raphael, Gabriel, and Michael, who were carrying a chalice filled with hosts (16). During this apparition to Maria, Our Lady predicted many events that would take place in the future, including saying:

> Like the Eucharist, the Sacrament of Holy Matrimony will be profaned in a multitude of ways, resulting in 'iniquitous laws with the objective of doing away with this Sacrament, making it easy for everyone to live in sin, encouraging the procreation of illegitimate children born without the blessing of the Church. The Christian spirit will rapidly decay, extinguishing the precious light of faith until it reaches a point that there will be an almost total and general corruption of customs' (16).

Even more recently, and as discussed in the Prologue and the central theme for this book, on May 13th, 1917, the apparition at Fatima, Portugal, occurred for the first time. The Church has approved that on this day, the Blessed Virgin Mary appeared to three young children while they were out herding sheep. This first visit was the first of six times that Mary appeared to the children, predicting and warning many things, with the last apparition taking place in October 1917 (16).

Two of the children went home to be with Jesus shortly after the last apparition. The oldest of the visionaries, Sr. Lucia dos Santos, lived until 2005. Before her death, she wrote a letter to Cardinal Caffarra, the cardinal appointed by St. Pope John Paul II to establish and plan the Pontifical Institute for Studies on Marriage and Family. Among many things she discussed in the letter, the most significant was the prediction she received from Our Blessed Mother, Sr. Lucia wrote the prophecy this book is based on and is mentioned previously:

> The final battle between the Lord and the kingdom of Satan will be about Marriage and the Family. Don't be afraid, because whoever works for the sanctity of marriage and the family will always be fought against and opposed in every way, because this is the decisive issue. Nevertheless, Our Lady has already crushed his head" (17).

Upon reading this, Cardinal Cafffarra went on to add:

> Speaking again with John Paul II, you could feel that the family was the core since it has to do with the supporting pillar of creation, the truth of the relationship between man and woman, between the generations. If the foundational pillar is damaged, the entire building collapses, and we're seeing this now because we are right at this point, and we know it" (18).

Scripture also describes the days we are living in 2 Timothy 3:2 – 3 also describes the moral decay we see in our society, saying:

> . . . in the last days will come perilous times of great stress and trouble . . . for people will be lovers of self and utterly self-centered, lovers of money and aroused by an inordinate desire for wealth, proud and arrogant and contemptuous boasters; They will be abusive (blasphemous, scoffing), disobedient to parents, ungrateful, unholy and profane. 3 They will be without natural human affection, callous and inhuman, relentless admitting of no truce or appeasement; they will be slanderers (false accuser, troublemakers), intemperate and loose in morals and conduct, uncontrolled and fierce, haters of good. 4 They will be treacherous betrayers, rash, and inflated with self-conceit. They will be lovers of sensual pleasures and vain amusements (19).

All describing what we are witnessing today.

The Apparitions Playing Out

Fr. Chad Alec Ripperger, an American Roman Catholic priest, theologian, philosopher, speaker, author, and exorcist, explains this breakdown described by the seers in his recent *YouTube* video titled, "State of the Spiritual Battlefield." In this recording, he explains the spiritual battle waged against marriage. First, he says that there are general demons in the spiritual realm, with the "principal end of the main demon named Baal, being to drive the destruction of marriage by the collapse of sexual morals" (20). He describes that "the free love of the hippies was the beginning of this moral decay, and once this happened, a cascade of events followed" (20). He goes on to explain further that, "Once you divorce conjugal relations from their end of having children and we divorce it from marriage, then anything goes" (20), even to the extent we have today in same-sex-marriage. Thus, although people do have free will, it is clear that the demonic spirit of Baal has been very successful in causing a collapse of sexual morals, causing an all-out attack on marriage as never before, just as the apparitions and Scripture predicted.

The Root of It All?

The moral breakdown leads us to the topic of contraception. I will make a bold statement by saying: it is perhaps the single most significant device the enemy used to initiate this. Following artificial contraception from its main debut in the 60's to today, has shown me that it is the root of "the cascade of events" that Fr. Ripperger said would happen when sex is divorced from marriage and from having children. I now understand why the Catholic Church has remained vigilant in its stance against artificial contraception. I firmly believe it is the main issue used to bring about the moral collapse, which ultimately has led to the crisis in marriage.

I understand that saying this is not a popular or well-accepted statement, especially when tying it to the marriage crisis. Still, I urge those of you who may want to put the book down at this point to please hear me out with an open mind. I have to say, this section was one of the hardest things I've ever written, and I'm certain that one reason is that there was a time in my life that I would have deemed this a ridiculous statement myself. The thought of not using birth control seemed absurd, backward, irresponsible, and naïve. I honestly thought not using birth control was too much for God to ask. I would think, *Did He really want me to have endless children, and how was I supposed to support all of them?* Having sex and using birth control seemed synonymous. I couldn't imagine one without the other, and I know I'm not alone in this thinking. This ideology is something children are taught as young as elementary school and is the primary focus in sex education classes.

Being raised as a Catholic, one would think I would have had a different outlook, as the Church is clear on its opposition to artificial contraception. But, like approximately 88% - 98% (21) of other Catholic women today who have used birth control at some point (21), this was a teaching of the Church I was willing to turn a blind eye to, thinking that the Church just wasn't in touch with reality. I didn't do any research to understand why the Church was so opposed to it, beyond thinking it was simply out of touch.

Unfortunately, the way I perceived this at one time is the societal norm even amongst Christians. An example to illustrate this was a situation a dear friend of mine experienced during her marriage prep classes in the Catholic Church. The priest who was counseling her advised her to visit a Catholic doctor who was a parish member. My friend followed through with this. While at the visit, the doctor told my friend she needed to get on the pill. He thought it was important she went on them right away to ensure she and her husband had time together before a baby came along. Taking his advice, she followed through with his suggestion. The priest, doctor, and my friend all went along with this, as I did, knowing that using artificial birth control was opposed to the Church's teaching.

"See to It That No One Misleads You" (22).

Researching and writing about all of this for this section has made me face that I had readily accepted something as life-altering as using contraception without doing an ounce of research to understand what it entailed, how it worked, the effects it would have on my body, how it would affect my marriage, and why the Church was against it. Although I didn't think about it consciously, I realized I had readily accepted and believed wholeheartedly the secular view that sex was primarily for pleasure, and children were a byproduct that you either planned or happened by accident. Of course, I always wanted children more than anything, so I wasn't against having them and have four. Still, I was entirely on board with the world's teaching about artificial contraception.

Unfortunately, I started taking the pill at 17, when I started dating my ex-husband (More expansion on this in later chapters.) but had to get off in my early twenties because it was causing me to have terrible migraine headaches. And, although I had a radical reconversion and born-again experience when I was 20, it wasn't until I was in my early thirties that I started feeling convicted about using birth control. At this time, I began using my version of Natural Family Planning haphazardly, without doing any actual research on how to use it effectively. After learning what I have for this book, I wish I had taken the time to research it in my teens. Also, I wonder why the sex-ed classes I had to take in high school didn't teach this information? Like today's classes, I only remember learning about different types of contraception, but not how they worked or what they were doing to my body besides preventing pregnancy.

Now, as a mother and teacher, I have witnessed firsthand that these classes today focus on discovering a plethora of perversions, such as sexual identity awareness and self-sexual exploration. And, unfortunately, they entirely leave out the emotional damage sex outside of God's plan has on the soul of a precious human being.

Planned Parenthood is behind much of this "education" that they use to solicit future customers and ensure abortion remains a booming business, ensuring that if abstinence or Natural Family Planning is mentioned, it is to discredit it. Unfortunately, teens, like me at that age, for the most part won't investigate, but will readily accept what someone tells them if it supports what they want to do at the time.

The research required for this chapter has made me realize more than ever the urgent need to get the truth out to our youth and to seek ways to ensure that sex education starts teaching a moral approach to intimacy that can be prayerfully implemented in mainstream education. I understand it's not an end-all solution, but it would be a start if the next generation can be empowered with the truth.

I also pray wholeheartedly that the Holy Spirit will use this book as one means to help shed light on the truth of this situation for any of you who, like me, didn't know or understand the grave consequences and destructive roots of artificial contraception or how it has been used as a primary device by the enemy to bring about the marriage crisis.

The History of Contraception

To better understand the truth about birth control and bring it into the light, it is essential to understand its origins. Birth control is referenced even in the Book of Genesis, with the "withdraw" method referenced in Scripture as "spilling your seed." The ancient Greeks used natural ointments as spermicides. In the mid-1800s, people were using a variety of contraceptives, including cervical caps, diaphragms, condoms, douching syringes, and sponges, only to have all contraceptives become criminalized in 1873. Yet, it continued despite being illegal (23).

In 1920, scientists working in Austria and Japan discovered the "Rhythm Method," and Pope Pius XII in 1951 announced that the Catholic Church would sanction its use among married couples as a natural form of birth control. During all this time, people were using different forms of birth control. However, it was not readily available, and in many states, it was still illegal and deemed as vulgar and obscene (23).

On May 9th, 1960, the FDA approved the pill as an artificial contraception. It had been in the works since the early 1950s by John Rock, a gynecologist at Harvard Medical School, and Gregory Pincus, a biochemist at the Worcester Foundation for Experimental Biology (24). Although it was officially approved, it faced significant opposition. Despite its popularity, with 2.3 million women now using it, it remained illegal in eight states for doctors to prescribe until 1964 (23).

On June 7th, 1965, Estelle Griswold and Lee Buxton from Connecticut, one of the states where the pill was still illegal, took their case to the Supreme Court. During this ruling, the Court found in the Constitution a "right to privacy" that extended married couples' rights to use the pill and found the prohibition to be a violation of this law. This same year, the number of women using the pill had reached 6.5 million, doubling by 1967 (23). However, it was not readily available, and in many states, it was still illegal and deemed as vulgar and obscene (23).

In 1968, the Catholic Church finally came out with its decision of birth control. A decision was made regarding its use in Pope Paul VI's encyclical titled Humanae Vitae (Of Human Life).

In this encyclical, Pope Paul VI wrote that the Church remains "unequivocally opposed to all forms of birth control except the rhythm method" and, before that, only abstinence was permitted (23).

The Catholic Church remained vigilant, yet the pill was officially launched in the 1960s, forever changing the moral fabric of our society. Although artificial birth control had been around in some form, beginning with the Book of Genesis, nothing had been as effective before preventing pregnancy. Knowing all of this, it shouldn't be any surprise that Roe vs. Wade would follow the 1965 Griswold v. Connecticut ruling less than a decade later. Baal/satan had his number one weapon to bring about his moral collapse, with abortion being one of its most devastating "cascade of events" to follow when sex was divorced from marriage and having babies. Jesus warns us in His Word that sin always leads to death.

The free love hippie movement Fr. Ripperger talked about was able to flourish with the introduction of the pill. It gave way to the "sex without consequences" ideology and supposed women's sexual liberation, making the primary purpose of sex to be for pleasure, and no commitment required. Advertisements, the entertainment business, and media all helped make what was once thought of as vulgar and obscene to become the accepted norm, cleverly keeping the devastating consequences that would result under wraps.

Facts Don't Lie.

So, now that we know the progression of birth control, what are these devastating consequences? For starters, *The Catholic Stand's* 2013 article, "Contraception Increases Rates of Divorce, Suicide, and Sexual Dysfunction," written by Dominic Pedulla MD, discusses a study that shows this correlation. This study by the "Royal College of General Practitioners' study (47,174 women), the Oxford/FPA study (17,032 women), and the Walnut Creek study (16,638 women)" showed that the divorce rate for those using oral contraception was double of nonusers (25).

According to another article, "Contraceptives Responsible for Increased Divorce and Abortion Rates," author Paul Buckley states that the divorce rate in America doubled between 1965 and 1975, right after the 1965 Supreme Court Ruling case. Buckley also says in his article that:

> A 1977 study conducted by Robert Michael at the Center for Economic Analysis of Human Behavior and Social Institutions examined this sudden jump. It concluded that a substantial portion of this increase could be directly attributed to the increased use of contraceptives. The correlation between contraception use and divorce rates is not too hard to see. People are able to have fewer children and have them later in marriage, they are able to commit adultery more easily, and it allows communication to deteriorate. All these things have been statistically shown to increase chances of divorce - and contraception makes them possible (26).

Marriage Is God's Design.

In addition to the correlations found above, what are the other main ways artificial contraception has been used as the most divisive tool to cause the marriage crisis predicted in the Marian apparitions of Fatima and Quito, Ecuador? Even before we can determine this, however, it is crucial to keep in mind that, as much as man has tried to take credit and control marriage, God, not man, established it. Marriage is not secular; it is spiritual. It is also one of the seven Sacraments of the Catholic Church. It is so sacred, created by God to mirror the Holy Trinity, which is a spiritual mystery that there are Three distinct Persons in One God. God the Father is the head with a bond to Jesus, the Son Who brings forth the ultimate expression of Love, which this Love manifests Itself in the Person of the Holy Spirit. In the Sacrament of Holy Matrimony, the husband, representing God the Father, and the wife, representing the Son, become one flesh. Through their bond of Love, a child, representing the Holy Spirit, is brought forth to complete an earthly trinity, sealed with the Sacrament of Holy Matrimony (27).

Gen. 2:24 confirms this when it says, "Wherefore a man shall leave father and mother, and shall cleave to his wife: and they shall be two in one flesh" (28), literally! So then, "from the beginning, the Lord commands them to be fruitful ("fertile") and multiply. A husband and wife fulfill God's plan for marriage in the bringing forth of new life, for God is life itself" (29).

So, the first thing that had to happen for marriage to be affected by contraception to the degree it has is that the definition of marriage had to be redefined from God's to exclude the most sacred aspect, which is to bring forth new life! Even in the Catholic Church, this revision has been made, despite its unwavering stance on contraception. In the original 1917 Canon Law, "(The body of laws and regulations made by or adopted by ecclesiastical authority, for the government of the Christian organization and its members" (30), the definition still included children. This original definition defined marriage "as an act of the will by which each party gives and accepts a perpetual and exclusive right over the body, for acts which are of themselves suitable for the generation of children" (2)(c 1081, § (31). Yet, in 1983, this was revised to read that marriage is "an act of the will by which a man and a woman, through an irrevocable covenant, mutually give and accept each other to establish marriage" (2)(c. 1057, § (31). It would still be a beautiful definition had it not omitted to bring forth life. I found it very startling that any mention of procreation was removed, which is in opposition to the Church's unwavering stance on this issue in marriage.

According to Cornell Law, the secular and legal definition has been drastically modified from the 1917 and even 1983 Canon Law definitions, reducing it to state, "The legal union of a couple as spouses. The basic elements of a marriage are: 1. the parties' legal ability to marry each other, 2. mutual consent of the parties, and 3. a marriage contract as required by law" (32). What a tragedy that marriage, the most sacred gift that God instituted for humanity has been reduced to such a robotic, castrated definition, yet it set the stage for contraception to be the norm and all other secular changes that have now desecrated the way God established this sacrament to be. The faithful

Archbishop Chaput said, "Evil preaches tolerance until it is dominant, then it tries to silence good," (33) a perfect way to describe how this has become the accepted norm. Anyone who doesn't go along with the new secular version is considered radical, extreme, and irresponsible.

Now that having children is not at the forefront of marriage, procreation in marriage doesn't have to be either. This "modern" version goes back to what Fr. Ripperger said, which I cannot state enough, that "once you divorce conjugal relations from their end of having children and we divorce it from marriage, then anything goes" (34).

"For the Wages of Sin Is Death . . ." (35).

Yet, man doesn't realize that something spiritual in origin cannot be redefined by man, no matter how hard he tries, without suffering severe consequences. God never changes, and His will for marriage and procreation in marriage has not either. Whenever people think they need to "help God out" and do things their way, it never turns out well, as I've experienced firsthand in my own life. Whether subconsciously or consciously, birth control is telling God, I, not You, know best how I should use my fertility, and it's not something I am willing to allow God to control. Although the world says it's being responsible and just part of having sex, it is disobedience, and willful disobedience to God's ways is sin, and sin always leads to death. The use of contraception is no exception.

Right from the Book of Genesis, God made His thoughts about contraception very clear. In Gen. 38:8-10, God killed Onan on the spot for "spilling or wasting his seed," (36) which is the "withdraw" method of birth control, and scripture goes on to say that God found his actions to be "detestable!" (36) One might say, "Well, I don't pull out. I use artificial contraception." But, when you understand how contraception works, all artificial contraception "wastes the seed" in one form or another, either into a condom, outside of the body, or into a woman's body that birth control has prevented from being able to conceive. Society calls this progress and liberation, but God calls it detestable and killed a man for doing it, and God never changes. He doesn't literally kill someone today as He did Onan, but how can God be pleased with the marriage bed if the "seed is spilled and wasted?" If God killed Onan for it, it's easy to see how it could cause "death" to a marriage, showing why it has been such a powerful tool for satan to use against marriage. Even though most people, like myself at one time, have no idea of the spiritual consequences.

Our God-Given Superpower!

Another reason contraception is such a massive contributor to the marriage crisis is your most sacred God-given superpower, the gift of procreation, is not part of your intimacy, which is what happens when using birth control. With this missing, there is no need for an eternal, "exclusive, and perpetual" commitment to your partner, even in marriage. Intimacy is then primarily about pleasure, and it can become primarily self-seeking, not the total giving of oneself. Please know I'm not against pleasure at all. It is a tremendous gift from God in this sacred act, but if sex always becomes about pleasure alone, the eternal commitment is not needed, and one cannot experience the full blessings and gift from this that God intended. This sacred act created by God can become distorted. The joining of two bodies into one flesh, as the Bible so beautifully described, can become significantly impeded, stop happening in intimacy, or not happen at all.

The best example I can think of to illustrate this is my personal experience after my ex had chosen to have a vasectomy. One time during intimacy, I had a complete revelation of the emptiness of sex without this God-given life-oriented power being present. I distinctly remember feeling like we were two people having sex, but we were both in our own world, not focused on each other, but our own pleasure, separate from one another. It's a bit difficult to explain, but I knew we were not bonded at this time the way God intended. I remember laying there thinking to myself; *he could do this with anyone. I'm just a vessel he is using for pleasure, and he is this for me; there is nothing special about me.* Even in marriage, it made me feel like an object, not a wife, not unique to him, and not one with my husband.

Sex in fornication and cohabitation, in most cases, is also purely for the intent of pleasure. There is little to no need for commitment, especially eternal. Like anything, when something is done solely for seeking pleasure, outside of God's laws that He gave to protect us, it almost always turns toward the gratification of self. This turning towards self in sex, which contraception allows for, explains the explosion of pornography, masturbation, and perversions of all kinds. Commitment is not needed, a complete sharing of oneself is not required, and the sacred, breathtaking, and holy act God created becomes profaned. Explaining why 2370 in the *Catechism of the Catholic Church* that talks about artificial contraception states:

> . . . every action which, whether in anticipation of the conjugal act, or in its accomplishment, or in the development of its natural consequences, proposes, whether as an end or as a means, to render procreation impossible is intrinsically evil:159 Thus the innate language that expresses the total reciprocal self-giving of husband and wife is overlaid, through contraception, by an objectively contradictory language, namely, that of not giving oneself totally to the other. This leads not only to a positive refusal to be open to life but also to a falsification of the inner truth of conjugal love, which is called upon to give itself in personal totality. . . 160 (37).

All of this shows how contraception makes marriage vulnerable and easy prey to attacks from the enemy.

On the contrary, when you have sex open to life, an undying commitment is required. You are saying to your spouse; I'm giving all of myself to you, holding nothing back, knowing that our intimacy might produce another eternal being that we will both be responsible for all our lives. When you give your procreative power entirely to your spouse, it takes commitment, "perpetual and exclusive." Knowing this makes a person very selective in whom they are willing to share in such a sacred act. It was designed by God to bond a husband and wife, that "the two would become one flesh," and I would like to add, one heart.

One might ask, but what about people who are not able to conceive? Or what about married couples that are past childbearing years? And I would answer, if they are surrendering their fertility to God's ways, they, of course, will reap all the marital blessings God intended even if they are not able to conceive. That is not something they are willfully preventing.

One of the most beautiful ways I've heard this expressed is from Cardinal Burke, in his article, "Marriage and Contraception." Cardinal Burke writes:

> What makes marital intercourse express a unique relationship and union is not the sharing of a sensation but the sharing of a power: of an extraordinary life-related, creative physical, sexual power. In a true conjugal relationship, each spouse says to the other: 'I accept you as somebody like no one else in my life. You will be unique to me and I to you. You and you alone will be my husband; you alone will be my wife. And the proof of your uniqueness to me is the fact that with you - and with you alone - am I prepared to share this God-given life-oriented power (38).

After reading this, it is hard to understand why anyone wouldn't want to receive God's fullness in marital intimacy! God always knows best and always wants our best! He is not trying to steal our "fun" by not wanting us to use contraception. He loves us beyond measure, and as the perfect Father, he wants to shower His children with all good things and protect us from being hurt through our disobedience. And, as much as one way hurts marriage and relationships, God's way strengthens it and makes it a mighty force and protects it from the enemy's attacks.

A Bitter Pill to Swallow

Finally, all the way back in A.D. 391, many of the great scholars of the Church had already recognized the devastating effects contraception can have on a marriage. For example, Jon Chrysostom, an early Father of the Church who served as Archbishop of Constantinople, had a bleak view of contraception regarding the marriage bed, even back then. One of his most famous sayings about this was when he said:

> Why do you sow where the field is eager to destroy the fruit, where there are medicines of sterility [oral contraceptives], where there is murder before birth? You do not even let a harlot remain only a harlot, but you make her a murderess as well... Indeed, it is something worse than murder, and I do not know what to call it; for she does not kill what is formed but prevents its formation. What then? Do you condemn the gift of God and fight with his [natural] laws? (39).

Contraception makes a wife a "murderess?" Isn't he going way too far? There was a time I would have thought this comment to be ridiculous, and it would have made me upset at someone for making such a correlation. When I was on the pill earlier in my life, I took it because I didn't want to get pregnant, and it never crossed my mind that there was a chance it could be abortifacient. It honestly never crossed my mind, as I'm sure it doesn't most people using artificial contraception. Yet, in researching this section of this book, I began to come across several articles that started to scare me, and I had to find out for myself. I had to know why Jon Chrysostom's Homilies on Romans 24 in A.D. 391, would make such a bold claim before all of the methods we have today were around. If he could make that claim then, what could our advanced methods be doing today?

I decided that I needed to find out from medical professionals how artificial birth control actually works, feeling upset with myself, that I have never taken the time before now to find out the truth, especially, with the fact that I consider myself 100 percent pro-life. What I have found from the medical professionals has made me weep and understand why so many in the pro-life movement say that you cannot address abortion without first addressing contraception. It made me lament that I had been disobedient to God's Will regarding my fertility, that in my pride, I thought I knew better than Him. I cried because I ignored what the Church taught that was for the protection and health of my soul and my ex-husbands. I wept because I didn't take the time to find out soon enough to tell my children. I cried for all the marriages, including perhaps my own, that might have survived if birth control wasn't on board. I wept for precious people, for our society, for our world, because I know that most people don't understand, just like I didn't, the grave sin that it is and what they are actually doing by partaking in it. God have mercy on us all!

With all of this said, I felt like it was imperative to let you know what I found out and provide you with the truth of how artificial contraception works for those who, like me, don't already have a good working knowledge of this. In addition, I felt it was also essential to determine if Jon Chrysostom's statement, as harsh as it sounds, had any validity regarding artificial contraception. Ephesians 5 admonishes people to bring all things to the light, exposing the darkness so that one can walk in wisdom. My prayer is that the following information will accomplish that and shed further light on how contraception has been so extensively used by the enemy, especially to wreak havoc on marriage in this final battle.

How Contraception Works

As I mentioned above, I went to medical professionals to give an unbiased, scientific explanation. First, we've already established that all artificial contraception wastes sperm in some form or another, and the purpose is to prevent life. Permanent birth control, such as a vasectomy for men, or tubal ligation for women, require surgical procedures. In a vasectomy, a male's sperm is sealed off, so that it is no longer present in the semen, and the sperm is absorbed (wasted) back into the body. A tubal ligation for women prevents pregnancy because the fallopian tubes have been tied, cut, or blocked, and an egg can no longer travel through them nor can sperm. With condoms or other types of barrier birth control, it's easy to understand how they prevent life. However, with other forms of artificial birth control, it is more complex.

In my research, I learned the birth control pill and other hormonal methods, such as some IUDs, patches, rings, injections, and the "Morning After Pill," work in the following three ways and are supposed to work in this order:

1. Prevent ovulation, 2. In case ovulation occurs, the cervix's mucus thickens, preventing the sperm from reaching the egg. 3. If fertilization of an egg occurs, the uterine lining has been thinned so that the fertilized egg cannot implant in the uterus (40, 41, 42).

Is Artificial Contraception Abortifacient?

When life begins must be established to determine if artificial contraception is abortifacient. According to the American College of Pediatrics March 2017 statement:

> The predominance of human biological research confirms that human life begins at conception—fertilization. At fertilization, the human being emerges as a whole, genetically distinct, in-

> dividuated zygotic living human organism, a member of the species Homo sapiens, needing only the proper environment to grow and develop. The difference between the individual in its adult stage and in its zygotic stage is one of form, not nature (43).

Second, what an abortion constitutes must be established, and according to the *Merriam Webster Medical Dictionary,* an abortion is defined as "the termination of a pregnancy after, accompanied by, resulting in, or closely followed by the death of the embryo or fetus" (44).

With this credible information, we can now determine what forms of birth control are abortifacient.

With sterilization, such as vasectomies and tubal ligation, although they are considered self-mutilation, they permanently prevent life and are strongly condemned by the Catholic Church; an egg is not fertilized, so they are not abortifacient.

Likewise, there is no egg fertilization with condoms and other barrier forms of birth control if they are working correctly, so no abortion occurs.

Now, to see how hormonal birth control works. For starters, and as shown previously, but well worth repeating, all hormonal birth control functions in the same way. 1. If there is no ovulation, there is no egg to fertilize. Therefore, no abortion occurs. 2. Next, if ovulation does occur, the thickening of the cervix's mucus will prevent the sperm from reaching the egg to fertilize it, so no abortion occurs (45). 3. The third way, however, does cause an abortion. If the first or second methods fail to work and an egg is fertilized, it cannot attach to the uterus, so this new life will starve and die, terminating the pregnancy (46).

How often does this happen? Considering the pill has a 9% failure rate for women getting pregnant (46), which seems high, it scares me to think about the percentage of babies aborted while using contraception without ever knowing. The tragic and heart-wrenching fact is that only God will ever know. If it only happened once, that is one too many. Even knowing this is a risk, a possibility, is an incredible tragedy.

Only God knows if any of my children starved and died when I was on the pill, and it is this that has caused me to weep the most. It is confirmation that Jon Chrysostom's words, as harsh as they were, accurately depict the tragic effects artificial contraception can create.

Not only is this happening in marriages, but cohabitating relationships, and the rampant casual hookups and one nightstand. It is absolutely horrific to know that there have been approximately 62,502,904 abortions reported since Roe vs. Wade in 1973 (47). I cannot even begin to think of how high the number of abortions actually is if the "silent" abortions were factored in.

I also weep for the holy innocents, all the babies aborted, as I know their blood cries out to our Lord! Is it no wonder marriage is in crisis? Dear Lord Jesus, we cry for Your mercy and forgiveness for our most grievous sins! How evident it is that the predictions in both Fatima and Ecuador have come to pass. The late Chief Exorcist of the Vatican addresses the moral decay of today saying:

> Divorce has been a disaster, abortion is a disaster. Each year 50 million children are murdered by abortion. And, euthanasia, the broken family, cohabitation . . . it is all destruction! The Lord gave us sex for a purpose and He also declared, 'May no man divide what God has joined.' One thing is sexual fun, another is love. Today there is much talk of love, but there truly is none! Precisely in Fatima did Our Lady say to the young seven-year old, Jacinta: 'The sin that brings the most souls to hell is the impure sin,' the sins of the flesh. She said this to a young girl, who did not even know what it was! We must listen to that which Our Lady says (48).

This destruction can all be traced back to what Fr. Ripperger said that this attack on marital relations will cause "anything to go with a cascade of events to follow," which we can clearly see the chain of events to be, "contraception, abortion, divorce, cohabitation/no marriage, same-sex, etc" (49).

The Truth Brings Freedom.

Please, know that I understand entirely how difficult all of this can be to take in. As I mentioned at the start of the chapter, this has been one of the most challenging issues I've ever written. I know it is because it has forced me to reflect on my own life and see how I so readily accepted the world's view. After all, it was easier. God's way, again, seemed so out of touch and like too much to ask. I've had to face the fact that I may have caused an abortion, even though I consider myself pro-life without exception. I've had to run to God and ask forgiveness for my willful disobedience and lament and weep for my sins and our whole world. Finally, the scales have come off my eyes, and I finally understand why artificial contraception isn't God's plan or will for us and how it has been the root of the marriage crisis.

Being a parent has taught me to realize that God never withholds things from us because He is a mean ogre who wants to keep us from having fun. Quite the contrary, He is a perfect Father Who wants more than anything in the world to keep us from getting hurt, hurting others, and out of harm's way. Any parent can finally understand this when they have children of their own. So, if God and the Church teach that contraception is "intrinsically evil" and a mortal sin, there is a good reason for it, and it is also for our good.

So, What Now?

So, what do we do with this knowledge? How can we go forward? How can we help with this? First and foremost, please, don't take my word for this. Yes, I've researched the heck out of this chapter because I was so afraid of not saying this in a way that God would approve. I never want to spread false information, but this is a soul issue, and only you, your spouse, and God can determine what you want to do with this information.

Next, if you resonate with what I have said and have used artificial contraception throughout your life as I have, especially ones that can be abortifacient, go to God and ask forgiveness. If you are Catholic, go to confession, and repent. There is no sin that God won't forgive and did not die for. Let God in His mercy forgive, heal, and give you the courage to turn from this and live according to His will in this area from now on. If you are married or sexually active and, in a relationship, share this information with your husband or partner. It can be harsh and painful if your husband or wife won't go along. I know this well. All you can do is present them with the information and then take it to prayer. I suggest also talking to a priest or counselor who can help guide you best in this situation.

Also, remember that knowledge is power, and know that God will use you to share what you now know, to help others not fall into the same trap that has, sadly, become the societal norm. St. Catherine of Siena said, "Start being brave about everything. Drive out darkness and spread light. Don't look at your weaknesses. Realize instead that in Christ crucified, you can do everything" (50). And she said, "Preach the Truth as if you had a million voices. It is silence that kills the world" (50). So together, we can take her great advice and get the truth out whenever the Holy Spirit gives us the opportunity!

God's Way Is Always Best!

Furthermore, God never closes one door without another being open, and this issue is no exception. Natural Family Planning is a beautiful replacement for artificial contraception. Most importantly, it allows you to express your intimacy according to God's plan. It will enable you and your spouse to be united and equally responsible for your combined fertility and allows you to entirely give to each other your procreative power "perpetually and exclusively." The seed is never wasted, it is never abortifacient, and it doesn't come with a plethora of potentially harmful side effects that artificial contraception can cause. Even for people who don't have a problem using artificial contraception, it is a healthier choice.

NFP is also very effective when wishing to avoid pregnancy. The *United States Conference of Catholic Bishop's* article, "NFP Effectiveness," notes:

> When wishing to avoid pregnancy, studies show that couples who follow their NFP method's guidelines correctly, and all the time, achieve effectiveness rates of 97-99%. Others, who are unclear about their family planning intention (i.e., spacing or limiting pregnancy) or are less motivated, will not consistently follow the method's guidelines and have a lower effectiveness rate of 80-90% (51).

Versus the Pill:

> Birth control pills are 99 percent effective with 'perfect use,' which means taking the pill at the same time every day without

> missing a dose. 'Typical use' is how most women take the pill, and then it's about 91 percent effective. Both combined oral contraceptives and progestin-only pills (also known as the mini-pill) have a typical failure rate of 9 percent (52).

As you can see, there is very little difference in effectiveness if used correctly. It does take more effort and discipline, but it is so worth knowing you are in God's will. In confession the other day, a priest said that obedience requires humility, and it made me think so much of this. It is a humble act to say to God, I trust You, not myself, with my fertility. Surrender to God in all things, especially this most sacred gift He gives us, brings true freedom.

The Catechism of the Catholic Church describes this so beautifully, saying:

> 2370 - Periodic continence, that is, the methods of birth regulation based on self-observation and the use of infertile periods, is in conformity with the objective criteria of morality.158 These methods respect the bodies of the spouses, encourage tenderness between them, and favor the education of an authentic freedom (53).

And, 1 Cor. 7:5 describes NFP when it states, "Defraud not one another, except, perhaps, by consent, for a time, that you may give yourselves to prayer: and return together again, lest Satan tempt you for your inconsistency" (54).

The time a couple is abstaining can be a time used to draw them even closer, increase their communication, and help their marriage stay God-centered, not just pleasure-centered. Knowing this helps to explain another incredible benefit of NFP. Research shows 58 percent lower odds of divorce among women who have used NFP in their marriage "as opposed to two times the odds of divorce and four times for cohabitation compared to those women who never used those methods. Use of periodic abstinence with NFP is the practice of marital chastity and is thought to strengthen the marital relationship" (55). But, of course, God knew best! Always!

Together We Can Effect Change!

If you are not Catholic, you might think *this is just Catholic legalism and doesn't apply to you.* But again, I urge you to look at the facts and data that support all that I'm telling you. Research it further for yourself. Study the Scriptures, and pray about it. I firmly believe you will see for yourself that it is indeed true and not a Catholic issue, but a soul issue. We must "have no fellowship with the unfruitful works of darkness, but rather reprove them" (56).

And imagine if only Christians started using Natural Family Planning and sharing how effective and healthy it is! Then, we could help start turning the tide on the marriage crisis, one marriage at a time! On our own, we cannot change the world. Still, we can do as St. Mother Teresa said, "Never worry about numbers. Help one person at a time and always start with the person nearest you" (57).

In doing this, we can help restore marriage and marital intimacy to all God had in mind for us in this most sacred sacrament! God says in His Word, "I call heaven and earth to witness this day, that I have set before you life and death, blessing and cursing. Choose therefore LIFE, that both thou and thy seed may live!" (58).

Chapter Three

"No-Fault?"

Although artificial contraception may be the most divisive tool satan has used to cause a moral landslide that has dramatically contributed to the marriage crisis, the no-fault divorce law might perhaps be a close second. We cannot adequately address the marriage crisis without a thorough investigation into this law, which comes as no surprise that its establishment was at the same time artificial contraception use was becoming mainstream.

In 1953, Oklahoma was the first state to put into practice the no-fault divorce law. This law had little effect on the rest of the country until 1970, when then-governor Ronald Reagan signed it into California law. Ronald Reagan, to this day, is one of my favorite presidents and had a remarkable overall effect on many aspects of our country. Still, one cannot deny that after this single historic signing, every state has instituted some form of the no-fault divorce, forever reforming divorce proceedings in America.

Colorado attorney Andrew Oh-Willeke describes it like this:

> The No-Fault Divorce Law simply means that everyone who wants a divorce may, in most states (including Colorado) without the consent of their spouse, end the marriage after going through the necessary waiting periods and court hearings. The courts don't care why you want a divorce in a no-fault case. Except for

> a handful of slight procedural nuances related to calculating deadlines and setting notices for court hearings, the courts don't care who actually filed for divorce in a no-fault state (1).

Naturally, this law has and continues to hold a great deal of debate and controversy regarding the effect it has had on the social, moral, economic, and legal basis of marriage and family in America. Many supporters of the law blame the divorce crisis on "other" factors. As we have discussed previously, it is not one single cause; however, it is undeniable that this law has played a significant factor in the substantial increase in divorce over the last 40 years.

According to the California Assembly Committee on Judiciary, the national divorce rate increased almost 40% in the five years following the establishment of the no-fault in California. Their studies show that through the 1950s and 1960s, the divorce rates were 400,000 per year. By 1975, they increased to over 1 million a year. And, again, today, as many as 42 - 45 percent of marriages end in divorce (2).

Of course, there are always two sides to every debate. According to California's Governor's Commission, the primary goals of the no-fault law were "to free the administration of justice in divorce cases from the hypocrisy and perjury that had resulted from the use of marital fault as a controlling consideration in divorce proceedings" (2). Proponents of the law also believed it was, and still is, a way for women in abusive marriages to get out of detrimental situations. Perhaps a worthy cause in theory; however, according to the commission, there is no substantial evidence to support that battered wives have benefited from the no-fault divorce whatsoever.

Battered spouses should never stay in an abusive marriage, and there are many other reasons why there are times when divorce is necessary. For example, I had a friend whose mother was having an affair with her husband. An unthinkable situation for endless reasons, yet some of her closest friends encouraged her to stay in the marriage! Also, a sign she needed to look for new friends!

Another friend of mine shared that her father was an abusive alcoholic. And she, her siblings, and her mother had suffered for years because of it. The abuse her mother suffered became so bad that she went to the ladies of her church, probably looking for permission (not that she needed it!) to leave finally. Their response was shocking! Even in this situation, the church's sweet little ladies told her that his abuse was her cross that she needed to carry, and she should go back and submit to her husband!

Circumstances that warrant divorce will always exist, but the no-fault law is not the answer when these situations arise. No-fault has not been beneficial or protected victims. What it does accomplish is a decision that a couple should make together, is decided by one partner alone, often resulting in an even more significant disadvantage for an abused spouse if their perpetrator is the petitioner. Proponents of the law believe that removing the blame will lessen the conflict, and the divorce proceedings will be shortened, making it easier on both parties. However, I have personally seen and witnessed for myself that just the opposite can take place. I have seen it, instead, provide the petitioner endless opportunities to continue forced litigation on the respondent, making a bad situation horrific.

I know of a woman who has had to endure over seven years of continued litigation. The courts allow her ex-husband to continue in endless court motions, with his sole motive being to significantly lessen or exterminate his obligations to pay child support, and to leave his wife penniless, even telling her, "I will put you into such a state of bankruptcy, you will never recover." The no-fault law allows this harassment to continue protecting his rights regardless of the situation or fault. The courts are not concerned that he abused her in their marriage, because like most abused spouses, she did not report him, nor are they concerned that he committed adultery.

Another gentleman I know came home after work to find his wife enjoying herself in bed with her boyfriend. Despite her infidelity, he was desperate to work it out for the sake of their two little boys. She, unfortunately, wanted nothing to do with reconciling, filed for divorce immediately after, and has spent the last ten years successfully keeping his boys from him as much as possible and petitioning the courts for continuous increases in her child support.

Before no-fault, issues like spousal abuse and adultery would have made it difficult for the petitioning spouse to come out victoriously. The courts would have found these issues to be glaring enough to ensure justice in both lives. Unfortunately, no-fault places all parties on equal playing fields, often doing more to protect those who are genuinely at fault than it has ever done to bring about justice in the lives of those who really need and are entitled to it.

Not only does it not provide justice to the appropriate party, but evidence also supports the idea that this law is responsible for creating divorce battles that are now primarily over child custody instead of the fault grounds. As a result, children are being placed in the crossfire as never before.

A lady I worked with spent year after year enduring child and family investigations that her ex-husband continually petitioned. He would petition the court for more custody with the children yet was never rewarded more than a few extra nights per month. As soon as the trial court would determine he did not get the fifty-fifty custody he had petitioned for, he would then start trying to lower his child support payments in other ways. The worst part of all was that her children were continually dragged through these investigations and had to live uncertain of what the next move or attempt at change would be. If "fault" had been allowed, the battles might have continued; however, they would have been between the parents and not issues with the children.

Although the no-fault law is certainly not the only factor for the alarming increase in the divorce rate, as we discussed in the previous chapter, several factors point to it having made a significant contribution. Author Maggie Gallagher states it well in her article in the 1997 August/September issue of *First Things*:

> When divorce is made quicker and nonjudgmental, more marriages fail. No-fault divorce is thus both a cause and a symptom of our current marriage crisis. When the law treats divorce as a unilateral right of one partner, culture can hardly take seriously the moral claims of marriage. Similarly, when as a culture, we begin to reclaim the lost ideal of marriage, we will certainly change our marriage laws to match (3).

In Colorado, a divorce can be final in 91 days. This limited amount of time gives the couples minimal opportunity to try and resolve their problems. Proponents of the law believe that it is too late to work out problems when a divorce is petitioned, and a judge may allow a divorce to proceed even if only one spouse is seeking it. In most divorces, one of the parties is often blindsided by the "news" as I was when my ex told me on our eighteenth anniversary, that he wasn't really into the whole "till death do you part thing," and wanted a divorce. Consequently, my anniversary happens to be on June 6th, also the anniversary of D-Day (June 6th, 1944, During WW II when US troops landed in Normandy.) which I have often thought, and even chuckle, thinking, how fitting.

Another lady I know experienced the devastation of the no-fault divorce law in her marriage as well. Several years ago, she was caught off guard by her husband's sudden interest in moving to Colorado. They were natives to New Jersey, their children were established in the schools, they had great jobs, and all their family was there. Yet, he kept on insisting that Colorado would be an excellent move for the family, and everything he told her about it seemed great. Finally, after several months of persistence, she gave in, thinking that it would be a fun change, so they moved to the state.

After just eight months of living in Colorado, she found out he was having an affair, and he petitioned for a divorce. She was devastated by the news, and even more so that she was no longer in the same state as her family for support. As the divorce proceedings began, she found out quickly why he had insisted they move to Colorado. Colorado is a no-fault state, and it made the divorce quick, easy, and benefited him financially. My poor friend not only had to suffer through all that divorce entails but had to realize that he had moved them to Colorado so that he could benefit from the no-fault laws. Like with my marriage and most in no-fault states, all he needed to claim was "irreconcilable differences," and he was free to start his new life with his girlfriend.

You would think that the fact they had been married 15 years and had three children together would slow the process, but the law also does not differentiate between a four-month marriage and a marriage of 40 years. It does not consider whether both parties want the divorce (four out of five divorces are decided unilaterally) and, in many cases, does not consider whether or not children are involved. Many times, the court will mandate counseling when children are involved, but not often enough. Children were involved in all the divorce cases I am personally familiar with, yet the court did not mandate counseling in any of them, including my own.

The petitioning party has little accountability and is not required to have any valid reason for requesting a divorce. There are no longer restraints to make a person think twice about getting a divorce or engaging in an extra-marital affair. "Irreconcilable Differences" is the patent reason. According to the courts, this is sufficient.

Before no-fault, you could get a divorce; however, the consequences and stakes were often very high. The courts protected women financially and with their children's care if the father was at fault, and vice versa. With today's laws, the petitioner often comes out better than the partner who was willing to honor their marriage vow for the sake of everyone involved and make it work, as in the case of the gentleman and lady mentioned earlier. The no-fault law has helped a me-first society flourish like a disease that afflicts a large portion of the population, with children being the group most affected.

Given the effects that the no-fault law has had on divorce, and society, particularly children, our judicial system must take a closer look at this law's reforms. More extraordinary efforts need to be made in rebuilding a culture of marriage instead of creating a culture of divorce with this law and the other contributing issues discussed in the previous chapter. The no-fault divorce law is definitely another weapon in satan's arsenal in his battle against marriage and the family.

Author and divorce expert Maggie Gallagher, sums it up powerfully, stating, "When the terror of a divorce delayed pales in our minds in comparison to the horror of seeing an innocent spouse dumped... then and only then will Americans have escaped the divorce culture we now inhabit" (3).

CHAPTER FOUR

"IT'S ALL ABOUT ME."

As we saw in the last few chapters, the enemy has used the significant decline in sexual morals, artificial contraception, and the no-fault divorce law to cause the marriage crisis we are facing today. But another byproduct of these is that it has caused people to more than ever become "lovers of self" above serving God and the needs of their mate and others. Scripture warned us we would see this in the last days.

The pursuit of personal happiness has, sadly, become another term often used to describe self-gratification. Perhaps as never before, we live in a society that teaches children before they even start school that it is a "right" to be happy. I've noticed this trend considerably in the classroom, having taught for the past 15 years. Please know, I'm certainly not against being happy and desire this for everyone, including myself, and I strive to be happy every day. However, true happiness is a gift from God and something we should strive for, but only from a Biblical perspective.

That said, what parents, including myself, don't long for their children to overflow with happiness in their life. Jesus Himself said, "... I came that they may have and enjoy life, and have it in abundance to the full, till it overflows" (1). Yet, in the Scripture immediately following, Jesus continues saying, "I am the Good Shepherd. The Good Shepherd risks and lays down His own life for the sheep" (2). It is clearly God's will that we enjoy life. It is one of the greatest gifts He offers to His children, but as Jesus states, we must also be willing to "lay down our lives for others," and our happiness should never come at the expense of others. Like so many other things, the world has perverted what true happiness entails. And people often spend their whole lives seeking it, but never find lasting happiness apart from God.

Moreover, we will never find the happiness God intended if we pursue it with only ourselves in mind, and this is sadly the primary focus of so many in the world today. The world's ideas of happiness, pleasure, and service to "self" have been elevated over and above others' needs and the desire to please God. We can see this so clearly in the moral decay. Please note that, as I say this, it is essential to understand that Godly self-care and self-love are crucial because we cannot give away what we don't have. If we don't love and nurture ourselves, we won't properly love others either; however, the world has distorted this concept as well. The scripture "Greater love than this no man hath, that a man lay down his life for his friends" (3) has become nothing more than a faded cliché to most of society, and the results have been especially devastating in marriage.

Doesn't Daddy or Mommy Have a Right to Be Happy?

A friend of mine, who had experienced divorce as a child, told me that when his father was breaking the news to him and his siblings that he wanted to divorce their mother, he posed the question, asking them, "Doesn't daddy have a right to be happy?" This young man said it took him and his sibling's years to forgive their father for asking them this question. In their mind, all they and their siblings could understand was that their dad had admitted he cared more about his happiness than the fact that he had just torn their world apart by his choice to divorce their mother. To make matters worse, his father would reinforce this belief by continuing to ask them this same question on many occasions when they were struggling with the divorce. In his effort to appease them, or perhaps justify it in his mind, he would ask, "Come on, guys, don't you agree that it all worked out for the best? I seem happier, don't I?"

A big problem is that people often enter marriage, thinking that marriage itself or their spouse will finally bring the everlasting happiness they are seeking. But the truth is, a mere mortal cannot give them something only God, through His Grace, can fulfill. Suppose someone enters a marriage thinking it will bring everlasting bliss. In that case, they are often let down when reality sets in, and they are faced with the harsh fact that marriage can be extremely challenging.

There are times it brings anything but feelings of happiness, and their commitment is challenged. Because their spouse isn't making them happy, they are filled with discontent when their spouse fails to fill this void. This lack of fulfillment and a flippant attitude towards marriage, in general, is a significant cause of divorce. It causes people to think they have fallen out of love, and despite the seriousness of their vows, they feel they have the "right" to find a person who will make them happy.

After 18 years of marriage, my ex-husband told me that he had realized he had never truly loved me, and that he needed to be with someone he could finally be happy with and truly love. You can imagine how deeply this wounded me. I went through a period trying to figure out why I was so unlovable. And didn't understand why someone would stay with a person for 18 years if they didn't care about them?

It's Not Your Responsibility.

Over the years, I've had several people tell me that their ex-partners have said the same thing. I realize now that the majority of those who said this had already given their hearts to another. In their lustful delusion and to justify their actions, they convinced themselves that they never loved their spouse. It also shows me how important it is to understand that if you are not happy before you get married, you won't be after, no matter who you are with. It is not your spouse's job to make you happy, nor is it your job to do this for them either. Once again, only God can truly bring this, and He designed it this way, so that you continually need to seek Him, and keep Him first in your life, even above your spouse.

Another thing we must be cautious of in marriage or any relationship is taking on a false sense of responsibility. For the first eight years of my marriage, I allowed my spouse to determine my happiness. If we were getting along, or he was in a good mood, then I was happy. If we weren't, then I fought depression, and continually looked for what I was doing wrong if he was angry or in a bad mood. I had assumed a false sense of responsibility for his happiness and spent years blaming myself when he wasn't happy.

Happiness is a Decision.

About this time, my mom gave me a book called *You Can Be Happy Now* by the late Pastor Merlin Carothers (4). This book, and all of Merlin's books on praise, were life-changing. For the first time in my life, I learned that through the grace of God, not only could I determine my thoughts, but that through His grace and praise, I could be happy regardless of my circumstances or the actions of other people. My happiness was my responsibility, and it was a choice I made. I no longer had to place this burden on my spouse or my children. The book taught me that if I would surrender the actions of others to God and thank Him for them, He would make them work for my good. I could choose to rise above my circumstances and let God's grace fill me with joy!

Merlin's teaching also taught me that I wasn't responsible for my spouse's or anyone else's happiness, for that matter. I had the responsibility to obey God's Word, which tells me to "respect and revere my husband, notice him, regard him, honor him, prefer him, venerate him, and esteem him . . . Praise him, love and admire him exceedingly . . . not pay back wrong for wrong, but always try to be kind to him" (5). But I was not responsible for his or anyone's happiness! Again, only God could provide this. I experienced such relief when I was able to truly let this go and give it to God. I had carried this burden of trying to make everyone around me happy since I was a child, and with this revelation, I felt the weight of the world lift off my shoulders.

It is a tragedy when people never learn this truth. Again, they enter marriage thinking it will be the magic key to eternal happiness. Over time, they often realize it's not, and divorce becomes a symptom of their failed search. They blame their ex-spouse and remarry, believing the next marriage will accomplish what the former marriage didn't. However, the divorce statistics for second and third marriages prove that a new marriage is not the answer either.

Marriage and Mashed Potatoes

Furthermore, our "me first" society has led men and women alike to lose the true meaning of sacrificial love, which is essential for experiencing true, Godly love in a marriage. As we discussed in chapter two regarding procreation, God never designed marriage to be an institution where we join to be strictly receivers of another's affections. It is a holy sacrament in which the self becomes extinct, and two individuals literally become one.

I recall hearing a talk once that likened marriage to making mashed potatoes. First, you find the potatoes, then you peel them with a knife, so that the insides are bare. You then cut them up and place them in boiling water until they are soft and pliable. Finally, you smash them up and beat them with a mixer on high speed until all the potatoes become one! A bit extreme, and humorous, I hope! BUT anyone who has been married will understand this fitting analogy! To make it work, we must continually, and daily, die to self, and like the potato, go through an awful lot, to ensure we are one flesh!

For marriage to last, we must commit to it being "perpetual and exclusive" despite how we "feel" for a day! The "in love" feeling is wonderful, I think there is little in the world that can compare, but what if a marriage goes through a time when the emotional feelings are dulled, or are not there for a period of time?

Marriage vows, at least traditional ones, don't leave room for such statements as "I'll stay with you if I feel in love with you and you make me happy," quite the contrary. Marriage requires a difficult commitment and is not for the faint of heart. The vows ". . . from this day forward, for better, for worse, for richer, for poorer, in sickness or health, to love and to cherish 'till death do us part. And hereto, I pledge you, my faithfulness" were not suggestions.

Again, God instituted marriage to be forever and an irrevocable covenant, and it will not last if it is entered into with your fingers crossed behind your back while reciting your vows to your spouse on your wedding day. Marriage should never be entered into flippantly, looking for an escape route before you even begin.

If I'm Not Happy, I Can Just Get a Divorce.

Several years ago, one of my co-workers was preparing for marriage. I remember a few of us women were sitting around after work, talking with her. One of the ladies commented that she didn't seem nervous. She responded very matter-of-factly, "Why should I be nervous? If it doesn't work out and I'm not happy, I can always get a divorce and find someone else who does."

I have never forgotten this comment because it was very foreign to everything I had been taught growing up. Although it might sound exceedingly naïve, I had not conceived the thought at the time that many people share her same philosophy and don't value "until death do us part," my ex included. About five years later, she decided she was not happy and divorced her husband. It was a glaring lesson that entering a marriage with such low expectations sets us up for failure from the start if one's focus is directed to what we can receive for ourselves in our marriage, rather than what we can give.

A more recent story happened to a wonderful young man that I know. A few years ago, he married the person he thought was the love of his life. This young man was financially well-off and had a great job, which allowed his new bride to stay home and take care of the household.

However, after just two years of marriage, she started complaining that he was working too much and was disappointed that he didn't have as much money as she had initially thought. He truly loved her, so he tried to cut down on his hours, but she continued to spend extravagantly, which made it difficult for him to do so.

One night, after a long day at work, he came home to find their apartment completely bare. She had taken everything and left a note on the kitchen table saying that she would serve him with divorce papers within the week.

As you can imagine, he was devastated, but for the sake of peace, he walked away and just let her have her way. He is now remarried, thankfully, to a wonderful lady, and they now have two beautiful children. Still, his first marriage is a glaring example of how greatly our self-serving society has infected marriage, and the destruction it is leaving behind. And, sadly, this sounds extreme, but I hear of stories like this more and more all the time.

The Survival of Our Society Depends on It.

Knowing that we live in a "me first" society makes it a bit easier to understand where millennials are coming from in their proposals to redefine marriage as essentially real estate contracts that provide an escape route if it isn't meeting their expectations. As we discussed in chapter two, many people today view marriage as outdated. They have lived through the horrors of divorce and have witnessed their parents and others they know, losing everything in the process; coming out of it emotionally, physically, spiritually, and financially bankrupt. You really cannot blame them.

Yet even though my marriage didn't last as I had planned, I still have great faith in marriage because I know Who is the Creator of it. The thread I keep seeing in everything we have discussed so far is how incredibly lacking education is in what a Godly marriage entails. I know my marriage prep classes, I'm sorry to say, were a joke. They were so light weight and did not prepare me anywhere near enough for what I was entering!

There is an urgent need to address these deep-seated soul issues, to spell them out, and pour solid Catholic teaching about marriage into our youth and those contemplating marriage, even if it's not their first time walking down the aisle. Because of the warning from Fatima and Ecuador, we know this is THE spiritual battle of all battles, and we must never give up fighting and praying for the restoration of this beautiful sacrament to be as God intended.

St. Charbel is quoted as saying, "The war of the Evil One against the Lord is his war against the family, and the war of the Evil One against the family is the core of his war against the Lord. Because the family is the image of God, from the beginning of the creation of this universe, The Evil one is focusing on destroying the family, the foundation of God's plan" (6).

This is the spiritual battle of all spiritual battles, and we must fight daily! The very survival of our society depends on it.

CHAPTER FIVE

"WHAT DOES GOD HAVE TO SAY ABOUT IT?"

A Match Made in Heaven

When I was a little girl, my favorite thing to do was play make-believe. I am not sure if it was regular childhood play, my overactive imagination, or the fact that I was the only girl with two older brothers, but I could shut myself away in my room and play for hours. As soon as the door closed, my room transformed into a faraway castle, I became a beautiful princess, and my stuffed animals became the cast in my land of make-believe.

I specifically remember my favorite story being one in which I would pretend to visit Heaven so that the Heavenly court, the angels, saints, Mary the mother of Jesus, Jesus, and God Himself could choose the prince I was to marry. It was a gallant affair, a true celebration beginning with the "court" choosing just the right dress I would wear to meet this perfect suitor. Next, my hair was styled just so, with the final event being the unveiling of my husband-to-be. It was literally a match made in Heaven.

I have often thought back on how as a small girl, I had an innate understanding that God was the orchestrator of marriage, and it should be God Himself that chose my mate. I marvel that my "little self" knew better than my "nineteen-year-old self" the importance of seeking God's will in finding a husband. After all, God is the inventor of marriage. He alone is the institutor of this sacred covenant, and Who better than the original Designer should we look to when selecting a mate for life?

Two of the best examples I can recall that illustrate how God answers prayers for this are from a young Christian man I know and one of my brothers. The young Christian man began praying for God to send him his wife, two years before he ever met her. When he finally met the girl he had been praying for, God made it clear that she was the one, and gave him confirmation that it was heavenly ordained. Because he was patient and waited, God blessed him with his wonderful wife, and they remain strong over 25 years later.

One of my brothers had a similar experience. After dating many of the "wrong" girls in high school, he decided to stay away from the dating scene and spend several years in prayer instead. While he was busy praying and serving the Lord, God was working behind the scenes, arranging a meeting between my now sister-in-law and him.

One of our uncles has dedicated his life as a volunteer for the Missionaries of Charity (the late Mother Teresa's order), and my brother often volunteered with my uncle as well. On one visit, the sisters had arranged for a birthday party to celebrate my uncle's birthday. While at the party, my brother took notice of a young Canadian woman who had also come to volunteer her time.

He describes that when he first saw her, his "spirit leapt for joy!" She was leaving to go back home to Canada the next day, and he knew he had to act quickly. He began praying to have a chance to talk with her, and his prayers were answered. After a brief encounter, and thanks to the matchmaking efforts of our bold grandfather, who was also attending the party, their "match made in heaven" was soon underway and is still going strong after 35 years of marriage.

We may never enjoy this type of assurance of God's involvement in choosing a spouse. Still, we must surrender this decision to God to the very best of our ability. Because of free will, God will allow us to choose whomever we wish to marry. Yet, with a decision as important as marriage, we should never enter it lightly or without gaining the best understanding possible from a Godly perspective of all that it entails beforehand. By the time we are old enough to get married, we've had so many worldly ideas thrown at us that it takes a conscious effort and deep study to try to undo all the deceptions of the world. If I could go back to my nineteen-year-old self, at the very least, I would encourage myself to read as much as I could about what the Church and God say about marriage, and then encourage my spouse to do the same, to ensure we shared the same ideas about it.

I'm not entirely sure I would have listened at that time, but I would like to think I might have. My nineteen-year-old self knew that marriage was intended to be for life. Still, I didn't have a clue about much else, and I certainly didn't understand what a holy and sacred covenant it was designed to be.

Over time, my life experiences have shown me so clearly that, short of your salvation in Jesus Christ, who you marry, and getting married, are the most critical decisions you will ever make in life. However, like many topics we've discussed, it wasn't until I wrote this book that I took the time to read about marriage in-depth. And I pray that in reading this chapter, if you are not already aware of how beautiful and sacred it is, your eyes will be open to the incredible beauty God has designed for His children in the Sacrament of Holy Matrimony and will give insight to those still seeking a mate or are engaged to be married!

God Has Everything to Do With It!

Our sophisticated modern society would consider my childhood games to be nothing more than children's folly. As we saw in chapter two, the secular trend states that God has little if anything to do with marriage, accepting that it is nothing more than a civil contract put into place to provide legal protections for both parties. Even Christians married in the church often choose to accept the authority of civil law over and above the teachings in the Bible and the Church, especially when it comes to the dissolution of marriage.

However, God promises in His Word, "And you will know the truth, and the truth will set you free" (1). And the truth is that marriage is far greater than any civil contract. It was created by God long before any manufactured institution existed, originating back to the creation of Eve. Genesis 2:18-25 tells us:

> Now the Lord God said, It is not good (sufficient, satisfactory) that the man should be alone; I will make him a helper meet suitable, adapted, and complementary for him . . . And the Lord God caused a deep sleep to fall upon Adam; and while he slept, He took one of his ribs or a part of his side and closed up the place with flesh. And the rib or part of his side which the Lord God had taken from the man He built up and made into a woman, and He brought her to man . . . This creature is now bone of my bones and flesh of my flesh; she shall be called Woman, because she was taken out of man. Therefore, a man shall leave his father and his mother and shall become united and cleave to his wife, and they shall become one flesh (2).

Adam was delighted when he saw Eve. Can you imagine? Adam might have thought, "She is for me, God? Wowee!" And, Eve was delighted with Adam, too! Yet, not only did He make them for each other, but He made them in His Image, blessing them and their union, and told them to ". . . increase and multiply, and fill the earth, and subdue it. . ." (3). And, through this, the first marriage came to be.

When Jesus came, He renewed the Sacrament of Marriage. During one of His discussions with the Pharisees regarding marriage and divorce, He refers to Genesis 2:18 - 25 when:

> answering, said to them: Have ye not read, that He who made man from the beginning, made them male and female? And He said: [5] For this cause shall a man leave father and mother, and shall cleave to his wife, and they two shall be in one flesh. [6] Therefore now they are not two, but one flesh. What therefore God hath joined together, let no man put asunder (4).

Also, in John 15:13, when Jesus said, there is no greater love than to lay down your life for your friends, He didn't only mean it for platonic relationships, but it was stating how a husband is called to lay down his life to make his wife holy, and the wife is to lay down her life for her husband in submitting to him (5). Often when people hear the latter part, it creates defenses to rise up. The statement to "submit to your husband" is often not popular in our modern world, especially when taken out of context, and, in all fairness, it has been abused. But, when you read all of Ephesians 5:22 through 30, it clearly shows that the wife's submission accompanies the husband loving her as Christ loves the Church. I encourage you to carefully ponder and meditate on each sentence of Ephesians 5:22 through 30 below, to grasp the fullness of these Scriptures and how God desires marriage to be:

> [22] Let women be subject to their husbands, as to the Lord: [23] Because the husband is the head of the wife, as Christ is the head of the church. He is the saviour of his body. [24] Therefore as the church is subject to Christ, so also let the wives be to their husbands in all things. [25] Husbands, love your wives, as Christ also loved the church, and delivered himself up for it:
>
> [26] That he might sanctify it, cleansing it by the laver of water in the word of life: [27] That he might present it to himself a glorious church, not having spot or wrinkle, or any such thing; but that it should be holy, and without blemish. [28] So also ought men to love their wives as their own bodies. He that loveth his wife, loveth himself. [29] For no man ever hated his own flesh; but nourisheth and cherisheth it, as also Christ doth the church: [30] Because we are members of his body, of his flesh, and of his bones (6).

As these scriptures tell, God places such a high value on marriage that it also symbolizes the relationship between Christ and His Bride. God begins the Bible with the institution of mariage, and the Book of Revelation completes this with Jesus our Groom, returning for His Bride, the body of believers. Marriage between a man and a woman was designed to provide the perfect balance for the family and the ideal environment for children to be nurtured and raised in the love and counsel of the Lord. God not only created man and women in His image, but He also designed marriage to be the image of Jesus' love and relationship with the Church.

So, as you can see, and as discussed in chapter two, marriage between two consenting adults is an expression of God's love for all humanity, a beautiful, sacred covenant between God and man, created to be a mirror of the Holy Trinity "confirmed by the divine law and caught up into divine love" (7). God created Eve out of the bone of Adam, and the two became one flesh. God made one for the other, no longer two but one flesh designed so that "what God has joined together, let no man put asunder" (8).

The Holy Family

The perfect example for us all to strive for in our marriage is the example of the Holy Family. God is the most masterful Creator, and always designs everything to have perfect balance. I remember being at a Marion Conference a few years ago, and on the stage, they had a large statue of St. Joseph on the right, a picture of Jesus in the middle, and a beautiful statue of Mary on the left. It was as if all three were radiating with the Holy Spirit, and I marveled at the incredible example God has left us with the Holy Family. They were three distinct persons, but all with a specific role, yet all united as one. It made such a lasting impression on me to see this visual example of how God desires each marriage and family to be. The Holy Family's appearance during the last apparition of Fatima clearly illustrated God's desire for all families.

What Does the Church Say?

One of the best places to read about the utter beauty and sacredness of marriage is in *The Catechism of The Catholic Church* and its alignment to Holy Scripture, even for those who are not Catholic. It is such a treat to read the explanations of marriage as God designed it to be. I found it so incredible that I did not want to risk paraphrasing the information and not conveying the fullness of its beauty, so I've provided select sections in their entirety. The website, *CatholicDoors.com* does a beautiful job of showing the scripture and the Canon Law reference to the text of the *Catechism*. Below is the section from the *Catechism* titled, "The Sacrament of Marriage," Part Two, Article 2, and defines "The Celebration of the Christian Mystery," including the references from *CatholicDoors.com,* as it pertains to the paschal mystery of the Church's Sacrament of Matrimony: (9)

THE SACRAMENT OF MATRIMONY

1601 "*The matrimonial covenant, by which a man and a woman establish between themselves a partnership of the whole of life, is by its nature ordered toward the good of the spouses and the procreation and education of offspring; this covenant between baptized persons has been raised by Christ the Lord to the dignity of a sacrament." [CIC, can. 1055 # 1; GS 48 # 1]*"

I. MARRIAGE IN GOD'S PLAN

1602 "*Sacred Scripture begins with the creation of man and woman in the image and likeness of God and concludes with a vision of "the wedding-feast of the Lamb." [Rev 19:7, 9; Gen 1:26-27] Scripture speaks throughout of marriage and its "mystery," its institution and the meaning God has given it, its origin and its end, its various realizations throughout the history of salvation, the difficulties arising from sin and its renewal "in the Lord" in the New Covenant of Christ and the Church. [1 Cor 7:39; cf. Eph 5:31-32]*"

Marriage in the order of creation

1603 "*The intimate community of life and love which constitutes the married state has been established by the Creator and endowed by him with its own proper laws.... God Himself is the author of marriage." [GS 48 # 1] The vocation to marriage is written in the very nature of man and woman as they came from the hand of the Creator. Marriage is not a purely human institution despite the many variations it may have undergone through the centuries in different cultures, social structures, and spiritual attitudes. These differences should not cause us to forget its common and permanent characteristics. Although the dignity of this institution is not transparent everywhere with the same clarity, [GS 47 # 2] some sense of the greatness of the matrimonial union exists in all cultures. "The well-being of the individual person and of both human and Christian society is closely bound up with the healthy state of conjugal and family life." [GS 47 # 1]*

> *# 1604 "God who created man out of love also calls him to love the fundamental and innate vocation of every human being. For man is created in the image and likeness of God who is himself love. [Gen 1:27; 1 Jn 4:8, 16] Since God created him man and woman, their mutual love becomes an image of the absolute and unfailing love with which God loves man. It is good, very good, in the Creator's eyes. And this love which God blesses is intended to be fruitful and to be realized in the common work of watching over creation: "And God blessed them, and God said to them: 'Be fruitful and multiply, and fill the earth and subdue it.'" [Gen 1:28; cf. 1:31]"*

> *# 1605 "Holy Scripture affirms that man and woman were created for one another: "It is not good that the man should be alone." [Gen 2:18] The woman, "flesh of his flesh," i.e., his counterpart, his equal, his nearest in all things, is given to him by God as a "helpmate"; she thus represents God from whom comes our help. [Cf. Gen 2:18-25] "Therefore a man leaves his father and his mother and cleaves to his wife, and they become one flesh." [Gen 2:24] The Lord himself shows that this signifies an unbreakable union of their two lives by recalling what the plan of the Creator had been "in the beginning": "So they are no longer two, but one flesh." [Mt 19:6]" (9)*

Reading these words in their fullness left me awestruck. And, again, I have only included the paragraphs that stood out most! But, even with just this information, it is clear that God meant marriage to be the most incredible and sacred gift to man from our loving Father! Marriage is truly sacred! And, although I am a hopeless romantic, as can be seen by my childhood play, this made me fall more in love with marriage and God than ever before, and I pray it does you as well!

God Hates Divorce!

So, if marriage was created to be so beautiful, so sacred, so holy by God Himself, what happened? How can something designed so perfectly become so dysfunctional and, in so many cases, wholly separated from its original form? And, after reading the incredible beauty and sacredness of marriage, is it any wonder why this is what the final battle is over? satan and all his forces are well aware of how precious marriage is to God and know full well it is the very soul of our nation and all of humanity, so he and his demonic forces have waged an all-out war. The foundation of our country and world depends on the strength and stability of marriage and the family unit. If destroyed, the foundation of America and the world will crumble, which is what we are witnessing today.

As we've seen in previous chapters, divorce is the byproduct of the causes we've discussed. The enemy knows that it undeniably creates chaos and disorder in the family and society. "This disorder brings grave harm to the deserted spouse, to children traumatized by the separation of their parents and often torn between them and because of its contagious effect makes it truly a plague on society" (10). It alters the course of many generations, forces families to try and "blend" unnaturally, and as a dear friend of mine who went through a divorce years ago puts it "the consequences and repercussions if you have children never end!" I can attest to this personally. I witnessed it more when my children were younger, however, even now that they are adults, it affects every major milestone of their lives, mine, and my ex-husband's, in one way or another.

Moreover, knowing how God designed marriage, makes it easy to understand why He said, "I hate divorce!" in Malachi 2:16 (11). The chapter of Malachi expands on this statement and provides a clear view of God's stance on this subject:

> Why then do we deal faithlessly and treacherously each against his brother, profaning the covenant of our Fathers? . . . The Lord was witness to the covenant made at your marriage between you and the wife of your youth, against whom you have dealt treacherously and to whom you were faithless. Yet she is your companion and the wife of your covenant made by your marriage vows. And did not God make you and your wife one flesh? Did not One make you and preserve your spirit alive? And why did God make you two one? Because He sought a godly offspring from your union . . . let no one deal treacherously and be faithless to the wife of his youth. For the Lord, the God of Israel says; I hate divorce and marital separation and him who covers his wife with violence. Therefore, keep watch upon your spirit, that it may be controlled by the Holy Spirit that you deal not treacherously and faithlessly with your marriage mate (11).

I was the wife of my ex-husband's youth, "against whom he dealt with treacherously and to whom he was faithless" (11). Because of my experience, I understand why God is so bold in stating that He "hates divorce." I have lived through, and seen firsthand its devastating effects on my life, the lives of my children, my student's lives, and many precious people around me, as I know many of you have as well.

The fallout is like a war zone with bloody and wounded casualties, and lives ripped to pieces. I remember feeling like someone had literally stabbed me repeatedly, especially when it came to issues with my children. This illustration may sound dramatic; but it is how I felt. Yet, even looking at it from a less emotional viewpoint and perhaps a more matter-of-fact view, it is easy to see how it undermines the fabric of society. God's ideas of marriage were not suggestions because He understood the trauma that it creates. How could the God of love and justice have any other thoughts towards something that creates such tragedy in the lives of His children?

Results of a Fallen World

The question often arises whether if God so clearly hates divorce, is it ever justified? Because we live in a fallen world with rampant sin and immorality, the answer is yes. There are definitely reasons someone should get a divorce. Tragically, there are cases where people who should get a divorce stay or literally cannot escape marriages where they or their children are physically and emotionally abused and are in danger. There are many reasons why they might stay, which could be because of monetary reasons, they don't see a way out, are too emotionally drained to leave, or, again, are trapped against their will, either physically or emotionally.

One might automatically think that these things only happen to women, but recent studies have found that of those who are victims of domestic violence, 40% are men (12). The study also tells how the media and police will often ignore these claims with men and not take them seriously. I know this happens with women, too, but this particular issue, as bad as it can be for women, can be even worse for battered men, as they are believed even less than women. Abuse of any kind, to anyone, is never acceptable, not ever, and no one should ever have to live in a state of fear, terror, and danger. In chapter eight, we will be going over this issue in great depth.

With all this said, everyone must know that God sees all, and He is always fair and just, even with the issue of divorce. The problem lies not with those whose divorce is necessary but for those who, like in Moses's day, wanted a law established allowing divorce for any and every cause, which sounds a lot like the no-fault law. When the Pharisees asked Jesus about the issue of divorce, he answered by saying it was ". . . because of the stubbornness and perversity of men's hearts. . ." (13) that Moses made allowances for such divorces. Yet, it was still not acceptable with God. Jesus stated to the Pharisees that ". . . whosoever shall put away his wife, except it be for fornication, and shall marry another, committeth adultery: and he that shall marry her that is put away, committeth adultery" (14).

There are many Scriptures like this in the Bible where Jesus makes some sobering statements that reinforce just how serious and sacred marriage truly is. Unfortunately, our society has diluted the sacredness of marriage to such a degree that I don't think most people understand the total capacity of the covenant when they say their vows. As I stated previously, when I said my vows, I believed in "until death do you part," but, again, I had no idea of what serious business marriage was in God's eyes.

Is Remarriage Permissible as a Christian?

Another area of grave concern is remarriage. I've heard so many conflicting arguments about this in both the Catholic and Protestant realms. I know what the secular stance is, which is to follow the law of the land. I also know the Catholic perspective. However, in the Protestant realm, I've heard some pastors say that divorce and remarriage is no problem, but I've also heard from others that you can get divorced, but you cannot remarry, so I wanted to know the truth.

However, before we dive into this section, I need to say that I had quite a lot of trepidation in writing it. I would never want to say anything that is not correct or talk about something in a book that I don't know anything about, especially with such a grave issue as this.

So, when it came time to write this, in addition to doing research as I will always do, I immediately thought of talking to a wonderful, traditional, and conservative priest, an expert in the teachings of the Church, and a dear friend of my family. This priest has been Heaven sent from God. He has been very instrumental in helping all my family, my children, and my healing from issues from my childhood, marriage, divorce, and many situations that have followed, and I believe his words will bring healing and clarity to many of you as well.

The Catholic Stance

After talking with Father, I realize how complex remarriage is, far more than I ever realized. I will start with the Catholic stance and then go from there, as I am most familiar with what the Catholic Church teaches about this issue and learned so much more after talking with Father.

First, we must start by clearing up the misconceptions that lead one to believe that divorce is permitted in the Catholic Church today and that remarriage also exists within the confounds of its teachings. You might wonder, "Well, if these are misconceptions, then why do I know practicing Catholics that are divorced and remarried?" and "Why does current Pew research data show a 25% divorce rate amongst Catholics?" (15). Still considerably lower than the national average, but high for a religion that does not allow it. These are valid questions, but, again, from its very origins, the Catholic Church does not recognize divorce. How then do we explain those, like me, who have gone through the civil divorce process, and by the world's standard of law, are divorced?

The answer to this can be explained in a process called an annulment. The United States Conference of Catholic Bishops define an annulment as "a declaration by a Church tribunal (a Catholic Church court) that a marriage thought to be valid according to Church law actually fell short of at least one of the essential elements required for a binding union" (16). What exactly does this mean? Well, the way Father explained it to me is that in a valid marriage, God does something supernaturally. Two people agree to get married, and then God takes over and supernaturally creates the sacred, "eternal and perpetual" marital bond. Once a couple is married in the Catholic Church, the Church will always assume that this bond was created until proven otherwise. Once this bond is made, divorce cannot break it; only death can do this, hence, "till death do us part." In the Catholic Church, a divorce is simply a form of words that lacks substance (17).

A person married in the Catholic Church must still undergo the civil process, and once finalized, the couple is legally divorced. But again, in the eyes of the Church, this civil divorce is not recognized. Therefore, unless they also obtain an annulment, they are still married in the eyes of the Church and are not free to even date, let alone get married.

However, the Church views other unions differently than those performed in the Catholic Church, and it can get a bit complicated. For example, suppose a baptized Catholic marries a baptized Protestant in a non-Catholic Church, or two baptized Catholics get married outside of the Church. In that case, even if it's by a minister, their marriages are not considered valid because they lacked canonical form (18). They lacked proper form because the laws of the Church bind baptized Catholics to getting married in the Church, and when they don't, the marriage is not considered valid, so an annulment is not needed if their marriage ends in divorce. Such couples would only need a declaration of nullity if they got divorced and wanted to marry again in the Catholic Church the next time (18).

Another fairly common situation is if a couple from one of the unions mentioned above decides later to have their marriage blessed by the Catholic Church, they can do so. By doing this, their marriage then becomes valid (18). An example of this is a situation that took place between some dear Catholic friends of mine. When they were engaged, they visited Santa Fe, New Mexico, and fell in love with it. They both decided to get married outside at sunset in the beautiful field they had discovered during their visit, and they had their hearts set on it. Yet, when they inquired about getting married from the priest at their local parish, they discovered that a Catholic wedding could only occur inside the church unless there was a legitimate reason.

According to Fr. Joe Krupp from the Cleveland Diocese, the Church mandates this because "as Catholics, we believe that marriage is a sacrament: a sacred moment given to us by Jesus. Therefore, when you celebrate this wonderful sacrament, we hold it in a space that is dedicated, sacred and consecrated" (19). For these reasons, all sacraments usually will take place in a church. However, despite learning this, the couple was unwilling to change their location, so they hired a minister to marry them outside in this field of their dreams.

Years later, the husband said he started to feel very convicted that he had done this and talked it over with his wife, who said she had felt convicted about it for quite some time but was afraid to say something. They both went to their parish priest to talk it over and were quite shocked to learn that all the years they were married, the Church did not consider their marriage valid due to the fact they were both baptized, catechized Catholics, and were married outside of the Church. Again, being baptized and catechized Catholics, binds them to follow the teachings of the Church in order to have a valid marriage.

Thankfully, instead of them becoming upset, it became a very healing situation for them. They both attended confession for this and then had the marriage blessed in the Church. My friends both said that they felt a tremendous weight lift off them that they had shoved down for years once they did this. Of course, getting an annulment brings this same freedom as well.

A Dissolution of Marriage in the Catholic Church?

In addition to having a marriage blessed to make it valid, there are also two rare exceptions to having an annulment, where a dissolution is appropriate instead. These are called the Pauline Privilege and the Petrine Privilege, or Favor of the Faith (20). These are not new in the Church, but they are not widely known and are rarely used.

Before we discuss these, however, it is important to keep in mind that an annulment determines that a marriage never took place, whereas, a dissolution/divorce, is very rare, and will only be determined in the Catholic Church in a valid natural marriage. As we've discussed, in a valid sacramental marriage, dissolution does not exist, as a valid sacramental marriage is for life, and cannot be dissolved, except for death.

The Pauline Privilege

With that in mind, the first of these exceptions we will discuss is the Pauline Privilege, which is under Canon Law 1143. It is named appropriately after St. Paul and is taken directly from 1 Cor. 7:12 - 15, which states:

> For to the rest, I speak, not the Lord. If any brother hath a wife that believeth not, and she consents to dwell with him, let him not put her away.[13] And if any woman hath a husband that believeth not, and he consents to dwell with her, let her not put away her husband. [14] For the unbelieving husband is sanctified by the believing wife; and the unbelieving wife is sanctified by the believing husband: otherwise, your children should be unclean; but now they are holy. [15] *But if the unbeliever departs, let him depart. For a brother or sister is not under servitude in such cases. But God hath called us in peace* (Italics mine) (21).

In terms of Canon Law, this means that if two unbaptized persons get married, their marriage can be dissolved if one person decides to get baptized and married to someone else because the unbaptized person has left them (22).

My first thought when I learned of this was to question why the Pauline Privilege was needed if the couple was not baptized when they got married in the first place? So, I carefully researched this and was surprised to find that the Church considers marriages between two unbaptized persons valid, if there is mutual consent to a life-long relationship, it is legally performed, and the marriage consummated. It is important to note, however, that they are considered natural marriages, not sacramental (23).

With that question cleared up, I could then understand the purpose of this exception.

And the best way I could think of to explain this, is to imagine that two unbaptized people get married, and neither are concerned about it at the time of the marriage. Over time, however, let's say the husband has a real experience with Christ, so much so that he decides to get baptized in the Catholic Church. After doing this, he is a changed man and begins leading a devout Catholic lifestyle, but, unfortunately, his wife doesn't want to go along. It starts to cause a great rift in the marriage, and she eventually divorces him because she cannot handle living with her now converted husband.

The husband is devastated for a while but eventually meets a nice Catholic woman and wants to marry. So, he goes to the priest at his local parish expecting the priest to tell him he needs to have his first marriage annulled. Yet, when the priest starts to inquire about his situation, he discovers that he doesn't need an annulment to get married in the Church. But, instead, he needs to fill out an application for the Pauline Privilege to determine if he meets the criteria to receive a dissolution of his marriage. Then, if the Church finds that he does qualify, he can marry his new love interest in the Church.

Some conditions need to be met, which are (24):

1. This does not apply to the husband or wife that becomes baptized. As the scripture says, the believing spouse must stay in the marriage if the unbelieving spouse is willing to stay, and they would not be granted this if they had petitioned the divorce.

2. This also does not apply if both husband and wife get baptized after getting married. In this case, the marriage needs an annulment instead.

3. The unbaptized husband or wife must leave the marriage or become so antagonistic towards the Christian faith that they can no longer live in peace.

4. The unbaptized husband or wife must be questioned to see if they want to be baptized or stay in the marriage and live in peace accepting the newly baptized husband or wife's Christian faith.

5. The dissolution only occurs when the baptized husband or wife gets married. Otherwise, they remain married to their original spouse (24).

The Petrine Privilege

The last exemption, The Petrine Privilege or Favor of the Faith, is also not very widely known and is rarely approved. Like the Pauline Privilege, it is based on The New Testament, but from St. Peter, instead of St. Paul. The Favor of the Faith determines if a marriage between a Catholic and a non-baptized person or a marriage between two non-Catholics, one of whom is baptized, can be dissolved by the Pope, which is why it's named after St. Peter.

Like the Pauline Privilege, these are natural marriages, but not sacramental. The differences between the two Privileges lies in the baptism status at the time of the wedding. The Favor of the Faith must be requested through the diocesan bishop, who then collects the required documentation and sends it to the Congregation for the Doctrine of the Faith. They then forward the request for the Pope to sign the favor if all the requirements are met (25). Like the Pauline Privilege, there are many conditions. A few of these are:

1. The petitioner did not cause the marriage breakdown, and there is no possibility of restoring the marriage.
2. The civil and moral obligations were fulfilled toward the first spouse by the petitioner.
3. The dissolution of the marriage must be for the good of the souls involved (25).

Tom and Susan's Story

Although I don't personally know anyone who has received the Pauline Privilege, I know a lovely couple, Tom and Susan, who received the Petrine Privilege. Their story is unique, and like meeting the requirements for the Pauline Privilege, it is pretty involved. Twenty-five years ago, Susan's husband passed away from lung cancer, and she suddenly found herself widowed after 33 years of marriage. The first three years after her husband's death were brutal, as she had to learn to live life without him. After the first three years of mourning, she was still feeling so lonely, so she decided to take a chance and put her bio on a dating site.

Several men responded, but one in particular, who happened to be Tom, kept reaching out via phone, and she found herself enjoying the company. After about a month of phone calls back and forth, Tom finally got up the nerve and asked her out. Susan was as nervous as could be. She hadn't been on a date since she was 15 years old, and that was with her late husband. But, as anxious as she was, she decided to meet Tom for coffee.

They hit it off even more in person than on the phone. Susan couldn't believe how comfortable she felt talking with him, and Tom was so pleased as well. They talked for hours, sharing many things about their current lives, families, and their pasts. Through the course of the date, Susan learned that Tom had been married two times before. Jokingly telling her, "I'm a two-time loser."

His first marriage was to his high school sweetheart, and he had two boys from that marriage that lasted 15 years; she learned his second marriage also lasted 15 years, but he didn't have any children with this lady. Being a devout Catholic, Susan also asked many questions about his faith and these marriages' situations. She found out that his first marriage took place in the Catholic Church, but his second marriage was performed by a JP. Like Susan, Tom had been raised and baptized Catholic but was at that time attending a non-denominational church, which did concern her a bit.

After the first coffee date, Susan knew that the relationship had potential, but due to his two previous marriages, she was concerned whether she should go out with him again. So, she decided to talk it over with the priest at her local parish. She made an appointment and met with him, telling him everything she knew and was open to his advice and guidance. After hearing the situation with his former marriages, the priest said he thought Tom would get both of his marriages annulled. He also found the fact Tom had been raised and baptized Catholic to be a good sign and gave her the go-ahead to continue dating him.

Over the next few months, they were having such a great time getting to know each other and enjoying each other's company. Susan and Tom hadn't felt this happy in a long time. They started talking seriously about having a future together, and it was at this time, Susan explained that as much as she cared for him, she would not be able to marry him, unless he got his marriages annulled. Tom really cared for Susan, too, so he was willing to start the process.

They made an appointment with the same priest Susan had spoken to initially, and right from the start, Tom felt comfortable with this priest.

Tom began working on answering the questions right away, as he really wanted to marry Susan. In addition to answering the questions, he had to ask for a baptismal certificate from his ex-wife, but she wouldn't respond to his requests. The priest and the archdiocese tried to contact her, and she refused to answer. He also had difficulty getting his witness statements, as it had been so long ago since he was married to her. However, the priest kept encouraging him that based on his circumstances, he had a good chance of receiving an annulment.

Tom completed the application and sent it to the archdiocese. The waiting time was difficult for Tom and Susan, as their future together had to be put on hold until they knew the results. Finally, Tom received the results in the mail, yet they weren't what they were praying for. Tom's second marriage didn't need an annulment because he was married in the Christian Science Church by an authorized minister of this church and the state, but, because both he and his second wife were baptized Catholic, the Church did not recognize this marriage. However, for his first marriage, he was denied an annulment. Needless to say, Tom and Susan were devastated.

The priest who had helped them was so surprised that the annulment was denied. He was willing to petition it for Tom and Susan, but at the same time, he was also retiring. So, he encouraged them to have the new priest do so instead and urged them not to give up, as he had also seen initial decisions overturned with further investigation.

After hearing the news, Susan called her dad in tears explaining that Tom was denied. Susan's dad had always been a wheeler and dealer, so he set out to see what he could do. Her dad started first by telling a priest he knew well about the situation. This priest asked if he could review Tom's annulment. Tom was happy to send it to him and hoped that he could turn the situation around. After this priest reviewed Tom's information, he, like the other priest, said that Tom had grounds for an annulment. Instead of turning it back in to be petitioned, however, he told her dad that the head of the tribunal at the time was known for denying all annulments, and he felt he could marry them in good conscience without doing so.

Since both priests who had helped Tom with the process, believed he should have received an annulment, Tom and Susan started to plan their wedding, and approximately three years after that first coffee date, they were married by a priest in the Catholic Church without an annulment.

Throughout their marriage, Tom renewed his devotion to his Catholic faith, and he and Susan became very active in their local parish. Susan, however, began to have terrible dreams and increasing worry that they had married in the Church without receiving an annulment. She spoke to many priests in confession, most of whom told her that she didn't need to worry because a priest married her, but the worry persisted. Finally, Susan dared to talk to Tom. He initially tried to assure her it was okay, but as time went on, he began feeling convicted as well, yet neither of them was sure what to do. They would be fine for a while, but then the nightmares and worry persisted.

Finally, Susan couldn't take it anymore and asked Tom if he would go with her to talk to the priest at the parish they now attended. Tom wholeheartedly agreed and wanted to go as well. They both had become very close with this priest and were very nervous about telling him. He was a very conservative, traditional priest, and they knew he would be honest and tell them only what was best for their souls and what was right in the eyes of the Church.

They set up a meeting and sat down and told him their story from the very beginning. They also shared the annulment application with this priest. Tom was able to add an essential fact that he didn't know when he originally completed the application process. This was that he had learned that his first wife was never baptized. She was raised in the Christian Science Religion, and this never took place.

As they had expected, and as painful as they knew it was for him, this priest could not condone their marriage in the way it came to be. But he was able to offer them hope in what seemed like a hopeless situation. First, he began telling them about the Petrine Privilege or Favor of the Faith. Then, he explained that due to Tom's wife not being baptized and other requirements he met for the application, he thought he might qualify for a dissolution of his first marriage from the Pope instead of an annulment. Perhaps the most challenging aspect for Tom and Susan was that this priest explained that they needed to live as brother and sister to continue receiving the Eucharist and being a Eucharist minister. And, Father explained that there was no guarantee that they would receive this, which could mean a lifetime of living as brother and sister if it didn't come through.

The waiting period was a challenging year and a half for Tom and Susan. They didn't know what their future held. There were times they felt they couldn't continue, but their willingness to sacrifice for the Lord and make the original wrongs right revealed their true and eternal devotion to living their lives for the greater glory of God.

Finally, after a very long year and a half, they received the answer they had been praying so intensely for. All the way from the Vatican, Tom was granted the Favor of the Faith. His first marriage met the requirements necessary to have his marriage dissolved. He and Susan were free to get married again in the Church, this time, without ever fearing God for how they went about it. Susan and Tom could finally have peace over this, and they both said it was worth all the sacrifices for the year and a half to know their marriage was finally, validly formed by God.

Three years ago, and 16 years from their initial wedding, they married again. They repeated their vows before God and their family and friends in a joyous, beautiful, and sacramental marriage.

Necessary?

I'm sure as many read this, you might struggle thinking this is nothing more than Catholic legalism, there was a time I would have, too. But, when you put it in light of the fact that someone's eternal soul could be at stake, it is a bit easier to accept. The Favor of the Faith is rarely granted to anyone, and only granted if all requirements are met. Tom met all the requirements, in particular, the fact his first marriage was a natural marriage between a baptized and non-baptized person, and in this case, perhaps for the sake of two souls, both Susan's and Tom's.

Clearly, Susan was concerned for a reason, and she knew she was being convicted by the Holy Spirit. When it is the Holy Spirit convicting a soul, God will give the Grace and strength needed to make tremendous sacrifices to act according to His will. When we find ourselves in such situations, it is so important to put them in light of eternity. This life is temporal, but eternity is forever.

It is not an easy path to follow the teachings of the Church or Christ in general. Matthew 7:14 makes this very clear, stating, "How narrow is the gate, and strait is the way that leadeth to life: and few there are that find it!" (26). And I have found that every time I resent one of the teachings, and decide to follow my way instead, it never turns out well, just like with the issue of birth control. Disobedience never bears good fruit. After a time of going my own way, I always find out that the teachings all find their root in Holy Scripture, and they are in place only with the good of our soul in mind and for the greater glory of God. We must constantly go against the tide of the world, if we are to live a life pleasing to God. Jesus gives us choices each day, saying, "I call Heaven and earth to witness this day, that I have set before you life and death, blessing and cursing. Choose therefore life, that both thou and thy seed may live!" (27).

What Exactly Is an Annulment?

With all of this said, what exactly happens in an annulment? As the definition above stated, it is an investigation to determine if God placed a bond on the marriage at the wedding; to determine if it is valid in the eyes of God. If the Tribunal (A Catholic Church Court of Justice) finds that it was not a valid marriage, meaning the marriage "fell short of at least one of the essential elements required for a binding union," (28) then this Catholic Court of Law would grant an annulment. Meaning, the Church determined that a marriage never took place, the ceremony did, but not a marriage, so the term "divorce" is a moot point (29). Also, this answers the question and misconception of remarriage. If a marriage never took place between two people, then there can be no remarriage. So, if the annulled person decides to get married after a civil divorce, the Church treats them as never married before.

On the other hand, if the Tribunal determines that the marriage is valid, an annulment will not be granted, and neither couple can marry again. Doing so is considered a grave sin; as the Scripture says, they would be committing continual adultery or fornication as they are still married. This ruling seems very harsh, and many people have turned away from the Church because of it and remarried elsewhere or become bitter towards the Church. Or they have gotten married outside of the Catholic Church yet continue to receive the Blessed Sacrament. Yet to partake in either of these is considered a mortal sin in the Church, which is a grave sin committed with deliberate consent and full knowledge that it is a mortal sin. If not confessed to a priest before a person dies, a mortal sin is so severe that it can lead to the soul's damnation, and it causes separation from God's saving Grace. As I mentioned earlier, following Catholic teaching is not easy, especially in our secular world. Yet, every single one of the teachings is designed to save our souls, let our communication to God stay open, and always allow our lives to be lived for the greater glory of God! Living in continual mortal sin, destroys this, as sin always leads to death.

However, as I say all of this, please know that I genuinely do understand the dilemma and the struggle. Being told you can never get married again is like receiving a death sentence to some, especially if you didn't choose the divorce in the first place. It can seem like a punishment, especially if it's not because of our choosing. This potential dilemma is one of the reasons why it is of the utmost importance that a couple enters marriage understanding as much as possible, precisely what is involved in saying, "I do." It won't guarantee that a marriage will last, but it would cause many more people to be a lot more cautious, myself included, if we understood all that we've discussed here before getting married. Unfortunately, too many don't understand the gravity of their decision when they get married, and I was one of them.

How Can the Church Decide?

I know this process can bring a great deal of skepticism if it's not fully understood. You might wonder how on earth does a mere mortal determine if God has bonded a couple in marriage, and how can the Church even claim to do so? How does the Church have the right to deny someone to get remarried or to have an annulment? Other misconceptions I've heard that cause skepticism in the process is

"Doesn't that make the children illegitimate?" and "The Church does it to make money." And "It's nothing more than Catholic legalism."

Addressing the children first, an annulment in no way makes a child illegitimate any more than having a child out-of-wedlock does. All children are planned by God. The annulment is about the parents, not the children, so it in no way does this. As far as the cost goes, it generally costs no more than $500.00 total, and the Church will work with you. For example, I only paid $20.00 per month, but once my annulment was final, the diocese dropped the bill, even though I hadn't even gotten close to paying it off.

I will address the Catholic legalism misconception with my own story below, but I can assure you, just as we talked about earlier, the Church doesn't have rules or teachings that are not Biblically based.

Making It Personal

Before I went through the annulment process, I wasn't aware that all of the Church's teachings were Biblically based, and I asked all these questions and was full of skepticism. I remember after my divorce, I resented even hearing about annulments. After all, I didn't want a divorce, so I thought, why should I have to go through the horrors of the civil process and then put myself through another invasive, and I assumed, a painful process by the Church? It upset me tremendously.

I spent hours looking for a way out of this by researching Scriptures that justify why I could get around it. I found Scriptures, such as the one I referenced earlier when "Jesus stated to the Pharisees that '. . . whosoever shall put away his wife, except it be for fornication, and shall marry another, committeth adultery: and he that shall marry her that is put away, committeth adultery" (30). And 1 Cor. 7:15, which states, "But if the unbeliever departs, let him depart. For a brother or sister is not under servitude in such cases. But God hath called us in peace" (31), both of which, I thought, justified me and freed me from my marriage in God's eyes.

My ex-husband's infidelity, and the fact he was pretty much agnostic and walked away from the marriage, I thought, proved that I was free and clear to date if I should please without going through an annulment. And, at this time, I had never heard of the Pauline Privilege that talks about the non-believer walking away. Needless to say, had I known about it, I would have known that it wasn't an out for me, as my ex-husband and I were baptized at the time of our wedding; he was in the Episcopalian Church, and myself in the Catholic Church, disqualifying our marriage for this anyway.

Yet, as time went on, I started feeling more and more led in prayer to get an annulment. It wasn't because I was dating, I had been so busy raising my four children and surviving to have time for that, except for two nightmare dates that scared me single, and it seemed like anyone I was interested in was either not a Catholic (a non-negotiable for me post-divorce), not a believer at all, or mysteriously disappeared as soon as I became interested, which I now realize was God's protection. But I started to feel deep in my soul a strong desire to finally be completely free, and I knew the Holy Spirit was leading me in this direction.

Finally, the desire became so intense, that I contacted the diocese and opened my official case, but when I first did so, I didn't realize I could seek help from my parish, and the questions seemed so overwhelming as I was so busy, that despite the desire, I finally gave up trying to finish it, hoping I would be able to start working on it at a later time.

Thankfully, the later time finally came. About six years ago, which was 12 years post-divorce, one of my best friends who had gone through an almost identical divorce to mine, told me she was in the process of an annulment and was being helped by a deacon in our church. She explained how much he was helping her, so I decided to make an appointment and open it back up again.

Right from the start, the deacon helped me to believe that I could make it through this and assured me that he would be there helping me all the way through. What started out to be something I was dreading became a tremendous source of healing. As I walked through my life with him during our meetings, for the first time I began to see so much of what I had endured. My eyes were opened to the dysfunction of my marriage, and for the first time, I opened up enough about it all to allow an outsider looking in to validate me in all that I had gone through and help me bring it before Jesus to let Him begin to heal me. He also helped me to face my shortcomings in the light of God's mercy, and, perhaps most importantly, helped me see what and who I still needed to forgive, including myself.

Perhaps one of the most healing aspects was when I was able to read all my witnesses' testimonies. I had to read them in front of a witness to ensure I didn't tamper with them, but their responses were the most validating of all. It was so painful to read them, but at the same time, their words echoed all that I knew to be true and had for years shoved down and refused to acknowledge. Finally, this annulment was bringing so many wounds to the light so that Jesus could really begin to heal me. And, the questions that started with my childhood, helped me to start connecting the dots in my life and begin to show me why I would marry my ex-husband when everything in my nineteen-year-old self, was screaming not to. All issues we will go into in greater detail throughout the remaining chapters of this book.

Once I answered all 100 questions and the witnesses' testimonies were completed, the Tribunal conducted a very thorough investigation into my life. In some cases, the Tribunal will call in an expert witness for further analysis of the information, which is what they did in my case. So, in addition to the Cannon Lawyers, a licensed psychiatrist also reviewed my case. Deacon also explained that a nun who lives somewhere in Europe also reviews all the cases in my diocese, and her input is greatly considered as well.

Although Deacon firmly believed I would be granted an annulment based on what we had talked about, he cautioned me that there was always a chance I would be denied. He made sure I understood going into this process, that if I was denied an annulment, I would never be able to date or marry again, if I wanted to remain a practicing Catholic. Yet, as heartbreaking as I knew being denied would be, serving Jesus as a Catholic Christian is my very existence, so I was finally ready to face the outcome, whatever it might be. Besides, through the process, the annulment had become much more about being free than about ever getting married again. Something I know was a work from God, not a place I would have reached on my own.

Most importantly, I knew I could trust the findings, as I had witnessed how deeply each case is investigated, and the complex process it entails. I have also learned from our family priest that the Tribunal

Lawyers literally take a vow to put their eternal salvation on the line for their rulings with annulments. A civil judge may get a hand slap or demoted if they make a mistake, but Cannon Lawyers are willing to put eternity on the line (32). There truly are no higher stakes, and I was amazed to learn this. Knowing this gave me complete confidence in the ruling they determined.

Finally, on April 17th, nine months after I began the process the second time, I was granted an annulment by the Tribunal. Although, I have had to swear to not reveal any of the findings and reasons for their determination, they had determined that a marriage did not take place, meaning, God did not create a supernatural bond between my ex-husband and I at our wedding. Knowing this, also validated that I always felt like my ex-husband had remained a single man, single in his thinking, despite the fact we were "married" for 18 years.

This showed me that I had been correct, and I find it difficult to put into words the freedom I felt to the depths of my soul. I was finally free, and I finally understood why the Church requires this process. What I once resented, I now understood to be a true gift from God. And should the Lord bring someone in my life again, I will be free to date, and even marry them with God's and the Church's blessings. That again, is true freedom! On a final note, if you are Catholic and civilly divorced, I cannot recommend enough for you to go through this healing process. Find out who in your home parish handles annulments and get started as soon as you feel ready! I know you will be so thankful you did!

What Is the Protestant Stance?

In the previous section, we talked so much about the Catholic Church's teachings. Throughout that discussion, it is clear to see there is a central authority that practicing Catholics are to follow in the Catholic Church. However, as I say this, not all do. There are some variations in the rules between the different dioceses and individual parishes. These variations are one of the problems that the Church is facing today. Like all religions and the world in general, confusion has perhaps never been higher, which is unfortunate. However, nonetheless, there is still a central authority that its members are to follow (33).

So, you may wonder, what this has to do with the Protestant stance on divorce and remarriage? And that is a great question that leads me to open this by saying that there is no central authority within the Protestant Church, which makes it almost impossible to provide any one set of rules. A Protestant might argue, the Bible is the central authority, and, yes, that is true, but the Bible is often interpreted differently amongst different denominations. My family priest explained that each church and pastor is where people seek spiritual guidance, and this pastor is the authority. With that said, there is no one set of rules people are to follow regarding divorce and remarriage (34).

As I mentioned at the beginning of this section, I have heard many different schools of thought in the Protestant realm. Some will say it's okay to divorce and remarry. But I've also heard that it's okay to get divorced, but not okay to remarry. Some churches make different exceptions based on the situation of the individuals. For example, the Lutheran Church will allow a divorce to the innocent party in the case of adultery. However, there is no specific annulment process or Tribunal a Protestant church member has to go to have this determined even in this case.

Father explained that many Protestant members follow the law of the land concerning marriage and, for the most part, have no problem with remarriage (34). This view might help explain why the divorce rate is considerably higher than for other religions. According to Pew, the Christian divorce rate for those who regularly attend church is 38% and jumps to 60% for those who do not regularly attend (35). Because there are so many different churches, many with conflicting views, it would be impossible to talk about what each one teaches. You would have to go to your pastor to talk about the issue of divorce and remarriage. I know that many Protestant pastors understand how grave divorce is and counsel their members well, and others simply follow the law of the land.

From a Catholic perspective, following the law of the land, can be troubling for our dear Protestant brothers and sisters. The Catholic Church considers the marriage of two baptized Protestants who are married in their church to be a valid marriage unless proven otherwise. Father also told me that baptism doesn't necessarily have to be water baptism, as there is also something called a baptism of desire (34).

Father explained that baptism of desire often occurs at an altar call when a person gives their life to Christ and becomes born again. He further explained that this type of baptism is often more valid than a water baptism that is not done correctly (36). It all depends on what God has done to a person. So, there are probably many Protestants that don't realize they are baptized. If a Protestant person who has been validly baptized divorces and then wants to get remarried to a Catholic, even though they are Protestant, they would have to have their marriage annulled first (36).

If someone has been baptized and married in a church, divorce and remarriage are especially troubling. One priest explained that divorce from a valid marriage, even outside of a Catholic wedding, does not remove the bonds God put there, even if the parties don't believe this happened (37). In God's eyes, it's there until death do them part. In Matthew 19: 1- 10, Jesus was asked about divorce and responded by saying:

> And it came to pass when Jesus had ended these words, he departed from Galilee, and came into the coasts of Judea, beyond Jordan. [2] And great multitudes followed him: and he healed them there. [3] And there came to him the Pharisees tempting him, and saying: Is it lawful for a man to put away his wife for every cause? [4] Who answering, said to them: Have ye not read, that he who made man from the beginning, made them male and female? And he said: [5] For this cause shall a man leave father and mother, and shall cleave to his wife, and they two shall be in one flesh.
>
> Therefore, now they are not two, but one flesh. What therefore God hath joined together, let no man put asunder. [7] They say to him: Why then did Moses' command to give a bill of divorce, and to put away? [8] He saith to them: Because Moses by reason of the hardness of your heart permitted you to put away your wives: but from the beginning it was not so. [9] And I say to you, that whosoever shall put away his wife, except it be for fornication, and shall marry another, committeth adultery: and he that shall marry her that is put away, committeth adultery. [10] His disciples say unto him: If the case of a man with his wife be so, it is not expedient to marry (38).

As I mentioned earlier, this Scripture is taken to mean that divorce and remarriage are only permitted on the grounds of adultery. However, the term adultery is also heavily debated and taken to mean many different things, which still leaves this grave issue with great confusion when there is no central authority to determine this (36).

Furthermore, I have only touched on the Roman Catholic and Protestant views, but it is of grave value to seek the truth about this issue regardless of your religious affiliation.

"The Truth Will Set You Free" (John 8:32).

As I write this, I want to say very clearly that I am in no way claiming to be an authority on this subject. I am only reporting what I found through research and talking to my family priest and what I have heard and learned throughout the years. Divorce and remarriage are grave issues, and cannot be taken lightly, they have the potential to literally cost someone their eternal salvation. In saying this, I'm also not claiming to act as God and make judgment on anyone. Still, I cannot stress it enough that if you are divorced and contemplating remarriage, please, go to your parish priest or pastor and seek wise counsel, seek the truth, pray about it as you have perhaps never prayed before.

Don't be afraid to talk to an authority on the subject that won't just tell you what you want to hear and tell you things to make you feel better. Deciding on something as important as divorce and remarriage cannot be about feelings but must be about finding the truth. I tried to provide much of it here, to really address what God says about marriage and divorce. Still, don't take my word for such a grave matter, go and seek it further with all that is in you. Hosea 4:6 reminds us how crucial it is to seek Truth, saying, "My people perish for a lack of knowledge. . ." (39).

And, please, know that I am praying for all of you, as I understand full well how difficult, painful, and confusing this can be. And when you have finally reached your conclusion, I pray your decision will lead you to what is best for your eternal soul and for the greater glory of God.

God's Mercy Is Greater.

After all we have talked about in the last chapter, while I hope not, some of you may be feeling heavy, concerned, angry, confused, or in despair. And, although God's views on divorce are unequivocal and unchanging, I think it is critical to express that it is not the unpardonable sin as devastating as it can be. And, as I say this, you might not be worried about divorce, but perhaps remarriage. Or perhaps through reading this chapter, you have concerns that your current marriage may not have been performed according to canonical requirements or adequately in the eyes of God to be a valid and sacramental marriage in the eyes of the Church. But, regardless of what our sins are, no matter how dark they might be, or you think they are, Jesus died to cover all our sins, even the sin of divorce and sins associated with it.

The best thing we can possibly do to overcome any feelings of despair and conviction is to run to God and pour our hearts out to Him. Let the Holy Spirit show you what areas you need to confess and ask forgiveness for, and then admit them to Him and ask forgiveness. If you are Catholic, go to confession, and receive the graces from this beautiful sacrament. Don't run from God if you are afraid, or not address a situation if you are concerned about it. That is the worst thing we can do. Adam and Eve ran from God when they tried to hide from Him in the garden. But God already knows every thought, action, or word we utter, so instead of running away, we need to run to Him with all our might. Of course, He doesn't like everything we have done, just as we don't always like everything our children do. Still, He promises us in Romans 8:38-39 that "neither death nor life, neither angels nor demons, [a] neither the present nor the future, nor any powers, 39 neither height nor depth, nor anything else in all creation, will be able to separate us from the love of God that is in Christ Jesus our Lord" (40).

Yet, if we stay in sin and don't bring it before God, we cut ourselves off from His healing Grace, and we cannot be set free. True repentance is a must and gift to us, and thankfully, we serve a God whose mercy is endless. God promises us in 1 John 1:9 that "if we confess our sins, he is faithful and just and will forgive us our sins and purify us from all inequity" (41). Proverbs 28:13 promises "He that hideth his sins, shall not prosper: but he that shall confess, and forsake them, shall obtain mercy" (42). Confession brings true freedom and allows God to work in our situations.

After my divorce, I knew I needed to go and ask forgiveness, even though I didn't want the divorce. But to start to heal, I needed to confess things I did that led to the marriage breakdown that I was aware of, and I have continued to do so whenever the Holy Spirit reveals things to me that I need to confess. I have struggled with feelings of complete failure and guilt that my marriage ended. I have felt extreme guilt over what my children have had to endure and have had to mourn the loss of our future's as I thought they would be.

"If I had done this differently" or "that differently," he wouldn't have left. I've struggled with pride and desperately wanting to hold on to hate and unforgiveness. I have repented profusely and endless times for these sins, often through gritted teeth, until Jesus could soften my heart enough to really mean it. I've had to repent countless times, too, repenting for saying terrible things, hurtful things, unacceptable things to my children about their dad and stepmom, and had to apologize to my children more times than I can count.

Yet through it all, Jesus always, without fail, shows Himself faithful when we cling to His love and mercy and trust Him, and when we run to Him to heal us through our repentance. Even when our faith is weak, He shows Himself strong. Repentance and forgiveness have brought tremendous healing in my life and continue to daily, and I am eternally grateful and humbled for Jesus' endless love and mercy; even though I know aside from Him and His Grace, I am unworthy.

Tom and Susan and the couple that had their marriage blessed in the Church also found freedom in repentance and making their wrongs right before God and the Church.

Bring It to God.

I believe that repentance is between you and God and a priest if you are Catholic, and true repentance isn't just saying you're sorry and confessing but turning from the sin and turning towards God. It will most likely take years to repair the damage divorce has done, some things will never be the same, but this is the first step.

From this first step, God can move in and start to heal and mend the damage we or others have done and even take a seemingly evil situation and miraculously make it work for good "for those who love him and are called according to His design and purpose" (43). So don't wait another minute to let healing in your life begin. I have found that Jesus shows us things we need to repent of in stages, and as He knows we are ready to receive it. If He told us all at once, I don't think we could survive.

Get alone with Jesus today and pour your heart out to Him. Repent of everything the Holy Spirit puts on your heart. Do it often, and then look to His unfathomable mercy and receive His forgiveness, knowing that nothing can ever separate you from His love (44), and He will never leave you nor forsake you, not ever! (45).

How Will They Know If We Do Not Tell Them?

My divorce was final at the same time I entered school full-time to pursue a Bachelor of Arts with a teaching license. One of the classes I was required to take for my degree was speech. Having just been through a brutal divorce, I decided to give one of my speeches on the subject. However, because I was at least 15 years older than all the students in my class, I wasn't sure how they would respond as none of them were married.

I spoke with them very candidly about the subject, from the no-fault divorce law to divorce statistics to the reasons why it is better to stay married if at all possible. One story I shared with them is the story of my grandparent's marriage. Their marriage was highly dysfunctional, to say the least. My grandpa had been a raging alcoholic until he was sixty, and my grandma endured many years of literal hell because of it. She had every reason to divorce him, yet it was when that was not acceptable.

Finally, at sixty years of age, my grandpa received a miraculous healing from Jesus from alcoholism. Because of this, they were able to spend the next 30 years traveling and sharing with anyone that would listen to all Jesus had done for them. They spent every evening on their knees, wearing their rosary beads bare, praying for their children and grandchildren, and sharing with others struggling with alcoholism what Jesus could do for them. God was faithful to their prayers and commitment to their marriage and greatly blessed the last part of their lives. Their excellent example provided a strong unit for all our family, and my grandparents were not only my heroes but my best friends.

At 92, my grandpa became very ill and had to be hospitalized, so we all visited him. When we arrived in his room, my grandma was lying up in the bed with him. I will never forget that despite all they had endured together, that day in the hospital, they were like two newlyweds. These two people, who by all practical purposes should not have remained married, sat there spending their last days, whispering sweet nothings in each other's ears. My grandparent's affection towards each other was the most beautiful display of marital love I had ever seen. Their love had endured the test of time, and their 64-year marriage ended as God intended, "until death did them part."

After I was finished with my speech, the response I received from my classmates was overwhelming. Of course, many of them had parents who were divorced, so their interest was understandable. But I didn't expect the gratitude they expressed to me for talking to them about how harmful divorce is and how marriage is supposed to be forever. Many of them said that this was the first time they had ever heard this information. Everyone had to fill out note cards, and the comments that meant the most to me were those that stated, "Thank you so much, we need this before we get married, so we don't want to get a divorce" and "marriage is forever!"

My eyes were opened that day, that the believers within the body of Christ must be vigilant and better at doing their part to educate the youth to try and help reduce divorce in America. As I've mentioned before, a significant thread that keeps coming up is the urgent need for Godly education on marriage and its associated issues. It is crucial that this happens, especially before saying, "I do." Our youth must understand that next to salvation, who they marry is the most critical decision they will ever make, and that marriage is not a thing of the past but a sacred covenant with God "until death does you part."

Chapter Six

"Before You say, 'I Do'"

I have been asked many times since the divorce, if I had to do it all over again, would I walk down the aisle with my now ex-husband knowing what I know now? Whenever I am asked this question, it's as if a movie begins to play in my mind. I picture myself walking down the long, narrow aisle of Sacred Heart of Jesus on my wedding day, dressed in my beautiful flowing gown, all 150 of my family and friends smiling adoringly at me as I continue in perfect step with "Here comes the Bride."

At the end of the aisle, I see my dashing groom, waiting there for me, watching me intently as I make my way down the aisle towards him as a single woman, owned by no one but God. It is the picture of marital bliss; you can practically hear the Hallelujah Choir singing... then it happens.

Halfway down the aisle, I freeze, unable to take another step. It's as if everything is suddenly in slow motion. The crowd gasps, and I hear them whispering among themselves. "What is she doing?", "What's the matter with her?" All eyes are staring right at me, yet I still can't seem to move. I hear a loud voice inside of me shouting:

RUN FOR YOUR LIFE! RUN FOR YOUR LIFE!

I look up at my now-pale-faced groom; the voice inside me continues. I slowly turn around, still in slow motion, and begin to run back down the aisle. Before me, I see pictures of my children appear. At first, the images are brilliant, beautiful, yet I notice that with every step I take away from my groom, they begin to fade. I run faster, trying to grab the pictures to save them, but it's useless. The further I run towards the door, the further they fade. I scream, "My children . . . save my children!" All that is left of the pictures now is a faint shadow; I can't make out their faces.

In horror, I slowly turn around again to face my groom; I realize that without our marriage, I will never have my children. My most cherished gifts from God, the very people I love more than life itself, will never exist if I choose to run from the suffering and adversity, I know that my future holds and that I know I will suffer at the hands of their father. Yet for them, for my four beautiful children, I will endure it all.

Taking a deep breath, I look up towards my groom and begin slowly walking back down the aisle. With every step I take closer to my groom, I notice pictures of my children start to appear. Once I have reached my groom, I can once again see images of all four of my beautiful children.

With this movie playing in my mind, the answer to "whether or not I would do it all again, knowing what I know now" has to be a definitive answer, YES! Do I wish I could have had my same children without involving my ex-husband? Absolutely, but I realize that without this marriage, they simply wouldn't be, and that is unthinkable.

Yet, the same people who have asked me this question are often uncomfortable with my yes. They pursue the questioning further by asking, "You believe you were meant to marry this guy after all he's done to you and the kids? How can you believe this?" And, I have to admit, that even knowing the four beautiful lives God brought out of it, I have struggled to understand all of the pain as well. Still, I know that all the suffering my children and I have endured is in large part due to my disobedience and my own willfulness.

As a perfect Parent, God warns us over and over in His Word, teaching us the right way to do things, because He knows that to do otherwise will bring us great suffering, and He wants only the very best for us. So, when we choose to go against what He tells us to do, the Law of Reciprocity takes effect, (This also works for good.) which means we reap what we sow, even if we do it unknowingly.

Unequally Yoked

One law God commands us very clearly in both the Old and New Testament regarding marriage and choosing a mate is He tells us, "Do not be unequally yoked with unbelievers [do not make mis-mated alliances with them or come under a different yoke with them, inconsistent with your faith] ... for what has a believer in common with an unbeliever?" (1) To do so is acting in direct disobedience to God's Word. I don't recommend even going on a date with someone if you know beforehand that they don't share your faith. No one goes on a date (at least rarely) thinking "this is the one." I certainly didn't, and even though I was cautioned by a good friend not to go out with my ex-husband, I remember thinking to myself, "It's only one date, what can it hurt?"

Yet, why even start something if it is clearly against the principles in God's Word? Following this alone will eliminate a large percentage of potential candidates. And, as with all God's commandments, He doesn't say this to keep us from someone we are interested in, rather, to save us from heartache.

One big problem I faced with this, however, is that during the time I met my ex-husband, I was not following the Lord, as I talked about in the previous chapter. I had been raised as a Catholic Christian though, and I had witnessed the struggles my parents had gone through by being unequally yoked, and chose to ignore them. So, when I was born again (a month after my wedding!), not being able to share the most essential part of my life with my spouse, my faith, made for a lonely road. It was difficult for him as well, and instead of bringing us closer, it served to tear us apart.

I'm Married to a Non-believer, Now What?

As we also discussed in the previous chapter, being unequally yoked is not a valid reason for the believer to separate. My parents were unequally yoked in their entire thirty-three-year marriage until my dad experienced a "death-bed-conversion" just a week before he passed away from lung cancer, but this issue caused a lot of heartache, especially for my mom. As Scripture states, the believing spouse can win the unbelieving spouse to Christ; yet there is no guarantee. I know a lot of people might overlook this issue while they are dating, thinking, my spouse will get saved once we get married, yet, as I say all throughout this book, I urge you never to marry someone, thinking you will change them and their beliefs. If we choose to marry a non-believer, we must be willing to accept the fact that there is no guarantee they will ever convert, and we must be willing to accept and live with this reality.

There are circumstances where it works, and the marriage is happy and thriving, yet that is not the norm. Marriage is difficult enough without adding this monumental difference. So, if you have a choice to not be unequally yoked, it's best to avoid it. To willfully choose to do so often results in a great deal of suffering and loneliness (attending church alone, raising the children in the faith alone, or not being allowed to, etc.). It also creates a plethora of other problems, especially if you are unwilling to compromise your beliefs for the sake of your spouse. Or, worse yet, they will cause you to lose your faith and fall away to become equal to them in this area. Sadly, I've witnessed this happening in many cases.

I was fortunate to have my mom's example to follow when I faced the same situation. Despite being unequally yoked with my dad, she stayed true to her faith. She always took my siblings and me to church, and our faith was the most essential part of our lives growing up. Because of her example, it never occurred to me not to do the same thing with my children. We were both fortunate that although my dad and my ex-husband did not want to partake in this part of our lives, they did support us in raising the children in the faith, but I have known of many circumstances where the non-believing spouse is not supportive of this.

As discussed previously, it is crucial that we know God's laws, thoughts, and conditions even before we start dating, and even thinking about marriage. To do otherwise, opens us up to a life of suffering.

Don't Waste Your Suffering.

If just considering being unequally yoked with my ex-husband, it is difficult for me to believe that my ex was God's choice for me, but one thing I am certain of is that despite my disobedience and willful choices, God upheld His Word and blessed me beyond measure with my children. They are very much part of His plan. He took something that satan meant for my harm, marrying my ex, and blessed me with four beautiful eternal souls.

As I say this, I don't mean to condone my disobedience. My children are simply an expression of God's love and goodness despite my imperfections. God promises to make ". . . everything work for good for those who love God and are called according to His purposes," (2) yet even with this, the price I have paid has been more than I ever bargained for, and unfortunately, my children have suffered and continue to suffer as well.

I've heard it said that a marriage is only as strong as its weakest partner, and I believe this is a crucial component in why so many marriages today fail. Too many wounded and injured people are getting married before they have had a chance to become whole themselves, with me being no exception. Like me, they enter marriage with no idea of who they are, let alone who their spouses are. Their understanding of what marriage actually consists of in God's eyes is limited, and they have unrealistic expectations without any fundamental knowledge of what a healthy God-Centered relationship should look like. Then, in this fragile state, they bring children into the equation and mess often believing the children will somehow fix everything. I certainly thought they would make divorce unthinkable, but how wrong I was.

It was in the intolerable suffering of my children because of the divorce and all that it brought into our lives, that I felt compelled to write this book. The thought of 50 percent of America's children suffering as a result of divorce was more than I could bear. My original thoughts were to write the manuscript exclusively about the effects of divorce on children. Yet, as I began, I realized that they can't and won't be helped unless their parents have strong marriages and the tools to keep their marriages thriving. It was this realization that led me to understand that, to truly help children and people in general and try to make a positive difference with the marriage crisis, it had to contain so much more, especially trying to convey Godly truths about marriage that I wish I had taken the time to learn before saying, "I do!"

Danger Zones

A good example to illustrate what it looks like when two people are fractured, and not at all ready to get married, is from an incident that took place one month before I said, "I do." I had gone dancing with a group of girlfriends over the weekend, and my now ex husband was infuriated. "You know I don't like you going dancing," he raged on and would not believe me that my only partners on the dance floor were my group of female friends. In his continued rage, he punched me on my upper arm, leaving a baseball-sized bruise.

Unfortunately for me, the bruise completely healed by my wedding day, and no one ever knew what he had done. Yet, even more concerning than his treatment of me was what was in me, or not in me, that I allowed someone to treat me that way. Then, worst of all, I turned around and married him a month later without giving it a thought.

As I've mentioned before, God in His loving mercy provided me with a truckload of signs and red flags, yet I chose to ignore them all. Many friends warned me not to marry him. They could see then that he didn't treat me right. Even without them knowing he had physically hurt me, they were always trying to point out how he constantly flirted with other girls and how critical he was. Deep inside, I knew all of this was true, but I didn't know how to leave and truly felt that I couldn't.

The biggest warning I ignored came from a very holy, Spirit-filled priest from Switzerland whom my family had known since I was pretty young. I had always dreamed of having Fr. Boyer perform my marriage, so when my "ex" and I were engaged, I immediately set up a time for the three of us to meet. The meeting itself seemed to go pretty well, especially considering my ex-husband was not Catholic, nor did he have any real belief system of his own.

A few weeks had gone by after the meeting, and I had still not heard back from Fr. Boyer. Being anxious to book our wedding preparation classes and the priest, I decided to call him instead. He explained to me that he didn't want to talk over the phone and that he would meet with me at his office the following day. He asked my mom to join us and specifically stated that he did not want my fiancé there.

When we arrived at his office, he was not his usual jovial self. He ushered us straight back to his office and practically ordered us to sit down. My mom and I exchanged glances, wondering why he was behaving so out of character. He sat down at his desk across from us, not saying anything and looking down. I was so uncomfortable that I broke the ice first and got straight to the point.

"So, Fr. Boyer, will you be willing to marry us?"

He looked up slowly from the desk, his blue eyes looking straight into mine. I again felt very uncomfortable. It was as if he could see directly into my soul. What happened next still never ceases to shock my mom and me both and has haunted me on more occasions than I would like to admit.

This little 75- to-78-year-old priest, whom I had always thought was the sweetest, kindest, most gentle man in the world, began literally screaming from across the table, pointing his finger at me while he spoke, shouting, "I will NEVER, I repeat NEVER, marry you to that man. If you marry him, he will make your life a living HELL!" And with this last declaration, he proceeded to pick up a half-eaten sandwich off his desk and throw it across the room.

I was pretty shaken up, to say the least. I couldn't understand what my ex-husband could have said that led the priest to this conclusion.

Trying to remain respectful, I proceeded, "Father, how can you say this?"

"I just know," he said, pointing his finger in the air this time.

"I don't think you're giving him enough of a chance, Father," my mom said, trying to intervene.

"I don't think this, I am CERTAIN of this! Maybe after eight months of intensive marriage counseling . . . but I don't think so."

"Father, I don't understand?" I said.

"You just need to trust me."

And that was that.

Yet, sadly, I left his office that day, not thinking I needed to reevaluate my marriage plans, but angry at him for yelling at us.

"How could he say such things?" I ranted and raved to my mom.

I know now that Fr. Boyer somehow saw into the future that day and was trying very hard to spare "his little daughter" (Something he called me.) from misery and heartache . . . yet in my willful, rebellious, teenage mind, he was just an "old fool," and I found another priest to marry us.

Know Thyself

Clearly, I was not in any state to get married when I did, and I refused to see what others were trying hard to show me. I had a lot of issues I needed to deal with and heal from before I could be a healthy contributor to a marriage. In addition, I was fornicating with my now ex-husband, and this sin, in particular, blinds us from seeing the red flags and warning signs both in the other person and within ourselves. I desperately needed to let Jesus heal me, and reveal areas of weakness in me, but I didn't have the wisdom at the time to even ask for this. We can't change or heal ourselves, but Jesus can and will if we are willing to walk through some of these doors to let His healing power come in.

Although we will be working with Jesus till the day we go home with Him to Heaven, specific issues have to be addressed before you should ever agree to join your fractured self with another human being in the Sacrament of Marriage. When I first met my ex-husband, I was in probably the most dangerous and vulnerable time of all of my life. I was sixteen, not following the Lord, and had decided to drink rather heavily despite the fact that I had suffered all of my life from the effects of my own dad's alcoholism. I had always been extremely shy and wanted to be popular, and I found out very quickly that alcohol helps you to lose your inhibitions.

In addition to taking up drinking, I was also suffering from a very serious eating disorder called bulimia. Since the age of nine, I had been a competitive gymnast, and my coaches had given me the nickname "fats" in the gym. I was far from fat; however, at my level, there was extreme pressure to be very thin. Because I am rather short, and I was very muscular, I didn't appear as thin as they wanted me to or as I wanted me to. When I looked in the mirror, all I could see was a squatty, large, "disgusting" person looking back at me.

The bottom line was, I had no business even considering dating at this time in my life. In just two years, from about fourteen and a half to sixteen, I had gone from being a sweet, eager to please Christian girl that my parents' thought was practically perfect, to an insecure, self-loathing, rebellious, partying, lying, bulimic mess . . . and the enemy wasted no time in sending me my future husband.

It's a Matter of Heart.

I dated my ex-husband for three and a half years before we were married. Dating a fair length of time was a good thing, but despite the three and a half years, we were still only 19 and 20. Also, during those three and a half years, neither of us did anything to identify our weaknesses and try to grow as individuals before entering marriage. I was highly blessed to have received a miraculous healing from bulimia when I was almost eighteen, so that was a huge blessing from the Lord and a significant step in the right direction. Still, I hadn't dealt with the most critical issue regarding my relationship. I had never addressed or even faced what in me allowed him to mistreat me, even while we were dating, and why I felt compelled to stay with him. The fact that he could be hilarious, a true life of the party, and had a way of always smoothing everything over should not have been enough.

What was wrong with me that I would proceed to marry someone who had physically hurt me a month before our marriage, blatantly flirted with other girls when he was with me, avoided spending time with me, was often very critical, didn't share my faith, and with whom I shared very little in common? I often wondered why he married me! We could use the age card as an excuse. Still, the bottom line is that I had more signs and insecurities than anyone should ever have. If we were old enough to get married, we needed to recognize that we had issues that needed to be addressed to have a strong, successful marriage.

As I discussed previously, my family and friends have asked me so many times since the divorce if I knew I shouldn't marry my ex-husband. I generally become somewhat defensive because I can't change it now, and again, as I also stated previously, I wouldn't have my children today. If I am being truthful, though, I always had uneasiness about him and being with him, even throughout our marriage, that I suppressed so deeply it was hard to identify what the feeling was after a while. I knew he shouldn't treat me the way he did, but I always thought he would change once we got married . . . not good! How many of us enter marriage thinking we will change the person we are marrying?

I cannot state it enough, (You will notice this!) that you never marry a person whom you view as a "project!" It is a very selfish, prideful act, and is not fair to the other person. We often have an unrealistic image set in our minds of how the person is or how we want them to be, completely ignoring the truth. Only God can bring about change in ourselves and others; therefore, thinking we can accomplish this will only lead to a life of discontent and frustration. If you believe your future spouse needs a great deal of change before you can be happy living with them, they are most likely not the one. During the courting stage, these problems are often subdued. Yet they are magnified once the honeymoon stage wears off, during the marriage.

Although I wasn't in touch with this emotion at nineteen, I also believe my self-loathing created a dangerous aspect in me that I subconsciously thought I deserved to be treated poorly. How we see ourselves can be the difference between whether or not we achieve our God-given destiny. I grew up with an alcoholic father, and I now realize I somehow felt it was my responsibility to make him stop drinking. I was the peace maker in the family as well, and because there wasn't a great deal of peace when my dad was home, I was not doing my "job." You will read more about these issues in future chapters.

The fact that I was bulimic, I believe, was due in large part to my gymnastics. Still, studies show a high correlation between being bulimic and having an alcoholic parent. Each of these issues began to create this self-loathing within me. I felt ashamed because of my dad's problems, and my thighs were too fat! If it weren't for my mom and her family's strong faith, which she passed on to my brothers and me, I'm not sure how we would have made it.

When I started dating my ex-husband, another factor that I mentioned previously, added to my self-loathing. Despite how wrong I knew it was, I began to engage in premarital sex. Whether I liked it or not, I was willfully engaging in a sinful act, and it was laying heavy on my conscience. Not only had I not listened and dated a non-believer, I was now sinning against God's Words in the Bible. St Paul in the letters of Corinthians clearly states, ". . . now the body is not for fornication . . ." (3). I believe what makes premarital sex so dangerous besides the spiritual implications is the fact that it subconsciously and sometimes not so subconsciously lowers your self-esteem and can create self-loathing as I believe it did in me, and it blinds you from seeing danger signs in a relationship, as I will discuss further in the next section of this chapter. God tells us that ". . . the wage of sin is death" (4), and I was reaping its consequences in the death of my joy and better judgment not to mention my soul.

Needless to say, this was a critical place in my life because I was not following the Lord, and I wasn't praying for his Will to be done in my life. I had left myself wide open for the enemy to annihilate me.

I remember sobbing, daily about six months before my marriage. My mom even kept telling me that I didn't have to go through with it, that I could cancel all of the wedding plans that she and my dad wouldn't care. But I thought the tears were from the fact that I was moving to another state right after the wedding, and it would be my first time away from home.

I got really good at shoving those little checks down deep, and before long I wondered if perhaps, I didn't receive them as frequently anymore. Hindsight has been a great teacher in my life, however, and has shown me now; I should have been listening not only to those around me but to God's prompting and my own heart that was desperately trying to warn me.

I can't urge you enough, if you have these same "checks" and warnings or others that are just as pronounced, don't rush into marriage. Don't rush in believing the lie that no one else will ever come along. As the saying goes, "fools rush in." Take a step back, get alone with Jesus, pray, fast, seek prayer from others whom you value for their Godly wisdom, and then wait and rest in the Lord and let Him lead you on the path to fulfilling your God given destiny. All the things I didn't do then, but now realize how crucial they are. And, throughout this book, you will see how Jesus continued to shed light into my life and began to slowly reveal deep seated truths I needed to learn in order to continue to heal. I pray, with everything in me, that this book will be used by Jesus as a vessel to do the same for you!

The Hook-up Generation

The first deep-seated Truth Jesus had later revealed was a better understanding of why premarital sex is so damaging. I knew God said it was wrong, but I didn't understand its full implications. We talked about the dangers of separating procreation from the sex act in chapter two. Still, because of the devastation I witness fornication having on our world today, especially our youth, I wanted to isolate this issue, and explain even further why God, in His wisdom, tells us to stay away from it, and to save His beautiful creation of sexual intimacy for the wedding night.

As mentioned previously, premarital sex, aside from the spiritual aspect, and besides the risks of STDs and pregnancy, is also very dangerous as it blinds you to the truths and even dangers that could exist in another person. Sex can simply cover them up. Being blinded by sexual intimacy is not just my own experience, but research proves this.

When we engage in sexual activity, our body releases the hormones and neurotransmitters oxytocin, often called the "love" hormone, dopamine, which produces feelings of pleasure and euphoria, serotonin, which regulates emotions and moods, and, finally, norepinephrine, which, like dopamine, creates feelings of euphoria and arousal. God knew exactly what he was doing when he masterfully made our bodies. All of these work together to help us bond and see our partner in a glowing light, which is excellent in a marriage. But in the dating realm, this can be dangerous, as it can skew our perceptions, causing us to overlook dangerous "red flags."

Premarital sex has always been a thing, but in today's world, it has become even more problematic, especially for the "hook-up generation." As a college teacher, I hear students say, "Dating means you have sex first, and if it goes well, then you decide to date." Not only is this spiritually dangerous to one's soul, it is physically and mentally dangerous as well. Women, especially, were not physically designed to have numerous partners. Women emotionally bond in the sex act, generally more than men, so when it is treated as a one-night stand, this fractures them emotionally and spiritually, even if they don't realize it, and the more sexual partners they have, the harder it is for them to be able to bond to one man for life.

Over the last decade, the Centers for Disease Control and Prevention (CDC) has found a 60% increase in depression and 31% increase in anxiety among adolescents and adults (5). Although there are numerous causes for this, based on how God created our bodies and souls, "hooking up" is undeniably a significant factor. Well-known Catholic speaker and priest, Fr. Jim Blount, makes the bold claim that the lack of purity and chastity in our world:

> is one reason the United States and, indeed most of the world, is crumbling to the ground because we must be chaste, all of us, priests, and people, men and women, adults and teenagers. We must be virginally pure. We have to return to sacred purity, as St. John Paul the Great said, 'Without purity, joy is impossible'. So we see in our country a depressed country. We have depressed teenagers and a depressed country because we are not chaste, and chastity and purity are a gift from Heaven (6).

Fr. Blount asks us to beg Jesus for a return to chastity in our world stating again that purity is joy.

We know Fr. Blount is simply stating what God tells us in His Word. The world promises us happiness in lust, self-sexual gratification, fornication, pornography, perversions of all kinds, and all things outside of God's Laws, but the current state of our world and marriage proves otherwise. A 2023 *PR NewsWire* report confirms this with the findings in their study which state that, "Sexually inexperienced individuals who have only had sex with their spouse are three times more likely to have a highly stable marriage than sexually experienced individuals" (7). To break this stat down further, they found that:

> Married men and women who have only had sex with their spouse have a nearly 45% chance of reporting a very high level of relationship stability in their marriage, compared to only 25% of married individuals with 5-9 lifetime sexual partners and only 14% of married individuals with 10 or more lifetime sexual partners (7).

You might say, this doesn't address whether or not they had premarital sex with their current spouse, but we have to look in the Word of God to know that following God's law and design of abstaining from sex before marriage are put in place to bless us and our marriage!

Surprisingly, even the secular world unknowingly agrees with God! In a National Library of Medicine study, they state, "Premarital sex predicts divorce, but we do not know why?" and further state, "We find the relationship between premarital sex and divorce is highly significant and robust even when accounting for early-life factors" (8). They state that it is a highly complex issue, but they readily admit they don't know why it increases the chances for divorce (8). But as Christians, we do understand, as God tells us over and over again, not to fornicate by having premarital sex. Research proves that not doing so is a great way to help divorce-proof your marriage, and a significant commitment to make before marriage!

God condemns self-fornication as well, which is rarely considered actually fornicating or even a sin. To not partake in masturbation contradicts our society's massive push for self-sexual gratification and exploration, but, again, God always asks of us what He knows is best for us!

The *Catechism of the Catholic Church* tells why it is a sin, and a mortal sin at that when it states:

> Consequently, masturbation is a sin against the Sixth Commandment, (Thou Shall Not Kill) because it violates the God-inscribed unbreakable bond between the love-giving and life-giving aspects of the marital act (see CCC 2366-70). Instead of the intimate and mutual self-giving that is the hallmark of the marital act, masturbation—and whether within marriage or outside of marriage—is an act in which one turns selfishly inward" (9).

And, further it states:

> Consequently, the Church has always definitively taught—and will always teach—that masturbation (CCC 2352) is 'an intrinsically and gravely disordered action.' And when committed with full knowledge and complete consent (CCC 1859), it is a mortal sin (see CCC 1854-64)" (10). (A mortal sin, if unconfessed, can damn you to hell.)

This act and having premarital sex with another person both seek to pleasure only ourselves, and fail to consider the eternal implications, and both separate sex from the life-giving gift God designed it to be.

Renewed Virginity

You might think, as I have, well, there is no way I can go back. I cannot become a virgin again or undo sins I have committed or am currently committing. Technically, this is true, but as a believer, you can repent and rededicate your sexuality to God and begin to live in sexual purity. If you are single, you can start to abstain until marriage, or remain celibate if you never marry or remarry. And, if you are married and are not living in sexual purity, you can commit to starting now.

Easy, no, possible, yes, with God's Grace only. Worth it, completely and eternally! Living in sexual purity in mind, body, and spirit will bring you closer to Jesus. If you give your sexuality to Him, He will help fill that void and provide the Grace to stay faithful. He will provide you with other outlets that are pure and holy. Jesus would not ask something of us unless He knew with His Grace we could do it.

Staying pure and abstaining from premarital sex is one of the best ways to prepare for marriage and is one of the greatest gifts you can give a future spouse. My brother and sister-in-law do Catholic marriage prep classes. Many, I might even say most, of the couples are living together when they start their classes. Part of the prep is to abstain from intimacy during the preparation, and wait to join together again, in the sacred and beautiful act from God, until their wedding night.

My brother has told me that most couples agree to do this and come back and tell him and my sister-in-law that abstaining was the single most powerful part of the preparation. It made their wedding night sacred, holy, and as if it were their first encounter with each other. Their feedback serves to show how beautiful marital intimacy is when performed according to God's design, the Creator of all.

I can speak from experience that there is incredible, indescribable freedom, peace, and joy that comes from living in sexual purity. No, it's not easy, and at times, it can seem unbearable, but it is at those times, you can bring it all before the Lord in prayer, and He will give you the strength to stay faithful.

Even if you are currently intimate in a dating relationship and not married or engaged, it is never too late to reclaim your virginity. I know it's scary, thinking *my boyfriend or girlfriend will surely break up with me!* Or, *I don't want to* or *I don't think I can stop.* I also know from experience that it is not easy, and it may be one of the hardest things you will ever have to do, but I've heard it said also that, "No one or no thing is worth going to hell for." I've also heard the expression, "The trash will take itself out," and that might sound harsh. But, taken in the context of true love, Godly love, it means you don't want to do anything to anyone, yourself included, that has the potential to send you or someone else to hell. Asking a boyfriend or girlfriend to do this, is a real test of whether a person is committed to God and doing what is best for you, or in gratifying themself. When I viewed it in this light, it clicked. I realized the world's view of love isn't love at all. True love, Godly love only wants the best for another and would never want to partake in something that jeopardizes eternity for our partner or ourselves.

Our Part

Once we give our sexuality to Jesus and ask Him to renew our virginity, we still have a part to play in being able to remain faithful to our commitment. We need to have a plan in place to hold us accountable for times we are tempted to fall into this sin, or it will be extraordinarily hard to keep this commitment. A plan I use for myself and highly recommend is as follows:

1. We must go to Jesus and confess our sins. For a Catholic, this means going to a priest for confession. Without taking this first step, we don't stand a chance. I've heard exorcist priests say that one confession is more powerful than an exorcism. Confession can literally break the power of sin off our lives.

2. Officially tell Jesus that you are rededicating your sexuality to Him if you are not a virgin, or dedicating it to Him if you are, and ask Him to use it for His glory. Write down in a journal or your Bible the date you do this, and look back on it if you are struggling.

3. Forgive yourself and others. Ask Jesus to show you the areas you need healed so you can avoid repeating and falling into these sins again. I highly recommend going to a priest and having him pray over you to break soul ties with anyone with whom you have had sexual relations or even an intimate sexual conversation.

4. All sin starts in our thoughts, and that is where the battle is either won or lost. You must replace the thoughts the minute they try to invade your mind with the Word of God or powerful prayers for spiritual warfare. Memorize Scriptures that you can speak out loud during times of temptation. Ask the Blood of Jesus to cover your mind and desires, over and over again, until the temptation stops. You can also pray powerful prayers, such as the Prayer to St. Michael, or St. Benedict's Prayer, which is also a favorite of mine and is very powerful. The initials for this prayer are engraved on a St. Benedict medal, and they are V.R.S.N.S.M.V.-- S.M.Q.L.I.V.B. The initials stand for the prayer in Latin, but the English translation says, "Begone, Satan! Never tempt me with your vanities! What you offer me is evil. Drink your own poison!" All of these are very powerful at thwarting the enemy, especially when spoken aloud.

5. Set aside time daily to spend with Jesus, in prayer, seeking His will, and reading the Bible and other prayerful books that will fill your mind and soul and provide protection from attacks from the enemy. Make it a consistent routine, so you form the habit of doing this. The Bible tells us very clearly in Psalm 119:9, "How can a young man keep his way pure?" By keeping watch [on himself] according to Your word [conforming his life to Your precepts]" (11).

6. Pray the rosary daily. Our Lady of Fatima told the little children that they must pray many rosaries and asked them to tell the world to do the same. It is THE weapon for this final battle!

7. Stay away from movies, TV shows, music, pornography, sensual reading material, videos, or anything else that sets you up for failure. You will never be able to stay pure by ingesting impure things.

8. Use Holy Water and wear other sacramentals, such as a blessed crucifix, blessed medals, or a St. Benedict bracelet every day.

9. Frequent partaking of the Eucharist at least once per week if not more. I suggest weekly confession. Frequently spending time in Adoration before the Blessed Sacrament. Weekly, or even daily, if possible, Mass attendance. These will greatly protect you and keep you strong in Spirit. They are our lifelines.

10. Take time meditating on the beautiful gift your virginity is to your future spouse and future children, and to God. If you already have children, this is also a wonderful gift to them, and your Godly example will speak more on the value of being pure than words ever could.

11. Set up boundaries within the confines of a relationship. Decide ahead of time what action with a boyfriend or girlfriend will lead you to fornication and impure acts, and draw that line ahead of time. Convey that to them as well, so they know from the start what your needs are to stay pure.

12. Be sure that you have someone who will keep you accountable—a good friend, sibling, parent, priest, or pastor.

I Gave It My All and I Fell.

Despite our best intentions and doing everything right, we sometimes fall. Yet, it is at this time that we must run, and I mean run, back to Jesus, repent, seek help, and do everything we can to get back on track. If we have backslidden for some time, we may need the help of someone else to help us get back on track, such as speaking with a priest or pastor, a Christian therapist, etc. We also must forgive ourselves and give ourselves grace, and then begin again.

The worst thing we can do is give up, run away from God, give in to a sinful lifestyle, and stop trying to do things God's way. To live in willful, habitual sin can lead us literally to hell. So, please, if you fall, know that God is not surprised or mad at you. He already knows anyway. He loves you just as much when you fall as when you are staying on track. He truly knows and sympathizes with how difficult it is for us to remain faithful. But, at the same time, He does want more than we can ever imagine, for us to run to Him and to try again, and again, and again! We have never failed unless we give up trying!

"With God, All Things Are Possible" (Mt. 19:26).

With all we have discussed in this chapter and the previous chapters, it is clear that a great deal of the work needed to try and divorce-proof a marriage begins before you ever say, "I do." The world's skewed view of marriage and sexuality is terribly disordered and in complete contrast to the way God intended it to be. The world's message has been loud and effective, which is why we have witnessed the breakdown of the family. That said, with God, ALL things are possible, and through conversion, prayer, good teaching, resources, and speaking out, we can all do our part to educate and change our world's view back to God's.

I think back to the students in my speech class who hung on every word of my speech on the no-fault divorce law, leaving me notes saying thank you for informing them of issues surrounding marriage and divorce before they are even dating, for some of them. As with so many issues that need change in America, marriage will change if the people who make up this country are given the tools, support, and courage to raise a standard and realize that it is God, not man, who created marriage! It cannot be redefined, changed, or made "modern." It is not a legal contract but a sacred covenant signed with the angels as witnesses in the Courts of Heaven.

The best divorce proof policy is doing what I did as a little girl and celebrate the fact that God will arrange for your spouse if you will let Him, let Him also show you areas where you need to be healed, learn all you can what God has to say about marriage, and make a commitment to do it His way, not the way of the world, so that when your flesh becomes one with your spouse, you are joining two healthy spirits that will be able to thrive together in the manner in which God intended and provide a home where both the parents and children can thrive.

What Should I Ask Myself Before I Say, "I Do?"

Although there are a myriad of questions and things to consider while you are praying for a spouse and once you are considering marriage, I have listed several things that are important to think about:

Before Meeting Someone:

- Am I putting God first?
- Have I prayed to the Lord to send me a spouse?
- Have I written a list of the qualities and characteristics I am looking for in a spouse and brought it before the Lord?
- What insecurities, hang-ups, and issues do I need to bring before the Lord for healing so that I can be a healthy contributor in a relationship?
- Am I striving to be a faithful spouse in my actions and words while I'm waiting?
- Decide ahead of time what your "deal breakers," are and don't compromise once you are in a relationship.

Considerations before Marriage:

- Are they a believer?
- Do you share a common faith and dedication to Jesus and the Church?
- What are their thoughts about sex?
- Pray to the Lord to reveal anything that needs to be exposed in you or the person you are considering marrying.
- Is this person responsible with their finances?
- Are they a hard worker and responsible for employment?
- Do they want children?

- Do they agree to raise your children in the Faith?
- Do you share many things in common and have common interests?
- Have they been faithful in actions and words?
- Have they ever physically hurt you?
- Are they emotionally abusive or overly critical?
- Does this person respect and value your beliefs and opinions?
- How does this person treat their family and yours?
- How does this person act around members of the opposite sex?
- Does this person have any destructive habits or addictions?
- Have you continued to pray and seek Godly wisdom?

Again, these are just a few to get you started. I highly recommend reading further than the pages of this book to learn more about what the Catholic Church says about marriage, contraception, and raising children. Many of these issues were discussed in the last chapters, but reading that should just be the beginning.

If you haven't met someone yet, use this time of waiting to work on becoming as healthy, spiritually, emotionally, and physically as you can. Once you're engaged, be sure you find a good marriage prep program. Contact your parish or church, as they will help you with this. As said previously, it is uncanny that with one of the most important decisions in life, there is often very little preparation put into it beforehand, and this has to change.

The bottom line is; however, we are all flawed people, and nothing will be perfect, but if you make Christ the center of your relationship, follow His blueprint and design, you stand a much greater chance of finding the mate He has for you, and having a beautiful, sacramental marriage that will last "until death do you part."

Chapter Seven

"The Broken Promise"

I think suffering through a divorce is similar in some ways to what we will face at the end of our lives. This comparison might sound strange. But I have heard many people who have experienced near-death encounters say they see their whole life flash before them as if it is on a movie screen. Some parts reflect moments of great joy and happiness, while others, let's just say, are moments in time we would like to forget and never have to remember.

I spent at least a year or two, maybe more, replaying my life with my ex-husband over and over again after my divorce. The "movies" would play continually, and now even 20 years out, while very infrequently, I still do this from time to time. My emotions are on a roller coaster when these "movies" are playing. I swing from experiencing moments of the most intense anger and hatred to heart-wrenching sadness to feelings of utter rejection and failure, guilt and remorse, and happiness and joy, especially the memories with our children.

This chapter of the book has been one the most difficult for me to write, for several reasons, one being that it has forced me to revisit areas that I would just as soon forget. Yet it was important for me to write about them, because I want you, the reader, to know that I understand, and I hope you will find validation through these chapters.

Although I know there are millions out there who have suffered much greater circumstances than I could ever imagine, I have lived through pain and hurt caused by a dysfunctional marriage and going through a divorce. I have lived it personally, and it is out of this pain and the pain of so many others that I am passionately committed to trying to help stop, or at least reduce, this insanity. I have spent many nights crying to God to use me and my life to help others. I don't mean to sound dramatic, but I want to make a difference on a larger scale by affecting marriage and divorce in our nation. I want to be on the frontlines of this final battle. The effects it has on our youth and future generations must improve.

While I say this, I have a grave responsibility not to hurt anyone with my words. That includes my ex-husband and especially not my children. As with any divorce, there are always two sides to every story. Although I didn't want a divorce, I, too, had a part in the breakdown of my marriage. Therefore, I have had to accept responsibility and deal with guilt and remorse over my actions that were not favorable during my marriage and in my dealings afterward. I remember hearing once that even if you only had 10% of the responsibility, it is this percentage where you must place your focus. You can't change another person, but you can work with God to fix this portion of yourself.

One thing I am sure of: without forgiveness, healing and restoration cannot come. It is so important that I felt the need to dedicate a large section to it later in this book, and I will revisit it in most chapters. God, in His mercy, has dealt with me repeatedly about the power and necessity of forgiveness. It is a continuous process that I struggle with and have to choose daily. I often remind myself of the mercy and forgiveness God has given me, even though I did nothing to deserve it.

As I take you on a journey into a small glimpse of my life, I hope it will fill you with faith and hope that there is light at the end of the tunnel. And that your life, no matter what you have been through or how deep a pit you feel you're in, can turn around and be something beautiful if you give it to God. One of my favorite Scriptures in the Bible is Romans 8:28 (I mention it often!). This verse says, "And we know that to them that love God, all things work together unto good, according to His purpose . . ." (1). I humbly pray that Jesus, in His Grace, will use this book in its entirety to bring healing and life to marriages, families, and all who read its pages.

A Glimpse into My Life

When I reflect on my marriage, I remember that the first two years were really great. Right after our June wedding, we packed up a U-Haul with our meager belongings. Then, we headed to Santa Barbara, California, to begin our new lives together. My ex-husband was registered to attend college there in the fall. So, we left early to get settled in our condo, so I could start working at a local travel agency in July.

Along with the excitement of a new marriage, moving to California also made me realize one of my biggest dreams of one day living by the ocean. The condo we rented was less than a block from the beach, so I felt like my childhood dreams were coming true.

Because we were just nineteen and twenty, neither of us had ever lived away from home or our families or friends. For the first time in our relationship, all we had was each other. I believe this is mainly why our marriage was better during this time. We looked to each other more, and less to friends and family around us, to meet our needs. We were in a new environment, wholly separated from our old lives, which freed us to begin making a new life together.

Just about a month into our marriage, I experienced another event that would change my life forever. I was raised in a devout, Catholic, Christian home. Still, as I mentioned earlier, I had not been serving the Lord for several years. I had to go out of town to Dallas, Texas, for a week of training on the American Airlines computer program for my job with the travel agency. I remember the week being tough. I had left my brand-new groom in Santa Barbara, my family was home in Colorado, and I was utterly alone for the first time. I struggled to make it through the week. Not only was the training very intense and challenging, but I also didn't like how vulnerable and alone I felt.

Although the training was excellent, the week couldn't have ended fast enough. I remember wanting to run onto the plane to get home and hoped I would sleep to help speed the process of getting there. Thankfully, just as I generally do, I dozed off to sleep the minute the engines started. However, when I awoke halfway into the flight, I felt disappointed that I hadn't been able to sleep longer. So, to try and help pass the time, I began writing in my journal. I wrote about all of the loneliness I felt, my fears and insecurities about starting a new life, and how even though I was happy to be married and living in Santa Barbara, I really missed my family.

As I continued writing, I was suddenly overwhelmed with a presence that filled my entire being. It was as if this presence I couldn't see had immersed me in and filled me with the most intense love, like nothing I had ever felt. I was so overwhelmed, and it was so intense that I began to sob uncontrollably.

The gentleman beside me was trying hard not to look at me, and I was so embarrassed that I was crying like this, yet I couldn't stop the tears if I tried. I never heard a voice speak to me to confirm this. Yet, I knew at that moment on an American Airlines flight from Dallas to Los Angeles that the Holy Spirit had just done a miraculous work in my life. Without even asking, I had become born-again. Jesus had come into my life in a way that I still don't understand today, and I would never be the same person again. I boarded the plane as one person and exited as a new creature in Christ.

When I arrived in California, I didn't share this experience with my ex-husband. Although I knew I was a new person and knew that Jesus was now living in me, I wasn't sure he would share my enthusiasm. He was not a believer, so I was afraid to tell him. Besides, I didn't even understand what had happened to me enough to be able to explain it. However, after this happened, I did start going to church again, and little by little, he began recognizing the change in me. I wish I could say he felt it was a positive change and wanted to join me.

Unfortunately, because of my upbringing, we were unequally yoked at the time of our marriage. But after this, it began to create a chasm between us. And this chasm would only continue to grow and be a source of conflict and separation between us for the rest of our eighteen-year marriage.

After being extremely homesick for six months, I finally started to feel better. I began to love California as much as I always knew I would. My childhood fantasy of living by the ocean had come true. And for the next two and a half years, I lived less than a block from the beach and was there as much as my work schedule would allow me. I was also in love with my ex-husband, Jesus, and our lives there. I had a good job, made great friends, thoroughly enjoyed my new church, and never wanted to leave.

With all that said, I've heard the expression that love is blind. As I look back over this time, I realize that I was blind to red flags already surfacing. Such as he was gone most of the time even then. He would choose to study at his buddy's house instead of ours, knowing I was often home alone, among other things.

However, I didn't let it bring me down. Instead, I would fill the time he was gone going to a Bible Study. On weekends, I would spend hours swimming in the ocean with the sea lions, praying and talking to Jesus. I didn't let myself acknowledge his absences and would rationalize them, making excuses for him. I loved living in California and hoped we would make a life together there.

On the other hand, my ex-husband wasn't nearly as enthralled with California as I was. He didn't like living there and wanted to move back to Colorado as soon as he received his schooling. He said he just couldn't live in a state where sand got on everything. His loathing for sand makes me laugh, but as I reflect on this, I realize there was no discussion about it. He decided he wanted to move back and started making plans.

I cried, telling him I didn't want to move back. Still, he insisted we had much more opportunity in Colorado for our future than in California, and he was probably right about that. He then told me to start applying for jobs as well, and once I had a job secured and he had finished as much schooling as he wanted, we were "out of there" as he put it!

He sent me and our cat Lollipop back on a flight to Denver a week before him, so I could begin working at my new travel agency job. My parents had put a down payment on a condo for us. And, within no time, we were once again living in our native Colorado and back in our hometown. I have often wondered if our lives would have turned out differently if we had stayed in California. But as fate had it, we moved back, and I guess I will never know.

Old Habits Die Hard.

As the saying goes, "old habits die hard," and my ex-husband was no exception to this rule. All his friends were thrilled that their "long lost buddy" had finally come home. They didn't waste a minute occupying all of his time. In California, I shared him with his college buddies. He worked every weekend in addition to going to school, yet this was different.

In Colorado, I soon became a weekend widow to his friends, and in addition, he took night jobs during the week. Granted, we desperately needed the money as we lived on this part-time income and my meager wage at the travel agency. He was trying to start a business, yet it didn't change the fact that I was always alone unless I was working or with my parents.

Things became so rough during our third year of marriage that I talked to a family priest (not the one who had warned me not to marry him). I desperately needed counseling. I knew things were not at all okay. We were not getting along, and he was literally never home. I wanted out of my marriage at this time, yet I couldn't find a place in me morally where I thought it would be okay. I didn't believe in divorce, but I didn't want to live like this either.

The priest talked me out of divorcing, explaining that the third year was often rough. He explained that the "honeymoon" was over generally by the third year, and reality sets in, making for a difficult transition. However, he assured me if I kept praying and loving him, we would make it even if he didn't love me back.

I took this priest's advice and went home, determined to make my marriage work. But unfortunately, despite my efforts, my ex-husband didn't start being home more or spending more time with me. He seemed much more like a single guy than a married one. Yet still, I truly believed it would get better.

Lifelong Dream Comes True

Two years later, we welcomed our first baby, which was the most miraculous moment in my life. When I was a little girl, people would ask me what I wanted to be when I grew up, and I would always say, "A mommy." They would repeat the question, "No, what do you want to BE?" In my innocence, I would think they didn't hear me the first time, and I would repeat myself, "A mommy." My career choice may not have seemed wildly ambitious to some, but on this day, my biggest lifelong dream had come true. I thought I had surely died and gone to Heaven when my precious little boy was laid in my arms.

I enjoyed being a mom so intensely that I couldn't wait to have more. So, two years later, our second child was born, another beautiful baby boy! When our first child was born, I started working for the travel agency out of our home. Yet, when our second was born, we made a mutual decision for me to quit work and invest my energies full-time into being a mom. I was so thankful that my ex-husband supported this decision.

This united decision made me hopeful for a positive change in his behavior. I had convinced myself that having our children would make my ex want to be home more. But unfortunately, the situation only worsened. I couldn't understand why someone wouldn't want to spend time with a family that loved them. I continually cried to him to please spend more time with us, but it seemed to fall on deaf ears. He seemed to like the idea of having a wife and children. Still, he did not show interest in actually experiencing it.

Thankfully, the pain of his absence wasn't as bad as before the kids were born. Now, I had them, and they had me. They and Jesus were indeed my refuges. We did everything together, and despite his absence and my sadness that he didn't seem to care whether he spent time with us, my two precious little boys and I lived very happy lives. Each day was a new adventure, and despite the problems in my marriage, I was a stay-at-home mom and living my dream.

Change Is One Thing We Can Count On.

When our second oldest son was two and a half, my ex-husband took a job traveling with a major phone company sponsoring the Rolling Stones Come back tour. I didn't want him to take the job because it meant he would not only not be home but would now be out of town for ten-day stretches, home for two, and then back on the road for ten for over eight months. However, he insisted that it was an opportunity of a lifetime that he couldn't turn down. The pay was excellent, and he thought it might lead to other, more permanent options, so he was adamant about taking the position.

In addition to this significant change, right before he was scheduled to leave, I discovered I was pregnant again with our third! I'm sure this begs the question that if he was already so uninvolved, why would I continue having children with him? I honestly don't know the answer to this, except perhaps I had grown up in dysfunction, and as hard on me as it was, I was used to functioning in dysfunction. It was customary and comfortable for me. Also, despite my marriage issues, I was getting to live my childhood dream of being a mom. That part of my life was absolutely glorious. I adored being with my children, and having more little angels to spend time with, was always a welcoming idea. And, I married for life, so despite it all, I didn't let divorce enter my thinking.

So, the discovery of a new little one on the way made me not want him to take the job more than ever, but he had already committed to the company, so off he went. I remember crying and crying. I think in addition to the realization I would be on my own more than ever, my spirit sensed the dangers that lay ahead for our marriage that was already dysfunctional and vulnerable to anything satan wanted to bring.

As the tour progressed, he became even more detached from our lives. The kids and I were living our lives, with a new baby boy growing in my womb, and he was living his life in a concert every night in a different city. I was mentally living a married life, and he a single one.

When he came home, he didn't want to be with us. Instead, he wanted to be with the new friends he was working with, and one of them happened to be an attractive female.

He had always been flirtatious with other women, but this one was different. I remember waking up in the middle of the night in cold sweats one night, trying to reach his hotel room. Over and over, I dialed the number, crying and sobbing the whole time. I couldn't prove anything, but I genuinely believe the Holy Spirit gave me confirmation about what he was doing. Finally, at four a.m., he answered his phone and had no excuse for why he hadn't answered. He could have been sleeping, but I could tell from his voice he had not.

Many other signs, including excessive phone calls to her number, confirmed that he was more than likely having an affair with this woman. I remember lying there one night on my living room floor, my pregnant belly swelling, feeling like I was being stabbed from the pain. The rejection, pain, and hurt were more intense than anything

I had ever experienced, and I genuinely felt like I was going to die. The worst part was that I knew the baby in my womb could feel and experience it all. I couldn't bear to think my emotional state was causing him to form in such a state of utter rejection.

Life with the "White Picket Fence"

Through all of this, I continued to believe and pray diligently that my marriage would get better. I now had three little boys with no way to support us and had to make my marriage work. He never admitted to having an affair with this woman. Through God's Grace, our marriage managed to survive this tsunami, with the next three years being the best years of our marriage. Through God's Grace, I could also trust him somewhat again, but I made a vow to myself during this time that I would never let a person take me to such depths of despair again.

After this disaster, I believe my ex-husband, for the first time except for perhaps our first two years, was trying hard to have a good marriage. During this time, we sold our little 1000-square-foot house in town and purchased a brand-new home in the country. It was indeed a magical time in my life. Although he was still gone almost every night, he would at least come home for dinner to spend time with the kids before returning to the office. So finally, I resorted to the fact that this was my life and had made peace with his absence.

A time that stands out as being particularly good was when we first started landscaping our new home. We bought the house as much for its large 1/3 of an acre yard as we had for the house itself. We both agreed we wanted a large yard for the boys to play in. We also knew that landscaping a yard this size would be costly, so my ex-husband decided he would plant the grass from seed. He had worked in landscaping when we were younger, so I felt confident in his ability to take on such a big feat.

It was quite a production, but one that I loved to observe. My ex-husband had rented a small tractor. Every night for a week, he and "his boys" would hop on and begin to till the ground, preparing it for planting until sunset.

Because we were the first family to move into the neighborhood, not many houses were built yet to block the incredible view of the mountains. And the beautiful August sunset's brilliant pink and orange colors never ceased to amaze me. I would sit outside watching my four men working so hard, all with smiles in tow, until the colors in the sunset faded. I was filled with joy, believing that my prayers were finally answered. I was blessed with a wonderful husband, three beautiful boys, and a house with the "white picket" fence. In my mind, everything I had ever dreamed of had come true.

Just after two months of being in the house . . . you guessed it; I was pregnant with our fourth! Despite the HUGE surprise, we were both genuinely happy. I was in a different state than when I was pregnant with our last child. I remember fighting feelings of guilt that our poor little boy was formed in such a state of turmoil. Yet I was so thankful that this baby would not have to endure the same situation and would be born into a happy, healthier home.

In August of the following year, our little GIRL was born! I hadn't taken a peek because I didn't want to be disappointed if the ultra-sound was wrong, so when my first and only little girl was born, I couldn't quit crying! God was blessing me abundantly; I could barely take it all in. My marriage was much stronger; we had four beautiful and healthy children and a new house. I was sure it would only get better from here.

Pie Crust Promises

Unfortunately, these were the last good years we would experience as a family. Six months after our daughter was born, my ex-husband's absences began to increase again. It had never improved as much as I would have liked for it to, but I was willing to take what I could get for the sake of my family.

When our daughter was three, my ex-husband's attitude started changing even more. He was becoming increasingly short with me and didn't seem like he much enjoyed being around me again. He said his business wasn't doing as well as usual, so I assumed this was why. He had always supported me in being home with the kids full time. Yet, he was suddenly hounding me to get a job and telling me we needed to downsize our house and think about selling.

I could understand him wanting me to contribute, but selling the house? Selling our new home didn't make sense. We had gotten a super deal on it and wouldn't be able to find anything even close to comparable. So, to save money, he also let me know about this same time that he was going to have his cell phone bills sent to the office so the company could pay them.

Hindsight has shown me he was setting himself up to leave me. But I didn't let divorce cross my mind, especially given we had four children. So, I happily buried my head in the sand, telling myself that all these signs meant nothing except that he was doing what he said, trying to find ways to save money.

On June 6, the day of our eighteen-year marriage anniversary, my ex-husband, seemingly out of the blue, informed me he wanted a divorce. I knew something was wrong for quite some time, but he wouldn't open up to me. Finally, on our anniversary, I confronted him, and the only answer I got was, "We'll talk when I come to bed." Right after this, I went to my bathroom and washed my face for the night, crying to God that I was distraught that something was terribly wrong with my marriage, begging Him for an answer.

The answer came as I leaned over the sink to rinse the soap from my face. I heard God's audible voice tell me, "Anna, I'm doing a work in him; you've asked me for it." The voice was so loud that I almost hit my head on the faucet and immediately pulled away from the sink, stumbling backward, saying, "God is that you?"

I didn't hear another word that night, but what I heard made sense. My ex is not a believer, and my family and I had prayed for his conversion for years. I could not share my faith with him, yet I never stopped praying for the opportunity to be able to do so. For quite some time, I thought this word from God meant that we would reconcile. Still, I understand it to suggest that this "work," whatever it might be, will be done between him and God, with us leading separate lives.

This night, the night of our 18th anniversary, was when everything came crashing in, and he had broken his promise "until death do us part." I had become so good at "seeing things as I wanted them to be" rather than how they were. My ex-husband's "overnight" decision to divorce me was a complete shock, turning my life upside down and shattering my dream of ever after. From this day forward, my children and I have had the ride of our lives, facing the final battle firsthand.

God promises in His word that, ". . . your sin will find you out (2), and Mark 4 states, "[22] For there is nothing hid, which shall not be made manifest: neither was it made secret, but that it may come abroad" (3). The Scriptures certainly rang true in my situation. It became apparent right after our separation that my ex had been having an affair for quite some time.

They didn't waste any time getting the ball rolling. They were engaged one month after our official separation and married two months after our divorce was final. Yet, despite this glaring evidence, my ex would never admit that he had been having an affair. Instead, when I confronted him, he would say, "You just cannot accept that I just couldn't stand being with you and had to leave because of you, not because there was anyone else." And it wasn't enough to divorce me. He and his new wife proceeded to petition what seemed like endless child and family investigations and court litigations, lasting eight long and traumatic years, that I will go into more depth about in the next chapters.

I am fully aware that the only reason I have survived, and the kids have come out as well as they have despite often very adverse circumstances is from the boundless, unmatched love, support, and generosity from my family and God. We would have never made it, at least not well, without this love and support. God is faithful to His Word. He has hidden us under the shelter of His wings. We had to live day-by-day, fully trusting Him, and God always proved Himself faithful! He is our Provider, our Refuge, our Comfort, our Strength, our Shield, and Protection . . . our Savior in every way, and he is yours, too!

If you haven't already, reach out to Him, believe with me that He will turn "all of our ashes into beauty," and He promises all provisions for those who put their trust and hope in HIM! A man or woman, father or mother, may have failed, abandoned, rejected, abused, hurt, and mistreated you, BUT GOD NEVER will! He will turn our messes into miracles if we give them to Him. My life is a living testimony to this. I pray that my story provides validation to any of you who have suffered this path, and that it shows you that it is not you; you are never alone, and God will see you through if you ask Him to.

Chapter Eight

"Sleeping with the Enemy"

A beautiful poem often used as a wedding prayer describes the shelter, safety, and security that marriage was intended to provide to those who partake in its sacred union, saying:

> Now you will feel no rain,
> For each of you will be a shelter to the other . . .
> Now you will feel no more loneliness,
> For each of you will be a constant companion to the other.
> Now you are two bodies,
> But there is only one life ahead of you. . .
> enter your days of togetherness (1).

As I reflected on this beautiful prayer, the verses that stood out most are, "for each of you will be a shelter to the other," and ". . . Now you will feel no more loneliness" (1). These verses really stood out to me as precisely what God intends for marriage to be! He intends it to be a "warm shelter," providing life-long companionship for His people to enjoy on this earth; a beautiful gift, a provision of safety and security for nurturing the husband and wife and the children that follow, all are a reflection of Christ's relationship with His Bride, the Church.

Yet, sadly enough, the enemy of our souls has invaded this ideal for marriage in far too many cases, coming only to ". . . steal and kill and destroy. . ." (2). Marriage in too many instances has become a breeding ground for fear, insecurity, and, yes, even abuse. Anything but a safe haven. In too many cases, women and men are often literally "sleeping with an enemy," lying down at night beside someone who physically, sexually, verbally, or emotionally abuses them.

Abuse of all forms exists in our world, and a book on marriage and divorce would not be complete without at least touching the surface of such a tragic epidemic. satan has wasted no time in using this as one of his weapons against marriage and the family. As I write this chapter and throughout the book, I am in no way claiming to be a counselor, an expert, or a professional qualified in this area. I can only write what I have learned through research, witnessed, and experienced in my life.

When thinking of domestic violence, physical abuse generally comes to mind. Yet, many other forms of abuse don't leave outward bruises, so they often go undetected. In my quest to understand this topic more, I looked up the definition of abuse. Some of the explanations used by *Dictionary.com* are: "to use wrongly or improperly"; "misuse: to abuse one's authority"; "to treat in a harmful, injurious, or offensive way"; "to speak insultingly, harshly, and unjustly to or about, to malign," "to commit sexual assault upon"; "to deceive or mislead"; "to inflict physical or emotional mistreatment through negligence or neglect often and on a regular basis"(3).

As I looked over this list, I realized that divorce itself should, in most circumstances, be considered abuse and generally is, not to mention all the other forms that typically lead up to the breakdown of a marriage and continue, in some cases, long after the decree is final. However, people don't often realize when they are in abusive situations in their marriages. When you experience it firsthand, your body, mind, and soul have the amazing ability to disassociate somewhat from the full impact of the trauma. Dysfunction becomes the norm, allowing you to survive unbelievable situations without fully realizing how abusive a problem may be. The frog in boiling water analogy is very true. God has given humans an incredible capacity to endure extraordinary conditions and survive.

I know in my own life; I generally don't fully realize how bad a situation is until I am removed from it. I have had this experience growing up with an alcoholic father. And now that I am twenty years removed from my divorce, I have realized how dysfunctional my marriage was. I did not acknowledge or recognize my situation to be abusive when I was in the thick of it.

How Prevalent Is Domestic Violence?

Sadly, domestic violence is far too common. According to the Center for Disease Control and Prevention, one in four women and one in seven men will experience domestic violence (Intimate Partner Violence) in their lifetime, equating to approximately 10 million people per year (4). Yet, as sobering as this statistic is, it does not consider the, perhaps majority of cases, like those I know personally, who will never report their abuse. Nor does it consider those who suffer from non-physical forms daily in their marriage or intimate relationships.

What Gives?

Why is domestic violence an epidemic? How can this be? Although it is a complex issue, studies have shown that one of the reasons domestic violence is rampant is because it often goes unreported, and people get away with it. Furthermore, it knows no race, no color, no sex, no class, no background, or religion. The victims so often continue to suffer silently, believing the enemy's lies that they are alone and are trapped for numerous reasons in their situation. The isolation and shame are a breeding ground for deep-rooted insecurities, a loss of self, fear, and an acceptance of worthlessness. The victims feel powerless and unworthy of being loved, positioning them right where their abusers want them, in a position where they can be controlled.

One lady I know admitted after her divorce that her ex-husband had physically abused her on three occasions during their thirty-year marriage. Yet, she never reported him nor told anyone about it while they were married.

The first incident happened early in their marriage, before they had children. She did admit to me that after this first instance, she thought seriously of leaving him but believed his promises that it would never happen again.

Ten years later, however, while questioning him about his relationship with a female co-worker, she again became his victim. She explained that he proceeded to kick her repeatedly, causing a bone in her coccyx to be broken and permanently displaced! Despite the injury, she once again did not report him. She had small children by this time with no way of supporting them on her own, so like many women and men in her situation, she felt she had no way out.

After the second event, she once again suffered silently, telling no one, not even her family. Perhaps the saddest part was that she remembers feeling responsible for his actions. "If she had been a better wife, he wouldn't have sought out another woman, and the argument would have never taken place." Instead, the affair (he never admitted it) and the "incidents" were swept under the carpet. According to her, life just moved on as if it had never happened. However, she knew if it happened again, for her safety and her children's, she would have to leave him, yet she didn't want her children's lives torn apart.

About eight years later, the "next time" did come. But because the abuse wasn't nearly as "bad" as the first or second time, she rationalized it again. She told herself that it wasn't severe enough to tear her children's lives apart. Three times throughout her marriage she chose to cover his transgressions, with her ex willing to go along with her and take no responsibility for his actions.

Ironically, she had not considered him an "abuser" because it had only happened on three occasions over 30 years. It was not until she disclosed it to a professional after the divorce that she was able to recognize it for what it was. I remember her breaking down when she described how she had lived her life fearing the "next time." She had spent years "walking on eggshells," afraid of her ex-husband's temper, learning to very cautiously confront him or avoid confrontation altogether.

With all of this said, I am a huge supporter of marriage and do not wish to advocate divorce, but what this lady suffered is unacceptable. Women and men need to know that any time someone physically hurts them, even if it's one time, it is abuse and must be reported and dealt with. Unfortunately, this lady believed that "only three times" wasn't the definition of a "true" abuser, given that millions of women and men suffer from domestic violence like this and much worse regularly. Whether it happens three or fifty times, fear grips people in this situation. The enemy is right there whispering to keep it a secret, telling them no one is there to help, and no one will believe them.

As with this woman, the enemy is a master at filling victims with shame and guilt, convincing them it's their fault; if only they were a better spouse, this wouldn't happen. But this wasn't her problem. It was his. Her ex-husband needed to be held accountable for his actions and obviously needed help himself. Perhaps if he had been forced to face his actions from the beginning, he would have gotten the help he needed, and their marriage might have survived and not ended in divorce. Ironically, her ex, not this woman, petitioned for divorce because he had finally found his "soul mate!" in one of his co-workers.

Two years after the divorce was final, this woman found the courage to admit what had happened to her. She revealed the abuse for the first time during a child and family investigation her ex-husband had petitioned to attempt to receive more custody of their children.

Although the investigator helped her confront what she had suffered, her testimony did not hold up in court because she had not reported it. It was considered hearsay, and it was ignored. At the recommendation of the Child Family Investigator, her ex-husband was not awarded more custody. Still, she was forced to face a hard lesson of the importance of reporting abuse right when it happens.

Years later, she was asked again in court if she had ever reported her "alleged" abuse, and because she hadn't, she was again made to feel like it was her fault. In the court's eye, an unreported abuse incident is viewed as a non-issue, especially considering the no-fault divorce law. And worse than this, it often costs people their lives.

Sexual Abuse in Marriage?

Another form of physical abuse that is prevalent in marriages is sexual abuse. When mentioning sexual abuse within a marriage, people are often surprised that this is valid or that it occurs. When people think of sexual assault, the first thing that generally comes to mind is this abuse coming from a stranger, not within the confines of marriage.

Some people even deem it "impossible," and throughout history, a large majority of societies believe that men are entitled to sex with their wives at any time, whether it is forced or consented to. This way of thinking has led to an uphill battle legally and within society for those victims of this very real aspect of domestic violence. It is even more underreported than other forms of abuse, and in today's world, it happens to men as well.

The definition for marital rape according to the National Online Resource Center for Violence Against Women (VAW.net) can be defined as "any unwanted intercourse or penetration (vaginal, anal, or oral) obtained by force, threat of force, or when the wife or *husband* is unable to consent" (5) (Husband added to the quote by me.). This situation is not a matter of a wife having a headache and a husband ignoring this fact and still pursuing sex with his wife; this is a grave issue, and in many cases, it is life-threatening and even results in death.

In their article, "Marital Rape: New Research and Direction, for VAW.net," Dr. Raquel Kennedy Bergen, with the Department of Sociology at Saint Joseph's University, and Elizabeth Barnhill, the Executive Director at Iowa Coalition Against Sexual Assault in Des Moines, Iowa, report that marital rape is not confined to any specific "age, race, ethnicity, social class, or geographic location" (5) However, the article does report a slightly higher incidence among African American women. The studies were based on women living in urban areas of the United States. Approximately half of the women in the survey had been raped by their partners (5).

Although some cases are isolated strictly to sexual abuse, marital rape generally accompanies other types of physical and emotional violence as well:

> Marital rape often involves what is described as "battering rape": severe physical violence, threats of violence, and the use of weapons by people against their partners. A spouse may beat their wife/husband and then force them to "make-up" through forceful intercourse afterwards. Other types are sadistic or obsessive rape which involve torture and/or perverse sexual acts are often physically violent often including pornography by spouses who force their partners to view this or enact what is depicted in pornography.

> Spouses experience physical effects, such as injuries to vaginal and anal areas, lacerations, soreness, bruising, torn muscles, fatigue, vomiting, broken bones, knife wounds, miscarriages and stillbirths (due to abuse during pregnancy) bladder infections and infertility. Victims are kicked, hit and even burned by their abusers. And because there are generally multiple assaults, and the abusers are someone they once trusted, the rape survivors seem to suffer severe and long-term psychological consequences, even more than if the abuse came from a stranger or acquaintance (5).

This website *vawnet.org* (6) offers a wealth of information and resources to educate, inform, identify, and report these cases if you or someone you know is suffering from domestic violence of any kind.

It's difficult to imagine the examples listed above taking place, ever, let alone in a marriage that God designed to be a warm and safe shelter, as the wedding prayer stated. No living creature should ever be used for such atrocious purposes. As discussed in previous chapters, God created sex to be a sacred act between a husband and wife, not an act of horror. I can only imagine how it grieves God to see His beautiful gift, and His beautiful children, being profaned in so many ways.

Some forms of sexual abuse are more subtle and much less violent. Yet also go against all that God desired marital intimacy to be. One way is withholding the sexual act from one partner as a means of control, punishment, or manipulation. Scripture is very clear on this matter when it states in 1 Corinthians 7:3 -5:

> Let the husband render the debt to his wife, and the wife also in like manner to the husband. [4] The wife hath not power of her own body, but the husband. And in like manner the husband also hath not power of his own body, but the wife. [5] Defraud not one another, except, perhaps, by consent, for a time, that you may give yourselves to prayer; and return together again, lest Satan tempt you for your inconsistency (7).

When entering the marriage covenant, both spouses promise to surrender fully to each other, never as consent to abuse, but to give entirely of themselves in the conjugal act. When a couple is intimate the way God intended, it protects the marriage. But, to withhold sex for purposes of ill intent is wrong, and it provides a point of entry for satan to cause sexual temptation outside of the marriage. There is already plenty of this in our world, so we must do everything we can not to invite it.

On the other side, using your spouse for the sole purpose of a sex toy is also abusive. It is natural for one spouse to have a higher sex drive than the other, but that is not what this is referring to. One spouse having a higher sex drive is a natural occurrence that doesn't involve using one's partner abusively for sex and shouldn't be viewed as a bad thing or something to criticize your spouse for on either end of the spectrum.

A perfect example of what I am referring to happened with a young girl I once worked with. She confided in me that her husband only showed any interest in her when he wanted sex. He worked very late nights, and would come home most nights, often around 2:00 or 3:00 in the morning, wake her up from a dead sleep, and demand sex from her. He would get irate if she were too tired, telling her, "It was her duty to give him sex whenever he wanted it."

To make matters worse, even when they had sex at ordinary times, he would leave her to watch TV in another room immediately after. She said she would be left alone in bed, crying and feeling unloved and used. He demanded sex from her daily, often more than once a day. She thought perhaps this was normal until she got up the courage to talk with some other married women about it. Thankfully, they let her know that what was happening was not right and was abusive. They encouraged her to seek counseling immediately. Unfortunately, she left our place of employment shortly after this, and I never knew what ended up happening to her. I pray that she was able to get the help she needed and confront her husband and that they were able to work through this.

Sticks and Stones May Break My Bones, But Words Will Never Hurt Me?

The adage, "Sticks and stones may break my bones, but words will never hurt me," couldn't be further from the truth. Verbal and emotional abuse is even more challenging to prove and identify. It often goes hand in hand with physical violence or is a precursor. Those who have suffered through it state that the wounds go deeper than physical bruises. Words contain great power. This is a spiritual law: what you sow or speak in this instance, you will reap either for good or for evil. The Bible says, "Death and life are in the power of the tongue . . ." (8). According to Genesis, God spoke the earth and everything into existence!

When negative, abusive words are repeatedly spoken over a child, a spouse, etc., these words begin to create and take shape and form. They often shape what the person believes about themselves and, even more frighteningly, can be what they become. Words can change the course of destiny. Many people's lives have been permanently altered by the words spoken to them, especially by those with whom they are in a close relationship.

Like me, I'm sure many of you still remember negative, hurtful words spoken over you throughout your life, and the hurt is still there. Some of the most damaging words spoken to me happened when I was a child. I was a competitive gymnast growing up. Unfortunately, I had verbally abusive coaches that, among other critical words, gave me the nickname "fats." These words, along with my dad's comment that "chubby little girls didn't look good doing gymnastics," contributed to me developing a severe eating disorder in my teens. In addition, these words led to self-loathing. They made me vulnerable to attracting people in relationships, such as my ex-husband, that continued this abuse cycle throughout my life. I can personally attest that it takes a great deal of work, time, and healing to overcome the damaging effects of verbal abuse.

Neglect – The Often-Overlooked Form of Abuse

Although neglect is a readily accepted form of abuse, it is one of the easier ones to look over and not be as easily identified. Looking back over my marriage, I realize the emotional and physical neglect I suffered was abuse. When I say that my ex-husband was never home, I mean he was never home. He traveled a great deal for work, and when he was in town, more nights than not, he would spend his time at the office until late, often not coming home until eleven or later. I would cry, beg and plead for his behavior to change. Yet, it fell on deaf ears, and he would vehemently deny that anything was wrong with his behavior.

When we moved to our new house, things got somewhat better. He would come home for dinner, play with the kids for a while, and then go back to the office until late, and he would generally try to be home for most of the weekend. The kids and I had gotten so used to his absence that I remember it being almost difficult when he did start to be home for these times. The weekends were especially an adjustment for him, the kids, and me. By Sunday night, it was apparent he was ready to be back at work, and because he seemed rather unhappy by this time, I was ready for this too. When I began to see this pattern, I realized that perhaps his absence, as much as it hurt, was part of why our marriage lasted as long as it did.

When we divorced, our next-door neighbor told me she thought he traveled three weeks out of the month because she never saw him. A few other ladies from church also confided in me that they always felt very sorry for me. Explaining that they did so because I was always alone with the kids no matter where they saw me.

For years, his neglect and avoidance made me feel insecure, unattractive, abandoned, unlovable, and unloved. The enemy took full advantage of the situation by reinforcing that "there was something wrong with me." I was constantly striving to be a better wife, be more attractive, be more interesting, have a cleaner house, and so on. Yet, no matter what I did to "be more," the situation never improved.

Around my twelfth year of marriage, God began doing significant work in me on the importance of my thoughts and attitude. His Grace allowed me to finally surrender to the fact that my husband wouldn't change on my account. But I could choose not to let his actions or moods affect my happiness. Instead, I immersed myself further in my relationship with Jesus and my children's lives. Through God's Grace, I learned to be happy despite his absence. However, one blessing about the neglect is that once I was divorced, I was used to handling my children as a single parent. I was also used to taking care of my household independently. The children and I were used to living most of our lives without Dad. In his defense, some of the absence was justified because he was self-employed. His business required plenty of hours to sustain it, but even when he had the opportunities to be home, he chose not to be on most occasions.

Validation Is Healing

Dr. William Harley Jr. wrote an excellent article on his website, *Marriage Builders*, that further helped me understand the abuse of neglect I had suffered. The article also provided solid preventative measures to follow. While reading this, I was surprised to discover that women file for divorce twice as much as men. I found this interesting because, with few exceptions, the men petitioned the divorces in the ones I am acquainted with personally. Equally surprising was that the main reason women divorce men was not infidelity like I would have thought, but rather emotional neglect or mental cruelty (9). The article described this as "indifference, failing to communicate and demonstrating other forms of neglect" (9).

Physical neglect was reported as almost as high as to why women leave. According to the article, women rarely leave for issues, such as, "physical abuse, infidelity, alcoholism, criminal behavior, fraud, or other serious grounds" (9). Instead, the women in the article voiced complaints, such as, "He ignores me unless he wants sex" (9). Or "My husband sits and watches television when he could be talking to me" (9). Or "He rarely calls me to see how I'm doing" (9). Or "He travels all the time and is emotionally and physically detached from our lives" (9). Women need to be emotionally attached to their husbands. When this is not satisfied, unhappiness, lack of trust, and insecurities flourish (9). I can personally attest to these situations causing me to feel all the above in my former marriage.

Dr. Harley explained that men have no problem understanding domestic violence or verbal abuse as reasons women leave. Still, when he would try to explain "neglect" as an issue of abuse, the men generally would not accept this as a valid reason for women to leave. The article states that men, on the other hand, feel that women are too demanding and want to be involved in every aspect of their lives.

He said that most men felt there were "rooms," real or metaphorical, that their wives should not be allowed to come in (10).

Dr. Harley has an excellent method by which he helps men overcome their fears that if they let their wives in, they will lose themselves. He calls it the "Policy of Joint Agreement" (10). This policy encourages the husband and wife to consult and consider the other's feelings in their daily decisions. The couple cannot decide something unless both are enthusiastic about the decision (10).

Dr. Harley explains that when these walls begin to break down, the woman's emotional needs are satisfied, creating emotional bonds between the husband and wife. The husband then feels comfortable bringing their wife into their lives more as they see it as a mutual partnership, not a take-over and a loss of self. The wife begins to feel a part and a priority in their husband's life. The result over time is what every couple desires, a marriage built on mutual love, respect, and compatibility (10).

If the Abuse Continues, Why Don't You Just Leave?

Stockholm Syndrome and Trauma Bonding

I've often heard people say, "What is wrong with them that they didn't just leave?" or "They have no respect for themselves by staying in an abusive situation." Yet statements like this are so ignorant. Unless you've suffered in an abusive situation, you cannot understand how difficult it is to leave. Although there are multiple reasons why a person doesn't leave an abusive situation or seek help, something called Stockholm Syndrome or trauma bonding, is often what is holding a victim "hostage" and can make it virtually impossible for them to leave.

The difference between the two is that with Stockholm Syndrome, an abuse victim develops this because they fully believe their life is in danger. Stockholm Syndrome is the coping mechanism they develop to survive their circumstances (11). The most famous case of this was the newspaper heiress Patricia Hearst, who was kidnapped and later fell in love with her captures. This syndrome can happen in any relationship where life-threatening abuse is present, such as an abusive marriage, child abuse, and human sex trafficking (11). Despite the abuse, the victim develops an attachment, dependency, and even positive views about those abusing them (11).

Trauma bonding, on the other hand, is similar, but the bond is rarely life-threatening. Instead, it is an emotional attachment that develops from "a cycle of abuse and manipulation" (12). The same types of abuse can create this bond, but there are numerous other reasons, which can even develop from coaches (12).

According to Sheri Jacobsen, and her blog article, "What Is Trauma Bonding? Is It Keeping You In a Bad Relationship?," some signs of this are feeling stuck in a relationship that you cannot leave, like a force keeps you in the relationship. Having moments where you know deep down inside that something is wrong. Yet, if you are being honest with yourself, you may not even like the person, let alone trust them, but you cannot leave. They are always making future promises that keep you hanging in that things will get better despite that they never do. Promises are never kept and just keep getting pushed out further and further, yet you keep believing them, telling yourself it is right around the corner (13).

You go through periods when you decide to leave. Still, you cannot go through with it, as the thought of this makes you feel physically sick, like you would die or could never survive if you do. So, instead, you end up convincing yourself that you can change them, even though friends and family are literally screaming, telling you to get out of the relationship. But, again, you cannot make yourself leave. So instead, you find yourself defending them, the relationship, and the few of their actions you have revealed to anyone else and not kept hidden (14).

When writing about this, I realized for the first time that I have experienced this several times. Unfortunately, each time I experienced this was a textbook example of trauma bonding.

I first experienced this as a child when I had very verbally abusive gymnastics coaches. Yet, I couldn't make myself leave the gym and go somewhere else. I would cry to my mom about how awful they were to me. As I mentioned in a previous section, they nicknamed me "fats," calling me this in front of my teammates regularly and would play the chicken song when I was afraid to go for new tricks, among other things. Yet, when my mom would insist I leave this gym and move to another one, I would beg her not to make me. I just couldn't make myself go!

The same thing happened again with my now ex-husband. I knew in my heart I shouldn't marry him, but I couldn't leave the relationship. And, I mean, I couldn't leave, yet I didn't understand why? As I mentioned in an earlier chapter, I cried every day for six months before my wedding, but I kept telling myself it was just because I would be moving away from my family, ignoring the warning I knew my heart was telling me. I remember walking down the aisle, knowing I shouldn't go through with it, but, again, it was as if a force kept me moving forward. This same "force," as I called it, remained until he petitioned for a divorce 18 years later. I now recognize this "force" as trauma bonding.

It happened again years later after my divorce in an online relationship that I will go into in depth in the chapter on narcissism. It was a disaster, but I couldn't leave this relationship either, despite how toxic it was, and it took an act of God to finally escape. I am forever grateful to God and my amazing friends and family for helping me leave before the relationship could go any further and before there was nothing left of me. A beautiful friend who is also a fantastic psychotherapist helped me recognize my inability to leave as falling prey once again to trauma bonding. It has been freeing to finally understand that this "force" had a name and is an actual condition that often happens in abusive relationships.

No Respecter of Persons

In addition to the Stockholm Syndrome or trauma bonding, victims often believe they are alone in their suffering, whether physical, emotional, mental, verbal, or any other kind of abuse. When I was at one of the lowest points of my marriage, I remember watching a family at my church and children's school whose life appeared like a fairy tale. I would watch them from afar, intently longing for their seemingly perfect life. They indeed seemed to be the picture of absolute bliss. Every Sunday, they would attend Mass, dressed beautifully, with all three boys behaving perfectly. Although I knew the mother, I didn't like to sit too close to them during Mass. I didn't want her to notice that my ex-husband never came and that my four children were not always well-behaved. I remember watching the dad thinking what an amazing Christian father and husband he was and how blessed she was that he shared her faith.

They lived in a fantastic lakefront home to make them even more perfect. Every summer, the dad took most of it off to coach their sons in water skiing, and their middle son was ranked first in the nation for his age group. Everyone admired them for many reasons, especially their "amazing" marriage and strong faith.

Over the years, I became good friends with this lady and truly enjoyed her Christian fellowship. I never lost my admiration for her family, which only progressed as time passed. Then, about 16 years ago, I received a phone call from her I will never forget. A call that tragically shattered the perception of her "perfect life" I had so admired. I never once suspected that anything other than what I saw on the outside was taking place. Sadly, this "perfect" family was not as it appeared behind the scenes. I was heartbroken to learn that my dear friend had been suffering from the same things I had throughout my marriage and was now facing a divorce.

I couldn't believe it when this wonderful Christian woman began telling me her husband of 20 years had left her. He had taken the family dog and kicked her and their boys out of "his" house, failing to mention it was so his girlfriend could move in. To make matters worse, she had visited the home to retrieve some of her belongings, and while she was there, an argument broke out between them. Her "perfect Christian husband" became violent in a rage. He spat on her and pushed her down their steep and winding staircase. Thankfully, she was alright and ran to a neighbor's house that convinced her to call the police. He ended up spending a night in jail on domestic violence charges.

Soon after this, I met with her to have lunch. This woman whose life I had so admired and believed had a wonderful, charmed life sat there telling me of all the years of abuse she had suffered from her ex-husband. She had suffered physically on a few occasions. Still, mostly he would threaten to harm her, curse at her, and had thoroughly convinced her she was a worthless human being. But, tragically, like many abused spouses, she never told anyone. Instead, chose to suffer alone to try and keep her children's lives intact and stable.

This was such a powerful lesson and a wake-up call to remind me that things aren't always as they appear and that I shouldn't assume someone's life is perfect. Looking back, I wondered if I overlooked things I should have noticed because I had created such an image of what I thought her life was like. I was devastated by her news and heartbroken that I had not been able to provide this friend with support sooner.

Then, shortly after this, another friend's seemingly "perfect" 15-year marriage came to a crashing halt. She also suffered emotional and physical abuse throughout her marriage. The abuse started on her wedding day when her husband slapped her across the face because she didn't take a bite of the cake properly. Ironically, in both cases, their husbands filed for divorce. Yet, despite their abuse, neither of these women shared with anyone what they were going through throughout their marriage. Neither of them wanted a divorce or ever reported their incidents. It made me wonder how many spouses out there suffer alone and tell no one of the private hell they are living in in their marriage.

Although these are only two cases, it confirms my thoughts that the rate of domestic violence is much higher than is officially reported. You never know what people might be going through behind the scenes. satan wants to keep all things that hurt and control us hidden in the dark. He uses shame, fear, desperation, and isolation to keep victims from telling anyone, with people often developing the Stockholm Syndrome or trauma bonding mentioned previously. He wants you to believe it is your fault and that you are the only person this is happening to or experiencing these things. You believe satan's lies that something is wrong with you; otherwise, it wouldn't be happening, and things would change.

The things we suffer have power over us as long as they remain hidden and in the dark. But they lose their control once we tell someone we can trust and expose these "secrets" to the light. Once exposed to the light, we can bring them to the Lord and let Him heal us. Turning a light on in a dark room causes rodents and bugs to run and exposes them. My mom always taught me to do this with anything I was being tempted with as well, as it breaks its power over us. The same thing happens when we bring the things we suffer to the light.

For years, I didn't tell anyone about the hurtful things in my marriage. I thought I was alone in my suffering. For most of what took place, I became numb and lived like a frog in boiling water. But to those things I did acknowledge, I felt ashamed and embarrassed to tell anyone, especially the women around me whose lives appeared so perfect.

Once my friends who I thought had perfect lives told me what had been happening to them, it helped all of us. Once we could share everything we had been through with each other, it tremendously lessened the fear, shame, and desperation. We realized we weren't alone in our suffering! We had gone through almost mirror experiences in our marriages. Having each other's support and being able to confide in each other was a massive step in the healing process. We were then able to help each other heal and work through traumatic experiences without trying to handle them alone. I am confident that the Lord purposefully connected us all. The most important thing we all agreed upon was that Jesus alone had gotten us through. Aside from Him, we would have never made it, nor had the strength to have ever reached out to one another. By the Grace of God, support from each other, and our beautiful families, we didn't just survive but began to thrive!

Help Is Out There.

With all this said, domestic violence must be seen as the devastating crisis it is. It is imperative that society becomes much more aware and informed that this is a genuine problem and that it exists. Victims of abuse must be helped, protected, guided, and most importantly, believed and given the courage and resources to report such atrocities. I also cannot stress enough that you don't have to suffer alone if you are a victim. Don't keep the abuse hidden and in the dark. Bring it to the light by first giving it to Jesus and then finding a trusted friend or family member you can trust. If you don't have anyone, call a local church or your parish if you attend, and ask where you can get help. They can provide contacts of people and organizations that are professionals at handling these situations. There is also counseling available that provides income-based payment plans.

Contact your local safe houses and women's shelters if you or your children are in danger. Report your perpetrators to trusted authorities, and be willing to flee, escape, and run for your lives and your children's lives if you have them. Please, don't wait until it is too late! There is a lot of help out there. satan will tell you that things will never change, that you don't have the strength to reach out, or that it is your fault, but he is the father of lies. Instead, God promises us the following in Isaiah 61:3, 4, and 7 (15):

> (15) To appoint to the mourners of Sion, and to give them a crown for ashes, the oil of joy for mourning, a garment of praise for the spirit of grief: and they shall be called in it the mighty ones of justice, the planting of the Lord to glorify him.
>
> **(4)** And they shall build the places that have been waste from of old, and shall raise up ancient ruins, and shall repair the desolate cities, that were destroyed for generation and generation.
>
> **(7)** For your double confusion and shame, they shall praise their part: therefore, shall they receive double in their land, everlasting joy shall be unto them.

You have a Savior, Jesus, Who loves you enough to die for you, and you shouldn't have to endure another day living in fear as a victim or being used as an object. God's will for how a husband and wife should treat one another is very clear, and God holds us all to this standard:

> Husbands, love your wives, as Christ also loved the church, and delivered himself up for it: [26] That he might sanctify it, cleansing it by the laver of water in the word of life: [27] That he might present it to himself a glorious church, not having spot or wrinkle, or any such thing; but that it should be holy, and without blemish. [28] So also ought men to love their wives as their own bodies. He that loveth his wife, loveth himself (16).
>
> But now put away and rid yourselves [completely] of all these things: anger, rage, bad feeling, toward (**your husband or wife**), curses and slander, and foul-mouthed abuse and shameful ut-

> terances from your lips! Do not lie to one another, for you have stripped off the old (unregenerate) self with its evil practices, and have clothed yourself as God's own chosen one . . . [who is] purified and holy and well-beloved [by God Himself, by putting on behavior marked by] tenderhearted pity and mercy, kind feeling, a lowly opinion of yourself, gentle ways, [and] patience . . . Be gentle, forbearing with one another. . . readily pardoning others; even as the Lord has {freely] forgiven you. And above all these things, put on love and enfold yourself with the bond of perfectness [which binds everything together completely in ideal harmony] (17).

Can the Marriage Be Saved?

As a firm believer in marriage and a devout Christian, I always pray first for the marriage to be saved. I wanted more than anything to save mine, despite it all. I took my vows seriously and wanted "till death do us part." The last thing I wanted was my children to be in a broken home. Unfortunately, I was the only one who wanted to save our marriage; it takes two. I prayed endlessly that it would be resolved. Looking back, however, I firmly believe Jesus knew I would never leave, so He forced my arm. Still, saying this makes my heart break for all that my children have had to go through.

The good thing is that I have seen marriages survive the worst situations if both spouses are willing to do the work it takes to salvage it. One person can be working on the marriage for quite some time, but eventually, the other spouse needs to get on board. The main component I have seen heal marriages is prayer, especially if both partners are praying and, even better, praying together. Jesus is the only One Who can change anyone. Prayer works to soften the hearts of both people if they are open to His guidance and willing to do whatever He directs them to do to change and save the marriage. Those who were ready to change and do the needed work often say that once they resolved their issues, their marriage was better than it ever had been before.

With all this said, abuse adds a grave issue to marriage. If you are in danger, you must leave the situation, and perhaps you can work on your marriage from a distance if it is safe to do so. In a dangerous situation, it is crucial that you seek guidance from someone, preferably a professional, that knows how to deal with these situations. It is vital to seek help from someone you can trust to guide you correctly and in a way that will keep you safe. Unfortunately, when experiencing trauma, you make emotional decisions that are not often the wisest nor helpful. God would never want you to stay in a marriage that could cost you your safety or your life or put your children in harm's way.

There's Hope for Change!

Although I'm afraid I have to disagree with Oprah Winfrey on most issues, I came across an episode of one of her shows that I thought was perfect for this chapter. An essential aspect of healing is understanding why the abuse happens in the first place. *The Oprah Winfrey Show* featured a program called "Why Men Abuse Women." She interviewed author Kevin Powell who wrote the book, *The Seven Steps to Ending Violence Against Women*. Kevin was formerly guilty of abusing women; however, he is now an activist who works to end violence against them.

The men he had interviewed for his book stated various reasons why they had abused women, including having abusive backgrounds and insecurities. Still, the central theme I got from the show is that the wrong message had been perpetuated throughout these men's lives. Whether through their upbringing, friends, music media, all of these, or elsewhere, these men had it engrained in them that they can abuse women and that it is acceptable. To the men interviewed, women were viewed as objects to dominate, not as God's daughters with a right to be loved and respected (18).

The hope for change is that being a former abuser, Kevin Powell is more determined than ever to "turn the tide" on how men are taught to treat women. However, the fact that he is wholly and genuinely reformed provides hope to all men that they can change if given the proper steps and training. I would also add that this means that women who abuse men can change if given the appropriate steps and training (18).

His book, passion, and willingness to commit his life to the cause are precisely what America needs. His type of training needs to start early on with boys and girls. They must receive this training before the world has a chance to completely reprogram them in the proper way to view and treat people in relationships. According to Kevin Powell, it is time to:

> Create a new kind of man, a new kind of boy. Violence against women and girls will never end if we males continue to live according to definitions of self that are rooted in violence, domination, and sexism. I have been saying for the past few years that more American males have got to make a conscious decision to redefine who we are, to look ourselves in the mirror and ask where we got these definitions of manhood and masculinity, to which we cling so tightly. Who do these definitions benefit and whom do they hurt? Who said manhood has to be connected to violence, competition, ego, and the inability to express ourselves? (18).

And, with the growing number of women abusing men, women must gain this same understanding. And, I would add that teaching our children Christian values from birth will help affect change more than anything. They need to know Jesus as their Savior and Lord. Having a personal relationship with Jesus will enrich programs, such as Kevin Powell's and give it even more depth and understanding. Children need to grow up learning about the teachings of Jesus, Mary, and Joseph. They need to be taught about the Holy Family and have the perfect example of how to treat others, especially a spouse. Truly the answer and solution to all things!

In the following three chapters, we will discuss three other issues that can all be causes of abuse and are abuse in and of themselves.

CHAPTER NINE

"THE CHEATER"

Another issue that often causes abuse in a marriage and is abuse itself is infidelity. I wanted to dedicate a whole chapter to this issue, as, besides being an extension of the previous chapter on abuse, it is a leading cause of divorce, and yet another one of satan's greatest weapons in this final battle.

One thing I have found in common with the divorces I am personally familiar with, is they were all a result of infidelity. Not one of those involved admitted it initially, but as the divorce progressed, their sin had found them out. A recent study showed that of married heterosexual men in America, 20 to 40% admit to having an extramarital affair that included sexual intimacy, and 20 to 25% of American heterosexual women admit to this (1). And a glaring 70% of Americans have admitted to engaging in some type of infidelity! (2). Not all of these marriages ended in divorce, but these statistics are disheartening.

What I have begun to understand about infidelity is that, in addition to abuse and causing tremendous pain, it should be considered attempted murder if sexual relations are involved. Such a statement may sound like a radical claim, but common sense alone explains that this is precisely what it is. A spouse who cheats and then comes home and sleeps with their husband or wife has just exposed them to possible STIs that can be either life-altering or deadly, such as AIDS. It is a highly selfish act that can potentially put a person's life at risk.

A lady I used to work with had been married to the same man for over thirty years, and he had been her only sexual partner. When this woman found out she had contracted genital warts, she immediately confronted her husband. He denied that she had caught it from him, but he was the only man she had ever been intimate with, so it is unlikely that she could have contracted it any other way, but from him.

Another woman married to a supposed devout Christian man found out he was cheating with two women and was making pornographic films with them! Like me, she has four children. She initially found out he was cheating because she contracted a venereal disease, and she, like the other lady, had never been intimate with anyone but her husband. Because of her husband's infidelity, she has to live with this life altering disease the rest of her life.

In addition to the potential danger, it is one of the most hurtful and traumatic events that anyone will ever go through. The first time I discovered my ex-husband was cheating, I was pregnant with our third child. I talked about this in my chapter, "The Broken Promise." As discussed in that chapter, he was on the road for ten-day stints, and I was left home with our two little boys. I discovered he was cheating from his phone bill and emails, and he was not home for me to even have the opportunity to confront him in person. To this day, I suffer guilt because of the turmoil, rejection, and utter devastation I felt while I had my third little boy forming in my womb, knowing that the stress I experienced made for an unhealthy environment for him to develop, not to mention the dangerous health risk it put me and potentially our child in, especially while pregnant.

Its Generational Effects

In addition to causing marriage and relationship problems, it causes ripple effects that reach future generations. And it causes agony and pain for all caught up in its evil, self-serving web! I have witnessed this in my life and the lives of my children, in other people's lives, and in the lives of my students.

Regarding the lives of my students, I have to start by saying, I am so blessed in the school I teach that I can do a lot of character and virtue lessons, as it is an integral part of our curriculum. Before break let out, the students and I embarked on a sober discussion, and the kids opened up about serious issues they were going through. One topic that came up multiple times was the issue of divorce and how difficult it is, especially as a child, to deal with this often-tragic situation. Sadly, the common thread in these precious children's cases was adultery.

The Pig Pen

As I was thinking about the issue of cheating in a marriage or committed relationship, I thought back to when I was at the state fair and was visiting the pig's pen. It was feeding time when I was observing these nearly 300-pound creatures. All the pigs in the pen were happy eating from the trough that had just been provided for them until, suddenly, an onlooker's fruit bowl accidentally fell into the enclosure! I couldn't believe my eyes! All the pigs immediately left their trough and started fighting and squealing, practically screeching, for the "new and different" item that fell before them! They went crazy pinning to get something different when they were content with what they already had just moments before.

I have often heard of cheaters described as "pigs." After observing this, I realize it is pretty fitting. I love pigs, and don't mean to criticize the animal, but they act on instinct, so they have an excuse. From my observation of these pigs at the fair, I noted several things. First, pigs are self-seeking and have no self-discipline. They also give no thought to their actions and will hurt themselves and the others around them to have a chance at something new and different. And finally, they have zero problems rolling around in the dirt and mud—all things they have in common with those who cheat.

As I say this, I realize that things can happen that people regret, and not every person who cheats shares these characteristics. And it's essential to recognize that they can be forgiven and truly change, and a marriage can survive an affair. But it is also equally important to recognize that cheaters don't always stop at one. There are those who will be habitual cheaters. An old saying that applies to this type is, "Once a cheater, always a cheater." They discard people as objects as soon as something "new" falls in their pen. I am tired of seeing this issue trash marriages, relationships, children's lives, and society. Because, like pigs, people are often self-seeking and often think that the "new shiny" thing is what they deserve. In doing this, they disregard how their actions affect those around them, often for generations.

It is also important to note, that this is a people problem, and men aren't any worse about this than women. A woman is going along with every man cheating and vice versa. Men, it doesn't make you a "stud," and women, it doesn't mean you are more irresistible than others. It makes you both "pigs" in the general sense of the word. Pigs are innocent creatures, but people were given a conscience and soul to know the difference! And, again, I'm sorry if I'm insulting pigs, but I found the parallel to be uncanny.

Dangers of Porn

The internet and electronics have supplied many creative ways to commit adultery, with pornography being a multi-billion-dollar-a-year industry. Porn addiction has become a massive cause of divorce in America and has destroyed countless individuals and their families. People will justify claiming it is not "cheating," yet Jesus' words prove them otherwise. In Matthew 5:28, Jesus teaches, "But I say to you, that whosoever shall look on a woman to lust after her, hath already committed adultery with her in his heart" (3).

In addition to porn being adultery, it's highly addictive. It causes men or women to view members of the opposite sex as objects to be used for their pleasure. It goes back to what we discussed in a previous chapter when Fr. Ripperger said if you separate sex from procreation, it opens a door for satan to enter. Sex becomes about the pleasure of self, not what God intended for it to be. For those viewing porn, suddenly their wife or husband's body is no longer appealing or arousing to them. Before their addiction, their spouse satisfied their needs, but once they enter this trap of satan, they lose interest. People addicted to porn won't be satisfied with what they first started viewing either. They will need to keep increasing the level of perversity to receive the same effect. It will not only destroy a marriage but will destroy the person who is enslaved by the addiction.

Many people on death row have stated that they blame their addiction to porn for the heinous crimes they committed. Sadly, the internet has made it accessible to anyone with an electronic device that connects to the web. You are never too young or old for this temptation to overtake you. As long as you have a beating heart, this is something that can ensnare you. No one is above this.

It is a terrible epidemic. And it is also shown that the porn industry relies on human sex trafficking to keep it afloat. So, what might look like porn stars who are willing participants are often trafficked women and men – and even children - who are enslaved against their will in this evilest industry.

No One Knows, So I'm Not Hurting Anyone, Right?

Just because something is done in secret does not mean it doesn't cause catastrophic effects on others, both physically and spiritually. In the powerful book, *The Healing of Families: How to Pray Effectively for Those Stubborn Personal and Familial Problems,* by Fr. Yozefu-B. Ssemakula, describes how a father was watching porn in the family home regularly, and his son, who had never even thought of porn, started being tempted to watch it and began struggling with lust (4).

Mark 3:27 warns us saying, "No man can enter into the house of a strong man and rob him of his goods, unless he first binds the strong man, and then shall he plunder his house" (5). According to Fr. Joe (this is what he goes by), "binding the strong man" is a natural consequence of our "private" sins. These sins don't just bind the one committing them. They also allow the enemy to come in and plunder the rest of the household members, too, creating a bondage, called the "Open Door Principle," giving the enemy permission to infect the bloodline, inserting temptations from the (in this case) father's sins into the minds and desires of other members of the family, including the children, even if they are not currently partaking in the sin. Because of this open door, the other members of the family become vulnerable to this sin, and it is very common for these temptations to manifest in other family members and is even how generational sins or curses are started (4).

Fr. Dan Reehil, the well-known pastor of St. Catherine of Siena Catholic Church, Vicar Forane of the Southern Deanery, exorcist for the Diocese of Nashville, and the National Director of Radio Maria USA, recently explained during one of his broadcast talks, that this is not limited to only biological family members. He explained that we get affected by everyone's sins. He explained:

> You never know this more than when you live in a Religious house. You have 12 guys living there and someone falls to impurity, and those demons go through the whole house, and by morning, you have 12 angry guys coming to breakfast asking, 'Who the heck messed up last night? Because now, all these things are in the house!' It's real! If you are going to do things, and I'm especially talking to the dad's as head of the household of the family, . . . the whole family suffers a loss of Grace (6) and can be attacked.

Partaking in "secret sins," such as pornography, not only enslaves you but also causes significant damage to your family and even your whole bloodline. This is not limited, of course, to viewing pornography or adultery, but applies to any sin. This is also not just a male issue, but women's sins have the same effect. Imagine how all the sins in the world, my sins, your sins, everyone's sins, cause such harm to society. We genuinely don't realize the ramifications of what we are doing, and pornography is one of the primary spiritual cancers and weapons satan uses to attack the family and marriage.

Jesus tells us to flee from temptation, to run from it. Please do everything you can to keep from becoming enslaved and captured by its spell. If you are already addicted, I urge you to get help right away! Do everything in your power to break free! Jesus will help you! He goes so far as to say, "And if thy right eye scandalizes thee, pluck it out and cast it from thee. For it is expedient for thee that one of thy members should perish, rather than that thy whole body be cast into hell" (7). He knew the dangers of lust. Perhaps He didn't specifically mention pornography, yet He knew sins of this nature could consume a man to the point of death, death to his soul, his family, and his marriage.

God also very specifically tells us how to resist the temptation of lust or adultery in any fashion through the wise words of Solomon in the Book of Proverbs when it says:

7:1
My son, keep my words
and store up my commands within you.

2
Keep my commands and you will live;
guard my teachings as the apple of your eye.

3
Bind them on your fingers;
write them on the tablet of your heart (8).

6:21
Bind them always on your heart;
fasten them around your neck.

22
When you walk, they will guide you;
when you sleep, they will watch over you;
when you awake, they will speak to you.

23
For this command is a lamp,
this teaching is a light,
and correction and instruction
are the way to life, (9)

7:5
They will keep you from the adulterous woman, your neighbor's wife,
and from the wayward woman with her seductive words (8).

But also warns in Proverbs 6:25-29 that to do otherwise has the following effects on our lives:

25
Do not lust in your heart after her beauty
or let her captivate you with her eyes.

26
For a prostitute can be had for a loaf of bread,
but another man's wife preys on your very life.

27
Can a man scoop fire into his lap
without his clothes being burned?

28
Can a man walk on hot coals
without his feet being scorched?

29
So is he who sleeps with another man's wife;
no one who touches her will go unpunished (10).

Viewing pornography is very much adultery, and the sin of adultery in any fashion brings grave consequences to anyone who partakes. Yet again, God always gives us a way out, and tells us this is through meditating on storing up the Word of God in our hearts. He also promises us that "**13** no temptation[a] has overtaken you except what is common to mankind. And God is faithful; he will not let you be tempted[b] beyond what you can bear. But when you are tempted, [c] he will also provide a way out so that you can endure it" (11). Fr. Jo's book also provides powerful prayers for deliverance to break these patterns and heal family lines. Through God, you can overcome, through God, you can be free!

Social Media: The New Way to Have an Affair

Another way the internet has increased adultery is through social media. I was listening to an excellent sermon recently entitled "The Lure of Lust; The Danger of Divorce" by Pastor Jerry Rueb, from Cornerstone Church in Long Beach, California. During his sermon, he provided a stat that came as no surprise. He stated, "1 in 5 couples who are now divorced blame Facebook for destroying their marriage" (12).

I have often wondered how much social media has increased adultery. One thing is sure: it has opened up another avenue for people to cheat. A like or compliment can often lead to an innocent conversation, leading to another. And, before the two people realize it, they are starting to look forward to chatting more frequently. In fact, they enjoy it so much that the public conversation soon begins to take place in a private message or even a text. The next thing they know, they begin to share intimate details of their lives with this person, who is not their spouse. Before long, what started as an innocent conversation, develops into an emotional affair that frequently leads to the breakup of a marriage. And this is a big problem even among Christians.

An emotional affair is simply when one partner becomes too close with another person outside their marriage or relationship. Flirting is often viewed as harmless fun, but this is frequently how an emotional affair begins. Besides, being on the other end of flirting is terribly hurtful. For example, my ex-husband was an incurable flirt, and it caused me terrible heartache and made me feel very insecure and untrusting in our relationship.

Furthermore, if the flirting continues, it generally leads to sharing information about each other, which often leads to telling intimate details about your spouse to the other person. For example, I have a married friend who started a Facebook "friendship," and the guy started asking her details about her and her husband's sex life. Thankfully, her husband found out, and she unfriended this man, and her marriage was saved.

People are very forward, and there is a significant lack of respect and boundaries towards marriage and serious relationships in our society. I have witnessed many occasions in the break room at work where two married people are flirting and even telling dirty jokes to each other. It makes me so uncomfortable and worried for each of their spouses. I'm sure their spouses would not appreciate the interactions I am witnessing. Unfortunately, I see the same type of banter on social media publicly. I can only imagine how the conversations shift to being inappropriate quickly when they take place in Private Messenger.

Another big issue social media creates is relying on others besides your spouse to meet your needs. For example, if someone's wife posts a picture of themselves on social media, and 300 men like the post and make flirtatious comments, this can be very problematic. This attention can become something the wife starts to seek out and then isn't happy with her husband's compliments here and there. It can cause the wife to feel unsettled in her marriage and cause her to seek the attention of other men outside of her husband.

In addition, it can also cause the husband to feel insecure and jealous. It may make them not trust their wife and become suspicious of her social media activity. It works both ways, of course. A wife will feel equally threatened if the same attention is given to her husband's post. It is important to remember that infidelity doesn't have to mean meeting up with someone, kissing them, or having sex. You are already there if you have to delete messages and lie about who you are corresponding with to your spouse.

Flee from Temptation.

Dr. James Dobson always said that you shouldn't start friendships, conversations, coffee breaks, lunches, etc., with members of the opposite sex if you want to affair-proof your marriage. Unfortunately, today we have social media that provides a "private meeting" place with members of the opposite sex anytime we want. How is it any different to "meet on Messenger" than it is to meet for coffee. At least with coffee, it's out in the open.

Suppose you are married and use social media. In that case, I recommend doing all you can to protect yourself and your marriage from temptation. I know many married people will have a couple's Facebook page. I also recommend not using Private Messenger with people of the opposite sex. It is shocking how forward people are on this forum. It can be bad enough for a single person, and I personally think a "married status" is an extra challenge to people who are on social media to cause trouble and get their ego fed.

Cheating has always been a thing and, sadly, always will be. But social media has provided a new avenue that can create this atmosphere, even without people realizing what has happened, and it obviously is. As the sermon I mentioned at the beginning of the chapter said, "1 out of 5 people has admitted to Facebook causing the destruction of their marriage" (13). Studies have also proven that emotional affairs are often even more damaging than physical ones and that most will eventually lead to a physical affair (13). Emotional affairs are often the most common with a staggering 90% of women and 70% of men worldwide admitting to this type of infidelity (14).

Another thing to consider is that although it's not adultery, emotional affairs can happen between friendships with the same sex or family members. For example, a lady I know started feeling very jealous of her husband's relationship with one of his guy friends. Anytime her husband had off, he wanted to spend time with this friend. He would drop everything to help his friend. He even canceled events he had planned with her to spend time with or help this guy. This friendship made her feel insecure and not valued by her husband.

The bottom line is that your closest relationship should be with your spouse, and any relationship that becomes more important is out of balance. This is in no way saying you should isolate yourself from other people and not have other healthy relationships. Still, your marriage relationship needs to be first.

"Father, Forgive Them, for They Know Not What They Do" (Luke 23:34).

If people really understood what they were doing, I can't believe they would cheat. I also think most people don't set out to have an affair. Many people who commit adultery say they didn't realize what was happening until they were hooked. The Book of Proverbs needs to be read to any man or woman contemplating cheating in any fashion. Solomon was very clear when he described the consequences of these actions. In Proverbs 6:32 and 5:23, he wrote, "But whoever commits adultery with a woman lacks heart and understanding. He who does it is **destroying his own life**. . . he will die for lack of discipline and instruction, and in the greatness of his folly, he will go away and be lost" (15).

Paul Newman cannot be compared with Solomon, and it is rumored he may have been unfaithful at one point, but he made an excellent comment about his wife, JoAnne Woodward. When people asked him how he had stayed married to the same woman for so many years, he would explain, "Why go out for hamburger when I have steak at home." Sadly, many spend more time looking for or building a relationship with someone outside their marriage than with their spouse. Imagine what a great marriage and stability for children would be established if all of the attention, time, effort, and money were invested in the marriage relationship.

Spend time with your spouse, pour your heart out to him/her, don't confide in a member of the opposite sex, and don't engage in personal messages, texting, and lunch dates. Remember that "harmless" flirting on the internet and otherwise is never a good idea if you want to be able to resist temptation when it comes. If you're going to be married, don't settle for mediocre, have the best of everything: friendship, companionship, spirituality, love, sex, and family.

Anyone married long enough will admit there have been times when they were perhaps tempted to stray. Although I didn't have friendships with other men or have a physical affair when I was married, I sometimes would get little crushes on other men. I struggled with fantasies in my mind about them that were not Godly. According to Scripture, these were affairs. Although I wasn't talking with them, I'm sure they would be considered emotional affairs because of how I felt about them. I've realized now how wrong this was. I would excuse them because my husband was neglecting me. Still, sin is never justified because of someone else's actions toward us. We have to guard our hearts and thoughts constantly. Again, the Bible tells us how to resist temptation. "How does a young man cleanse his way? By taking heed and keeping watch on himself according to Your word conforming his life to it" (16). Love thy neighbor as thyself is another way when considered, in which the temptation will cease to be inviting if followed.

Action Steps to Take to Affair Proof Your Marriage

Your marriage is worth fighting for and doing all you can to protect it from the temptations of life and the enemy. But like Sr. Lucia of Fatima said, "The final battle will be against the family and marriage," and it is undeniable that the battle is raging. Below are steps you can take that will help affair-proof your marriage. A lot of these are similar if not the same as how to stay away from premarital sex, but well-worth repeating:

1. Have a personal relationship with Jesus Christ. - Set aside time daily to spend time alone with God and pray. We cannot expect to overcome temptation if we do not keep ourselves strong in spirit, and this can only happen by spending time with God and in His Word. Jesus tells us, ". . . for without Me,

you can do nothing!" (17). Three people must be present in a marriage to keep it strong: God, Husband, and Wife.

2. Pray with your spouse every day. - I saw the fruit of this with my grandparent's marriage. Nothing came in the way of them praying every night before bed, and their marriage lasted until "death do them part."

3. Go to Mass or Church – This is crucial. Husbands, lead your wives in this. Be the head and take your wife and your family to church. There is no more excellent prayer than attending the Holy Mass, especially as a couple and family.

4. Choose Love – Love is more of a commitment than a feeling. Feelings are fickle and can change daily, but a commitment is solid and unchanging, especially when God is first.

5. Read *The Five Love Languages* by author Gary Chapman. Communicate what you find with each other and work daily on fulfilling your spouse's language/s of love (18).

6. Set Boundaries – Communicate with each other what boundaries you need to feel secure, loved, respected, valued, and safe in your marriage, and honor these. This is especially important with interactions with the opposite sex and social media.

7. Communicate – This might seem repetitive, but it is a crucial aspect and cannot be overstated. Transparency in communication is essential. It takes humility, the willingness to be vulnerable, and to forgive, but is worth it all!

8. Don't Take Your Spouse for Granted – Each day, challenge yourself to find 10 things you love about your spouse. Keep your marriage fresh and allow for spontaneity.

9. Mutually Fulfill Each Other's Intimacy Needs – This is not limited to sex. This also includes affection and cuddling. Communicate your needs with your spouse and listen to what they need to be fulfilled as well. Set healthy boundaries and keep

your intimate life in accordance with God's Word and Catholic Teaching so that God can abundantly bless your union.

10. Have Accountability – Hold each other accountable. Keep in mind that you have an ordained responsibility through the Sacrament of Marriage to help your spouse gain Heaven, which needs to derive from a place of love. Obviously, it's good to have accountability with each other. Still, it is also good to have a trusted friend or family member who can also hold you accountable. Great men's and women's groups provide this and can help you bring temptations to the light that you might be facing. Frequent Confession is also a way to hold yourself accountable before God. It is my second favorite of the Holy Sacraments. **It is even described as a mini exorcism that can break demonic strongholds and temptations off your life.** If you won't make a good and honest confession with your parish priest, go to another parish to receive this sacrament so you won't hold back things that need to be brought to the Light.

11. Three is Not a Crowd - Avoid regularly socializing with only one other couple. Dr. James Dobson said that adultery often sprang from two couples getting too close. He said this problem was usually eliminated if a third couple was added.

12. The Golden Rule – "Do unto others as you want done unto you." This is always important to consider with our actions.

13. RUN, Literally RUN from Temptation - St. John Kronstadt once said, "Fear evil/temptation like fire. Don't let it touch your heart, even if it seems just or righteous. No matter what the circumstances, don't let it come into you. Evil is always evil!" (19). So, we are to flee from temptation, not invite it. satan always comes through the backdoor. It all begins with an innocent thought, that if you give heed to, can grow into a full-blown affair. Immediately reject this thought from its very onset and send it back to hell where it belongs. Replace it with a Scripture about the sanctity of marriage. Cover yourself, your spouse, and your marriage with the Blood of Jesus. Use

Holy Water and Holy Salts to protect yourself. We are in a war, and we must use our weapons! Your marriage is worth it!

14. Have A Plan of Action - Don't Let Your Guard Down – Decide ahead of time what you will do when temptation presents itself. I suggest talking with your spouse about coming up with a plan.

15. Habitual Cheaters are Going to Cheat – Sadly, there are situations where you are doing everything right, but your spouse still cheats. Their actions are not your fault. You are doing what you need to, and the sin falls on them. God will reward you in some other way for your efforts. We never go wrong by taking the high road.

16. YET - Marriage Can Survive and Even Thrive After an Affair – Infidelity does not always have to mean the end of a marriage, especially if it is a one-time offense. I have known several marriages where the couples have worked through an affair. In several of these cases, the marriages were stronger after the infidelity than before. With that said, it took both people's willingness, forgiveness, and humility to do the work necessary to heal the marriage and prevent it from happening again.

If you are struggling with forgiveness, remind yourself of all Christ has forgiven you for. Think of times you might have been tempted in this area or even had an emotional affair. This is your opportunity to exercise the mercy of Christ. Again, this is not giving the advice to be a doormat and overlook adultery. Still, if there is a way and a willingness to salvage your marriage after, it is worth the effort. It will take the Grace of God to do this, but it is essential to remember what Jesus said in Matthew 9:26, "[26] And Jesus beholding, said to them: With men this is impossible: but with God all things are possible" (20).

Chapter Ten

"The Addict"

To extend and dive into abuse further, it is important to also include a chapter on addiction. Growing up with an alcoholic father and suffering for several years with bulimia, I understand addiction. I don't claim to understand it from a professional standpoint, but I have learned what it entails from the school of life. My grandpa's and dad were severe alcoholics, and I have seen firsthand the devastation it creates in people's paths.

I liken addiction to possession or enslavement. When an addiction takes hold, it begins to take over the person, stripping them of their rights and it leads and rules their life. Everything they do in life becomes about serving the addiction. Tragically, people who are addicted often lose everything and everyone in their lives, but they still cannot kick it.

Although my dad's dad died when I was in second grade, and the few times I was around him, I don't remember him drinking as I think he may have stopped by then, he was nonetheless a severe alcoholic while my dad was growing up. And my dad suffered an abusive childhood because of it. My mom's dad finally stopped drinking when I was little; I don't remember him being an alcoholic, either. But I know my poor grandma, my mom, and her brother's endured years of hell because of it. And my mom, my siblings, and I suffered the effects of my dad's alcoholism until he finally stopped when I was 16. So, this is clearly a generational addiction in my family.

A Stolen Life

You might think my dad would not have drank because he grew up with it, but, unfortunately, this was not the case, as it so often isn't. Growing up, my dad would come home sloshed and "holding up" the walls more nights than not. He would then begin yelling at my oldest brother or would start an argument with my mom if she got on him about his obvious inebriation. She was good at avoiding fights with him and generally made it her goal to get him to eat dinner to take down the buzz. But, of course, eating also served another purpose. He would become extremely tired, go straight from eating dinner to his favorite chair, fall asleep, or pass out; I'm not sure which one.

So much of my time with my dad, not to mention his own life, was spent with him being intoxicated. I remember taking the shame on myself for his addiction. Although I wanted him to come to my school functions and gymnastics meets, it was better when he didn't. I felt so embarrassed and ashamed the few times he did show up and was obviously inebriated. I was also nervous about having friends over as I didn't want them to know and see my dad in this state. It made for a tumultuous childhood, and my brothers and I suffered significant consequences from his addiction. It's taken me years to work through it all.

It took a tremendous toll on my parent's marriage as well. I don't think it would have lasted if my mom had not grown up in that environment and she had not witnessed her mom staying in her marriage despite it all. Although my mom and dad's marriage was filled with trauma and the abuse that comes with living with an alcoholic, it was a comfortable environment for her. Trauma bonding had also fully set in; this is all she knew.

No one in a family escapes the trauma caused by addiction. I understand the person is sick, but it is difficult to not view it as a very selfish act. This is because they are drunk or high, while all the sober members of the family have to endure the pain of their actions.

The good times with my dad were when we spent time as a family in nature. He was an avid sportsman and was in his element when we were in the mountains, and he had his fishing pole cast in a stream or was hunting whatever game was in season. During these times, I saw the remarkable man he was minus the alcohol. My dad had many great qualities; he was a genius in math and at his trade of engineering. He was hard-working and taught us all to be. He was honest in his business. He also always had my mom's back when raising us kids. And even though he was agnostic until his deathbed conversion to Christianity, he supported my mom in raising us Catholic. I remember often thinking just how tragic addiction is, as it overshadowed these great qualities of my dad and turned him into someone completely different.

The fact that a person is hijacked, and the alcohol or drug takes them over is perhaps the biggest tragedy. They become a different person, not who God created them to be. From a little girl on, I realized how damaging addiction was not only to the person with the problem but to everyone around them. Everyone misses out, and a life is literally stolen. Everyone else pays the price for the addiction, too, and it creates an often fear-filled and shame-based atmosphere in which to live.

It Takes an Act of God.

I'm sure in this day and age, my mom would be criticized for staying with my dad. Yet, she had seen her mom put up with an alcoholic husband (her father), so staying in the marriage was a natural choice. Although despite the years of turbulence we suffered because of my dad's drinking, I am still thankful that my parents never got a divorce. You might think, "Why didn't your mom force him into treatment or give him an ultimatum?" Yet, this is easier said than done. As discussed in chapter eight, there are so many reasons why people won't leave abusive situations. And I know you cannot force anyone to become clean and sober. They have to be willing, and I think in almost all cases, it takes an act of God.

For example, my grandpa tried for years to stop drinking. But, still, he could never kick the habit. For years, Grandpa cried out to God to heal him, but he only worsened with each passing year. Thankfully, my grandma, her family, my mom, and her brothers refused to quit praying for him and holding out hope that he would finally be free one day.

One night on Holy Thursday when my grandpa was around 63, he stayed after Mass to be alone and pray. Kneeling at the altar, he began crying out to God and begging him to please finally take this terrible addiction away from him.

While he was praying, my grandpa said he heard the audible voice of God, but it wasn't what he wanted to hear. God clearly spoke to him that night, saying, "Warren, you will never have another cigarette." My grandpa was quite a character and responded to God by saying, "What the hell does that have to do with anything?" Feeling disgusted and let down by God, he left the church that night. He couldn't figure out why in the world God would say that to him. Yet, Grandpa was adamant that he had heard this.

Well, the words he heard from God that night came to pass. He was equally addicted to cigarettes. He said that after that night, the craving for them completely disappeared, and he never smoked again. God knew what steps needed to happen for my grandpa to finally be healed.

About a year later, my grandpa was admitted to the hospital after a three-week drunken binge and was declared dead soon after arriving. For the next ten minutes or so, all looked lost. Yet while the hospital staff thought they had lost him; he claims that he died and went to hell and specifically remembered smelling burning flesh. He said he knew what this smelled like as Grandpa had had a previous surgery where they had to cauterize him, which is where they burn the skin to seal it, and he said this was the same smell.

Much to the hospital staff's surprise, and by a sheer act of God, his life was spared. When he came to, he was miraculously speaking in tongues. Something he had never experienced before. From that day on, he was miraculously healed from alcoholism. He and my grandma got a chance to live their last years of marriage without the tragedy of this addiction.

I never knew my grandpa as an alcoholic as my mom did. Still, he was very open with all of us kids and anyone who would listen about the dangers of drinking and all God had done for him. My grandpa was one of my best friends, and I could trust him with any problem I was having, and he never made me feel ashamed but would pray with me and help me through whatever I was struggling with.

Instead of drinking, Grandpa spent the last years of his life telling other alcoholics what God had done for him. He had a special devotion to the Native Americans as alcoholism is such a problem for them. Grandpa often spoke on the reservations. He encouraged anyone that would listen to rely on Jesus and the Holy Eucharist to find deliverance from their addictions. He insisted that receiving Jesus daily in Holy Communion was key to his sobriety. He said, "A day without receiving the Eucharist was a day from hell."

My grandpa was also intensely devoted to the *Novena to the Holy Ghost* (1), the most ancient Catholic Novena and the only one officially approved by the Church. If you ever met my grandpa, you would have the novena in your hand. He would grab your hands, look straight into your soul with his beautiful blue eyes, tell you how instrumental it was for his deliverance from alcoholism, and encourage you to start reciting it.

What a tragedy it would have been if my grandpa had died in that hospital room and was not given a second chance by Jesus to be the person God created him to be. My grandpa was given the incredible gift of freedom from the hideous bondage that alcoholism brings. Instead of dying that night in the hospital in a drunken stupor and going to Hell, he died at 92 in the arms of my loving grandma as a redeemed and mighty man of God.

Alcoholism Runs in the Family.

Although my experience was not as dramatic as my grandpa's, I received a miraculous healing from the addiction to bulimia as well when I was 17 years old, as mentioned in an earlier chapter. It is common for children of alcoholic parents to develop an eating disorder. In addition to having an alcoholic parent, I was also a competitive gymnast. So, when I was 14, I started becoming anorexic to lose the weight my coaches insisted I lose.

After several months, the anorexia turned into a four-year-long battle with bulimia. Thankfully, my parents discovered I was bulimic soon into having this addiction and put me in counseling. And although my therapist was well-meaning, seeing her didn't help. I wanted to stop more than anything and tried often, but I couldn't. So, I spent the next four years lying and sneaking around to cover up my excessive binging and purging, even stealing money from my parents to buy food to binge.

Also as mentioned in an earlier chapter, in addition to the bulimia, I had also started drinking. Like with my dad, you would think I wouldn't go near alcohol after all the suffering it had brought my family and me. Still, once I started, I admit I liked the feeling of getting drunk. My grandpa had always told me that you can be an alcoholic before taking a drink, and I know this is true for me.

It was apparent from the very beginning, though, that I should never drink, as once the alcohol started flowing in my veins, I didn't have an off switch. A perfect example to illustrate this happened one of the first times I ever drank. I was only 15 and attended a party with some older people I worked with. For some unknown reason, they thought I would be a good bartender. So, they gave me a quick lesson on making Roman Cokes for all the guests. As people came to the table to get one, I gave one to them, and I drank one for myself. I had no idea there was such a thing as alcohol poisoning, and I soon lost track of how much I had drunk.

The last thing I remember was dancing foolishly and crazily before waking up later in the ER for a brief moment before passing out again. Apparently, I passed out at the party, and my co-workers took me to the ER as I was unresponsive. They called my mom and dad, and they met them there. The nurse in the ER told my mom that my heart had stopped. She explained that I was lucky to have survived, given the amount of alcohol I had in my system, especially with my petite frame.

I would like to tell you that I never drank again after that, but I continued to binge drink nearly every weekend for two and a half years. I quit gymnastics, and about a year into this pattern, I met my ex-husband. As I also mentioned in a previous chapter, I was 16 and in no condition to enter into a serious relationship, as I was in a terrible state. I was severely bulimic and binge drinking, to boot. We went to different high schools, so, for the most part, we only spent time together on the weekend, and our relationship revolved around alcohol. You cannot get to know a person very well when you are drunk nearly every time you spend time with them.

This destructive pattern continued and became a normal way of life. I even had one night that I completely blacked out and found myself walking around alone at night outside of a party, having no idea how I got there. Thankfully, by the grace of God, two of my ex-husband's friends found me and took me home.

On New Year's Eve of this same year, my senior year of high school, I was out with my ex-husband, and we were going to attend a party. We started to go, but a blizzard swiftly moved in, and the roads quickly became treacherous. Thankfully, we were close to his parent's house, so we returned there. Unfortunately, I lived across town, so his parents insisted I stay there for the night, as it was not safe to drive me home.

I was pretty close with his family as we had been dating for a year at this point, so I felt comfortable staying there. I also wasn't feeling well that night, so I was glad to be able to just go to sleep and not have to attend a party. His dad made a bed for him in the family room, and I slept in my ex-husband's room. I fell asleep quickly, but about two hours into my sleep, I had a dream that I am sure was a warning from Jesus. In this dream, Jesus came to me and told me that if I kept living the way I was, I was going to die soon. I remember waking up abruptly from this dream shaking, knowing that Jesus had spoken to me and that it was true.

The dream scared me so much that I didn't drink at all for the rest of the school year. I was able to stop drinking on the spot, but as much as I wanted to, I couldn't stop the addiction of bulimia. I was completely enslaved to this addiction and couldn't break free. It had consumed my life to such a point that I finally fully surrendered to the fact I would never recover and that it would kill me, but I couldn't get over it. I assumed that the warning from Jesus was referring to this as well, but again, I couldn't stop.

Like with my grandpa, I have a loving family that never gave up praying for me. Thankfully, my mom and grandparents' continued to pray for me, even though it appeared that I would never get better. My mom even sent a prayer request to a TV Evangelist, without my knowing it, who claimed to have the gift of healing. His ministry mailed her back a response and told her that I would be healed. And one week after she received this letter, I did receive a supernatural and instant healing from Jesus.

About a month and a half after I had received the warning from Jesus in my dream, I remember waking up one morning to go downstairs to start my day with my usual binge, but the desire had wholly left me. I remembered marveling all day about how I simply didn't want to binge when I had binged and purged uncontrollably at least four or five times every day for the past few years. Finally, after three days of the desire being completely gone, I told my mom something had happened. We both cried tears of joy when she informed me of the response from the ministry, and we knew then that Jesus had truly healed me.

As with my grandpa, I shudder to think what would have become of me if Jesus hadn't warned me in my dream. I am eternally grateful that He allowed me to stop drinking and miraculously healed me from my addiction to bulimia. I continued my relationship with my ex-husband, but I am incredibly thankful to Jesus that I didn't bring alcoholism and bulimia into our marriage. There were other problems that I've talked about, but thankfully these were not added to them.

Never Give Up Praying.

My dad, on the other hand, iron-willed it. He finally stopped drinking for good, not because he wanted to, but because he got a second DUI, which cost him a small fortune. Most people, however, cannot do this no matter how hard they want to be free. They may not need a healing to be as miraculous as my grandpa's. But, before deliverance from an addiction of any kind can take place, three things have to happen:

1. They have to admit they have a problem.
2. They have to want to stop.
3. They have to accept that they are powerless over the addiction.

In this surrender, the Grace of God can take over and set them free.

My dad, however, was in a different category and the rare few who can iron-will it. All of my life, my brothers, mom, grandparents, and I prayed for my dad to stop drinking, but to no avail. We often confronted my dad over his drinking and smoking, but he would never admit there was any problem. And although he had been baptized in the Baptist Church when he was little, he was a professed agnostic.

Thinking back, I'm genuinely impressed that, as I mentioned before, he completely supported my mom in raising us Catholic. Going to church was never open for discussion, even though he didn't join us and even mocked us at times for our faith. I've often wondered if, deep down, he wished he shared our faith and wanted us, kids, to have this even though he didn't seem to desire it or be able to grasp it for himself.

Despite seeing no light at the end of the tunnel with my dad's drinking, we never stopped praying. One thing we can always count on is that God is faithful, and our prayers are always working, and no matter how dark a situation might appear to be in the natural realm, God is always working behind the scenes in the supernatural. When we fully surrender a person to God, saying, "Whatever takes, Lord," we can be especially assured of His working as we have taken our hands off and given God full reign. If a person doesn't surrender gently, I firmly believe God will allow uncomfortable circumstances to occur in a person's life to encourage them to want to change.

God's Uncomfortable Discipline

When I was 11 years old, my dad got his first DUI. We all believe this was one of those uncomfortable circumstances sent from God. I'm shocked that it took all those years for him to get his first one, but he always took the back roads home when he knew he was too intoxicated to be driving. I can only imagine what the cop would have thought if my dad had had to open the passenger side door to get out to do the Field Sobriety Test. As a kid, I learned how to open the door very cautiously if my dad was dropping me off somewhere to avoid a cascade of beer cans falling to the ground outside the door for all to see. I still get a sick feeling in my stomach if I hear even a soda can fall out of a car onto the pavement, as it brings back this terrible memory.

After this first DUI, my dad stopped drinking for three months, as it cost him a small fortune. His stopping cold turkey was the first time I saw someone iron-will away an addiction. Regardless of how he did it, we were all so happy, and I remember this being a good time for my family. It was so wonderful not to have alcohol in our home for the first time. Unfortunately, though, his sobriety didn't last.

Approximately three months later, I will never forget seeing my dad come through the door that night, obviously intoxicated. I remember our faces dropping and feeling like my heart had sunk to the floor. My mom sheepishly asked him, "Have you been drinking?" Without missing a beat, my dad responded defensively, "Yeah, what about it?" And after this, he returned to drinking with a vengeance. Yet it was even more challenging to be around it after we had tasted life without it.

It also made it even more difficult because my mom had finished her college degree and started working full-time. She was a food service supervisor in a nursing home and had to work most nights. My mom, being gone, left my dad alone with all of us, without her to buffer his drinking. When my dad was drinking, he was verbally abusive to my oldest brother, and the fighting was terrible between them. I assumed the role of peacekeeper, always trying to deescalate my dad, but you cannot reason with someone who is drunk. My brothers just did their best to stay out of the line of fire, and we were all thankful when he finally passed out in his chair. These years were especially tough times of my childhood.

As I said before, God is always working even if it doesn't look like anything is happening in the spiritual realm. When I was 16, my dad got his second DUI. He told us, "I bet you were praying this would happen." And to be honest, we were. This DUI cost him more than a small fortune. In addition, he lost his license for six months. My second oldest brother had to drive him to and from work every day, and he had to go to jail every weekend for this time frame. It was right at this same time that I started dating my ex-husband. I told him that my dad had to go on business trips every weekend, which is why he was always gone. I chuckle at that now but am thankful that he believed me then.

My dad's stint in jail was the most uncomfortable experience God allowed to happen to him, and as the old saying goes, "It scared him straight." After the second DUI, my dad never drank again. I would like to say that he replaced his drinking with Jesus, as it had been for my grandpa, but, sadly, this was not the case. Grandpa always said that something will always replace an addiction once a person is free. And my dad replaced it, sadly, with depression and resentment.

A Dry Drunk

We were incredibly grateful that he had stopped drinking, but tragically, he was not a happier person because of it. I do think my dad experienced what is called a "dry drunk." *Alcoholic.org* describes this as follows, "A 'dry drunk' is someone who is sober but is struggling with the emotional and psychological issues that led them to have a problem with alcohol" (2). Alcoholism is a physical addiction, but it is also a Band-Aid for the emotional problems that caused the addiction in the first place. Until these are addressed, the habit might end, but these won't. Unfortunately, this was the case with my dad.

Furthermore, when a person stops drinking or doing drugs, they also quickly discover their real friends. My parent's "friends" no longer invited them to their parties or wanted to associate with them. I'm sure this was another painful aspect for my dad. However, it was a good thing as I don't think he would have stayed sober if they had continued to socialize with them.

Sadly, my dad became very depressed, making him more angry and bitter. I think my dad also had a sort of love affair with alcohol, and he resented the fact he had to stop. It had been his closest companion ever since he was about 16 years old, and my dad mourned the loss of it. Perhaps being sober also made him face emotional issues he had shoved down all his life.

I'm sure the fact that my dad kept everything inside made giving up alcohol even harder on him. He had erected a wall around him, rarely letting anyone in to know what he was going through. There had been a few times when he was drinking that he would share a few things here and there, but for the most part, my dad kept any suffering he was going through to himself. He wasn't the type to go to AA and find support in others, so I wonder what private hell my dad went through giving up alcohol? Perhaps the anger and resentment were also manifestations of his inner battle to stay sober? And how painful to think that he thought he had to do it all on his own.

My brothers were primarily out of the house by this time, so his anger shifted from my oldest brother to my mom. I was drinking heavily during the first few years after he stopped. And I was severely bulimic. I was too much into my own world with my eating disorder, working, school, my ex-husband, and my friends to pay much attention to it. But, looking back, I realize why my mom threw herself into her work. I wasn't available to her, nor were my brothers, and it was her escape.

At 19, I got married to my ex-husband and moved away to California. And although my mom and I have always been close, she didn't complain about the situation with my dad, so I wasn't aware of how bad it was during this time. My ex-husband and I were there for two and a half years and then moved back home to Colorado, so, again, I wasn't home to see everything that was going on. (Our time in California was discussed in depth in the chapter "The Broken Promise.")

When I moved back, I spent a great deal of time with my parents because my ex-husband wasn't home very often. My parents and I had a lot of good times together going to the mountains and boating. My dad was always at his best in nature, and we spent much time there together. As I mentioned earlier in the chapter, my dad was in his element there. The beautiful person God created him to be, shined through in nature. When we were back at the house, however, I noticed how critical and verbally abusive my dad was to my mom. He wasn't to me but witnessing how he treated my mom was heartbreaking. This treatment of my mom went on for many years, and it seemed there was no hope in sight. She was loyal to a fault, though, and to this day, never thought of divorce as an option.

In these next few years, I had my first two little boys. My dad was good to them and seemed to enjoy being around them. Watching him interact with them was fun. He enjoyed giving them rides on his backhoe and sneaking them cookies, as I didn't like them having a lot of sweets. Also, during this time, my parents were building their dream home. They had bought 10 acres, moved from my childhood home, and lived in the shop my dad built while they were building the house. This was one project that my parents seemed to enjoy working on together, and this, along with continued prayers, gave me hope that my dad would finally stop being so verbally abusive to my mom.

The day finally came for my parents to move into their new beautiful home. Seeing my dad's pride in this lovely house he had built was fun. However, it was also about this time that I started noticing my dad seemed out of it at night when I was over there. It started worrying me that he was developing early onset dementia or wasn't doing well mentally.

After the New Year, he also caught what we initially thought was bronchitis. He went to the doctor, and they sent him home with amoxicillin, saying it should do the trick. Well, the amoxicillin didn't do the trick, and about two weeks later, my mom had to take him to the ER as he had horrific pain in his chest. As I mentioned before, my dad always kept any suffering to himself, so for him to agree to go to the ER told us how much pain he must have been experiencing.

The ER doctor did a chest X-Ray, something that should have been done when he went in for bronchitis, as my dad had been a chain smoker since he was 16, and the X-Ray showed a giant mass on his lung. They sent him home with pain meds and oxygen and insisted he followed up with an oncologist the next day.

There Are No Atheists in Foxholes.

On February 1st, the day of my dad's 52nd birthday, he was diagnosed with stage four lung cancer and told he had eight weeks to live. The years of alcohol abuse and chain smoking had taken their toll. What I thought might be early onset dementia was a lack of oxygen at night, causing him not to be able to think correctly. I also wonder how much of his anger was caused by cancer that he must have had far longer than we imagined? I guess we will never know. However, we knew that short of a miracle healing, this man who always seemed infallible was given a death sentence.

After he heard the news, ironically, on his 52 birthday, he stopped smoking. He had never been able to before, but upon hearing this news, he quit cold turkey, just like he did with alcohol, but sadly it was too late. And although his cancer created terrible worry and sadness for our family, our biggest fear was that he had never accepted Jesus as His Lord and Savior.

My dad had to spend a great deal of his time in the cancer ward as he quickly became extremely sick. One night early on, while he was in the hospital, my mom confronted him in a panic. She asked him, "Are you really going to die without accepting Jesus into your life and risk your eternal soul? Don't you realize you don't have time to wait? It's now or never!" There is an old military saying that there are no atheists in foxholes. And it was at this time that my dad said He wanted to accept Jesus as His Savior. My dad was in a foxhole confronted with one of the greatest enemies of us all – death. And as tragic as this was, we knew this was a situation God allowed to bring this stubborn, strong-willed man to his knees finally.

Although it was devastating watching my dad suffering so terribly, there was an element of joy, perhaps even delirium, as for the first time in our lives, my dad was praying with us all. We could barely believe this. Our lifelong prayers were finally answered, and we were overjoyed. My grandparents were staying with my mom to help. And my grandpa, a Eucharistic Minister, was bringing my dad Communion daily, and we marveled at how much my dad looked forward to it.

People who came into his room in the hospital would say, "There's something special in this room." And we all knew that the Holy Spirit was present. We, of course, were praying for a miracle healing for my dad, but we had a level of peace now, knowing that if Jesus didn't choose to heal him physically, he would die a redeemed man.

My Last Precious Memories

A few days before my dad passed away, he was able to come home and spend a little time in the beautiful home he had built. I was there every day with my two little boys, and by this time, my brother who lived in another city and my sister-in-law were also there to help. My brother was helping my mom with the business issues, and my sister-in-law was helping me care for my dad.

The cancer had caused my dad's feet to swell horribly with fluid. This made it impossible to put socks on my dad's freezing feet and a blanket felt too heavy on them. My sister-in-law had the ingenious idea to sew two socks together to make one large one for each foot. I jumped in to help her make these.

I had just finished sewing the oversized socks to put on my dad's feet which were now so swollen with fluid from cancer that they looked like he had elephantiasis. I gently reached down to put the fresh pair of dry "booties" on the most fierce man in the world, who now used a wheelchair as cancer, in its final stages, persisted with a vengeance to wage war on his terribly weakened body.

"Does this hurt?" I asked as I finished pulling the socks over his freezing ankles.

"Not too bad; they feel warm," he said softly, barely keeping his eyes open as he spoke.

"Dad…are you scared? I mean, are you scared to die?" I asked cautiously, knowing that it was a great accomplishment if I could get him to open up to me.

This sun-weathered, beer drinking, cigarette-smoking man of steel had a great deal to share with the world, with me. Yet, some unseen force had always seemed determined to have him leave this world with it all bottled up inside. As I mentioned before, only on rare occasions, mostly when he had been drinking, would it allow him the freedom of opening up and sharing what he kept hidden inside. I went on speaking to him.

"Please tell me, Dad, are you afraid…please tell me."

"I don't want to die if that's what you mean, but am I scared? I guess I'm more scared to leave all of you here without me," he said, closing his eyes more tightly.

Suddenly he began raising his finger up and down, up and down, and then he would stop and begin this rhythm again as though he were keeping time to a metronome set to skip every fourth beat. He went on to explain.

"My heart, it's like it beats steady, and then on every fourth beat, it just stops…when it stops, I fall asleep, but just for a brief….," Not finishing the word moment, he dozed off briefly and then quickly opened his eyes again.

"Are you awake, Dad?"

"I guess so," he chuckled.

"You know, Dad, God, has it all under control." I was extra cautious with this statement, as discussing God with my dad was a new luxury.

Looking at me more sweetly than I had ever remembered, he answered me with the words I had waited a lifetime to hear.

"Anna, I do not doubt God has it all under control, but it's time for you to understand that."

With tears welling up in my eyes, I reached for his hand. Then, whispering, I quoted 2 Corinthians 4:16, saying,

"That's why we are not discouraged. No, even if outwardly we are wearing out, inwardly we are being renewed each and every day" (3).

I wasn't sure if my dad heard me, but his response told me he had.

He said back, "That's right. I'm going away soon . . . I'll be building a house for all of you."

He briefly dozed off, waking up just as quickly to again remind me, "Remember, Anna, God has it all under control."

This conversation was the sweetest one I ever had with my dad. This man, whose addiction had stolen most of his life, would not die in darkness. I realized then that we can never, ever give up on someone, not ever. We are here to pray for and help each other go home to Heaven when it is our time. Those with addictions and those without them. In the end, all that matters is eternal salvation.

Three days later, my dear dad took his last breath in the hospital. My mom was right by his side and was on the phone praying the rosary with my grandparents. He died peacefully in the arms of his faithful wife of 33 years and with her and her parents praying the prayer of angels to escort him, a sober and clean man, to eternity.

Only You and God Can Decide.

I pray that these very personal examples have given hope to those addicted or are married to someone who is! I focused on alcoholism and an eating disorder because these are my personal experiences. Their purpose is not to dismiss the horrors of drug addiction or other life-enslaving and life-altering addictions. Sadly, we live in a world where they are the norm. A great deal of people suffer from some addiction throughout their lifetime. But what I share in this chapter can be applied to any of them. You only need to substitute alcoholism for whatever addiction is affecting you or a loved one, and I pray my experiences will give you hope that there is a way to freedom.

Today Is the Day.

If you are an addict, I beg you to seek help. Don't let another day go by, allowing addiction to steal your life and the lives of your family. Alcoholics Anonymous (A.A.) (4) and Narcotics Anonymous (N.A.) (5) are excellent 12 Step programs that have proven effective in helping to get clean and sober. My grandpa attended A.A. frequently and appreciated the support and accountability from his fellow brothers and sisters in this program. There are great programs to help heal and recover from eating disorders as well. Regardless of the addiction, be sure to find a God-centered program. Studies have shown that those that are not God-centered don't often help long-term. Also, remember that you will most likely need to find new friends. Often the "friends" you thought you had will scatter when you no longer party with them. And if they don't, you may have to be the one to scatter as associating with them can drag you back into drinking or using. The "birds of a feather, flock together" analogy.

These following steps, if followed, can help you break free:

1. See and admit it as a problem – Drugs and alcohol are poison. Any addiction (Something that controls you) is harmful, self-defeating, and usually, time and life stealing.

2. Completely surrender yourself and the addiction to Jesus – You CANNOT do this alone.

3. Get into a Support Group – A.A., N.A., and Eating Disorder Support Groups, etc. that are God-centered and offer a 12-Step Program (6).

4. Assess how much you are drinking or using per day – Try to cut it down by 10% each day to avoid withdrawal. Take N.A.C., N-Acetyl Cysteine. N.A.C. helps to reduce cravings (1)

5. H.A.L.T. – My counselor gave me this acronym, which helps me to this day.

    H – Never let yourself get too hungry – This is important with addiction. Low blood sugar puts us in a weakened state, and we cannot make good decisions, making us vulnerable to temptation.

    A – Never let yourself get too angry – Getting too angry lowers our I.Q. Like being too hungry, we don't make good decisions, reduce our impulse control, and can be a trigger that sends us back to our addiction for comfort and coping.

    L – Never let yourself get too lonely –Loneliness is a killer. A wonderful priest, also an exorcist, says that he finds loneliness the number one reason people dive into unhealthy habits and relationships that ultimately move them away from God. But, like anger, loneliness can also cause us to turn to our addiction for comfort and coping.

    T – Never let yourself get too tired – When we are tired, we are vulnerable. Our emotions can get out of whack, and problems loom bigger than life. Being too tired also puts us in a dangerous place for resisting temptations.

6. Recite the Serenity Prayer Daily:

    God grant me the serenity
    to accept the things I cannot change;
    courage to change the things I can;
    and wisdom to know the difference.

    Living one day at a time;
    enjoying one moment at a time;
    accepting hardships as the pathway to peace;
    taking, as He did, this sinful world
    as it is, not as I would have it;
    trusting that He will make all things right
    if I surrender to His Will;

that I may be reasonably happy in this life
and supremely happy with Him
forever in the next.
Amen.
(Reinhold Niebuhr (1892-1971)) (7)

7. Recite the *Prayer of St. Francis* Daily:

   Lord, make me an instrument of Thy peace;
   Where there is injury, pardon;
   Where there is error, the truth;
   Where there is doubt, the faith;
   Where there is despair, hope;
   Where there is darkness, light;
   And where there is sadness, joy.
   O Divine Master,
   Grant that I may not so much seek
   To be consoled, as to console;
   To be understood, as to understand;
   For it is in giving that we receive;
   It is in pardoning that we are pardoned;
   And it is in dying that we are born to eternal life. Amen (8).

8. Pray Against Generational Curses – Like with our eye color, height, and hair color, sins can be passed on. It is important to pray prayers of deliverance for generational curses. The best book I've ever read on this, and mentioned in an earlier chapter, is by an African priest named, Fr. Jozefu B. Ssemakula, and the title of the book is, *The Healing of Families: How to Pray Effectively for Those Stubborn Personal and Familial Problems.* This book is intense and requires a lot of participation, but it is worth every minute of it (9).

And if perhaps you don't have a full-blown problem yet but find yourself going further and further into an addiction, try to stop now before you become enslaved in its trenches. I recommend never touching alcohol or drugs, as it is too easy to become addicted. Remember that if you never start, you don't have to stop!

Sobriety Is a Gift to a Marriage.

The greatest gift you can give to your marriage and to yourself is to get free from addiction. You are not in this by yourself; there is much help if you want it. But don't try to do it alone. Jesus is always there to help you. Also, remember that it takes courage to go through life clean and sober! And Jesus will give you all the courage that you need. Just ask Him!

If it is your spouse who is addicted and they are willing to get help and genuinely want to change, I suggest getting behind them and supporting them. First, seek professional and spiritual help, and then take the advice of a professional on working through this together. My personal life experiences have made me adamant about trying to give people opportunities to get free from addiction. I'm so grateful that my family didn't give up on me, my grandpa, and my dad. And my family is a testimony that lives can be turned around with the healing power of Jesus Christ.

As I say this, though, I know how difficult it is to live with someone with no interest in getting better and who won't even admit they have a problem. Not even God can force someone to change who doesn't want to. We begged my dad for years to stop and to get help but to no avail. So, if they won't get help, I encourage you to seek it for yourself and your children if you have them to help you through this. Pray and seek Godly counsel on the best action to take in this situation. Only God and you can decide what is best for you and your family to do in your case.

However, if you or your children are in danger, please seek help immediately. Don't let another day go by without doing so. Praying still for them to get help from a safe distance is okay. Whether or not you stay in the marriage, I suggest checking into Al-Anon (10). It is excellent for children of or those married to an addict. Seek help from your local priest or pastor and parish as well. Pray, fast, and turn the person over to Jesus. Thank Jesus every day that he will take this terrible situation and work it for good. I know he miraculously healed my grandpa and me. Then, if the addict is willing to be delivered, I believe a healthy marriage has the opportunity to follow.

Chapter Eleven

"The Narcissist"

Another form of abuse that has reached epidemic proportions and is affecting families, marriages, and society is narcissism. That said, it's hard to find any current relationship article that doesn't mention the term "narcissist." Although it is an actual epidemic, it is also unfortunate, this label is thrown around very flippantly, and people are being "diagnosed" as narcissists by individuals who don't understand what it actually is. As with each chapter on abuse, however, I do not claim to be a professional but can only speak about my experiences, what I have learned from professionals, and what I have learned in the school of life.

That said, the over-labeling of narcissism reminds me of the recent influx of people following a gluten-free diet. Comparing these two issues might seem like an odd correlation, but just as it often seems the whole world is suddenly narcissists, it also seems like the entire world is suddenly gluten-free as well.

For example, I have celiac disease, a complete gluten intolerance, and I am very severe. It only takes a smidge of gluten to make me very sick. When I order food at a restaurant, I always stress the severity of my gluten intolerance. Yet, I cannot express how many eye rolls and condescending tones I have experienced from servers, as they don't take it seriously. And consequently, eating out is like playing Russian roulette. Despite how hard I try to convey my needs to the server, I get sick more than I don't because they don't take it seriously.

The same thing is happening with narcissism. The flippant overuse of the term causes many to be labeled as something they are not, and also causes those suffering in a relationship with an actual narcissist not to be taken seriously. Not taking someone seriously who is in this toxic relationship is like eating gluten for those with celiac disease. It is dangerous. Excellent, perhaps for the narcissist, but not the person caught in their web. Therefore, one of the most critical issues in getting help is the validation that what you are experiencing is not in your head and is an abusive situation with an actual narcissist.

Although it is not generally possible to get someone besides ourselves diagnosed by a professional, before labeling someone as a narcissist, educating yourself about what it is and the signs to look for is essential. First and foremost, it is crucial to acknowledge that narcissistic personality disorder (NPD) is an actual disorder and a growing problem in our society. Education empowers you and opens your eyes to notice red flags that you once may not have been aware of before and might help you identify the root cause of patterns of abuse you might be experiencing. I cannot express how eye-opening and validating it was for me to do this.

To start at the beginning, the origins of narcissism come from an ancient Greek myth. The gist of this myth tells how the Greek hunter Narcissus, known for his beauty, saw his reflection in the water and fell in love with it. However, when he finally realized it was his reflection and that a relationship could not materialize, he fell into despair and committed suicide (1).

The obsession with self in the myth goes along with author Josephine Campbell's article, "Narcissism (Psychology)," when she states, "Narcissism refers to a series of characteristics including self-love, selfishness, and manipulative behavior" (2). It is important to note that everyone has some narcissistic character traits that are not all bad. They can even be beneficial at times. But it is when these traits become all-consuming, like with the Greek hunter, that the problem lies, and it goes from being a few traits to narcissistic personality disorder (NPD). There are actually ten different personality disorders, and narcissism is only one of them (3).

Education Is Power.

According to the *American Psychiatric Association's Diagnostic and Statistical Manual of Mental Disorders 5th Edition* (DSM), the primary characteristics used to diagnose this specific disorder are as follows:

1. Grandiose sense of self
2. Preoccupied with fantasies of unlimited success, power, brilliance, beauty, or ideal
3. Believes that he or she is "special" and unique and can only be understood by, or should associate with other special or high-status people (or institutions).
4. Requires excessive admiration.
5. Sense of entitlement, unreasonable expectations of favorable treatment or full compliance with his or her expectations.
6. Exploitative, takes advantage of others to achieve his or her own ends.
7. Lacks empathy: unable to recognize or identify with the feelings and needs of others.
8. Envious of others or believes that others are envious of him or her.
9. Shows arrogant, haughty behaviors or attitudes (4)

According to Katherine Allen, M.A., Psychotherapist, and Expert in Narcissistic Personality Disorder and Trauma Recovery from Narcissistic Abuse, the most pronounced trait of all these is a lack of empathy. This lack of empathy makes narcissists much more likely to commit domestic violence, cheat, and lie, as well as the other characteristics listed above (5). I heard one person say that if a narcissist is talking, they are lying. Narcissism also often goes hand-in-hand with other disorders. Stats from 2022 show that of those diagnosed, 40% suffered from substance abuse, 40% also had anxiety disorders, and 20% were also diagnosed with (6) mood disorders (7). The rate of substance abuse is likely so high because they are using it to cope with the deep-seated insecurities and emotional turmoil within them. It is essential to remember that this is not a personality flaw or a few annoying characteristic traits; it is a mental health disorder that has a varying degree of severity.

How Prevalent Is It?

This information leads to the question of how many people in the United States are diagnosed with NPD. Cleveland Clinic's 2022 stats show that up to 5% of people have NPD. Gender also does seem to play a role, as 75% of those diagnosed are men (8). 5% might not sound like a large percentage. Still, Sandra L. Brown, founder of the Institute for Relational Harm Reduction and Public Pathology Education, breaks it down to show how far-reaching this is. During her research, she estimated approximately 304 million people worldwide. Of those 304 million people, 12 million are diagnosed with a personality disorder. She then hypothesized that if the 12 million had approximately five partners each, over 60 million people would be subject to narcissistic abuse (7). Although this is a hypothetical calculation, it highlights just how far-reaching this abuse has become.

However, one problem with the 5% stat, Ms. Campbell's hypothesis, and even the gender percentage is that very few people with NPD will ever seek help, as they won't acknowledge they have a problem. And, for those who seek help, 40% drop out of treatment. Contributing factors to this are that reversing this process is slow and challenging. And they are most likely struggling to acknowledge the need or desire to change. They have perfected their manipulative tactics and they work, so why change? (7). Therefore, this statistic is likely much higher than it appears, and the number Ms. Brown hypothesized is even higher. This disorder creates abusive relationships as it "causes people to think, feel, and behave in ways that hurt themselves or others. Signs of personality disorders usually appear in the late teen years and early adulthood" (9).

What Causes Narcissistic Personality Disorder?

Although there is much debate about what causes NPD, and the precise cause is not known, there are certain factors that professionals agree on. According to Cleveland Clinic they are as follows:

- Childhood trauma (such as physical, sexual and verbal abuse).
- Early relationships with parents, friends, and relatives.
- Genetics (family history).
- Hypersensitivity to textures, noise, or light in childhood.
- Personality and temperament (9).

Katherine Allen, M.A., Psychotherapist, who is an expert in NPD and Trauma Recovery from Narcissistic Abuse, explains that it is essential to keep in mind that narcissists are hurting people. "They were at one time victims and are crippled and injured people who, because of this, go on to perpetuate this pathology, repeating the cycle." She explains further that many never want to change, as "they enjoy the benefits (power, control, success, accolades, etc.)" that this destructive behavior brings. Their tactics are perfected and work (10).

The Different Masks of the Narcissist

Over the years, people have tried to come up with different labels for narcissists because there are varying ways in which they manifest their symptoms. However, it comes down to three different types of masks they wear: the overt, the covert, and the community narcissist. It is essential to be aware of all three, as they initially will look quite different. But, when the mask comes off, they are all the same; sadly, predatory and looking for victims to feed their deep-seated insecurities. I am forever grateful to Katherine Allen for sharing her expertise with me that you will read throughout this chapter and below, that has been nothing short of life saving.

The Overt

The first mask is that of the overt narcissist. This type is the easiest to spot. They are typically loud, command the attention in a room, are arrogant, demanding, boastful, and feel superior to those around them (11). An example was when I had gotten myself tangled up in a disastrous online relationship. Every night, this guy would call me and talk for hours without stopping for a breath. He would boast the entire time, "teaching" me about his scholarly wisdom and knowledge. After a while, he would ask me how I was, but before I could answer, he was on to his next subject. He thoroughly enjoyed that I allowed him to have this monologue so he could hear himself continue on and on with his endless diatribe. He wasn't looking for a relationship, but a victim to "feed" his needs and deep insecurities. I will go into more detail about this later in the chapter.

The Covert

This next mask is the most dangerous, as this narcissist is known as the "Master of Disguise" because they come across as the complete opposite of the overt and are much harder to identify. They are professional at playing the victim, and they use this tactic to draw in the actual victim. They appear kind, caring, humble, and full of empathy, but it is a disguise to hide that they are inwardly selfish, cunning, controlling, angry, and vindictive. This type is looking for a victim to take care of them, as they are innately lazy. In addition, they are pessimistic, so they also seek a victim to provide the positivity they lack within themselves (11).

An example of a covert would be someone you are meeting for the first time for coffee, and within the first half hour of the conversation, they tell you about their abusive childhood and how it has affected their whole life. This story may be accurate, but they are using it as a means to an end. They have found that telling their victims about their traumatic experiences right from the start "hooks" them in to allow the manipulation process to start right from the beginning. It also weeds out those who don't show interest or empathy for their situation, so they don't waste their time (12).

The Community Narcissist, A.K.A. - "The Hero!"

This final mask of the narcissist is called the Community Narcissist. This type will most likely be the head of the church food bank, president of the PTA, or a company CEO. From the start, it is crucial to declare that I am not stating everyone in these positions is a narcissist, but that these are positions community narcissists are drawn to because of the image associated with them. All narcissists prioritize their image, but it is especially vital for this type. They regard themselves as nurturing, understanding, and empathetic, and cherish their status as "givers" and "doers" within their community or companies. They also believe themselves to be superior to the rest of humanity and take pride in proudly announcing how much they give to charity and do for others. Within the first 20 minutes of meeting a community narcissist, they will tell you how they are the head coach for both of their children's competitive softball teams, the youth pastor at their church, the leader of the men's ministry, and how they gave the most in charity over the past year (12).

A Narcissists Main Target

Hopefully, the information above provided helpful insight into understanding what a narcissist is and the characteristics of narcissistic personality disorder. And now, it is equally important to shed light on who a narcissist is seeking and who is most vulnerable to their tactics. The explanation for this is usually a bit less complex. As mentioned above, someone with NPD lacks empathy and compassion. So, they are looking for someone with these qualities that they don't have. This person is called an empath, which simply means someone with empathy and compassion. So, anyone with empathy and compassion can be prey to a narcissist (13).

Also, as mentioned previously, image is everything to a narcissist. Sadly, narcissists are incapable of truly loving anyone. They view people as objects and as a means to an end. Someone with NPD will seek relationships with someone who will make them look good and has beneficial qualities that will feed their ego. So, if you were the target of a narcissist, it is a compliment, of sorts, because they saw these great things in you (13).

Sadly, a narcissist is like a chameleon. They lack any real substance within and will change their personality to fit with whomever they are around. They are often the ones you cannot believe you have so much in common with when you first meet them. They copy the qualities they see in you to attract you, build your trust, and hook you in. Any unsuspecting person is vulnerable to this. A narcissist thrives best around people who have never heard of this disorder and have no idea what they are dealing with, let alone how to set up boundaries to protect themselves (13). That is why awareness and education are so important. "A narcissist's worst nightmare is an educated empath" (14).

The Most Vulnerable

Although any empath can be a target, some are especially vulnerable and, sadly, some are even drawn to a narcissist. These are empaths who have, in most cases, suffered narcissistic abuse as a child or at other times in their lives. They've experienced the "tricks of the trade" personally, and although toxic and even dangerous, it is familiar, so it feels "right." Therefore, awareness of what makes us incredibly vulnerable is as important as learning what a narcissist is. If we know our weaknesses, we can also learn how to safeguard ourselves from them (15). According to Katherine Allen, M.A. Psychotherapist, a few of these traits are as follows:

1. Trained, Usually as a Child – An empath who had a narcissistic parent or another significant family member knows what it is like to be the victim or how to play the game. They speak and understand the language of a narcissist, so there is an immediate attraction. As mentioned above, it feels "right" because dysfunction is what the empath understands. However, this is dangerous as it causes you to enter relationships with toxic people.

2. Forever Trying to Please the Narcissistic Parent or Significant Family Member – A common saying is that you will marry

your father or mother. A child with a narcissistic parent or significant family member will seek these same qualities in a mate and other relationships in the hopes of finally being able to please this person. It is generally not something done consciously but subconsciously.

3. The Caretaker – Empaths, especially those who grew up in an abusive environment, often have an insatiable desire to please and help others, even to their detriment (15).

The Final Outcome

Regardless of who you are, if you stay in a narcissistic relationship long enough, the outcome is generally bleak. Either the narcissist will discard you for one of the often many interests they've been pursuing on the side. Or, you may have to escape the relationship finally and pray that you can get out of it before there is nothing left of you: your identity, self-worth, respect, trust, often your finances, family, friends, and so on.

People who finally escape feel ashamed that they let themselves get involved in such a manipulative and dangerous relationship. Thinking, *how could I have been so stupid?* But it is essential to understand that people with NPD are professionals at reading people, identifying their vulnerabilities, and using a very effective pattern of manipulation to trap their victims. They usually have had years of practice (16).

The average person doesn't function this way or even think to do such things, so they are easy prey, and the narcissist counts on this. So please, if you are beating yourself up over this, take this time to bring all the hurt to Jesus instead and let Him heal you from the trauma and abuse you have suffered. And as I say all of this, I don't advocate for divorce, but if you are married to a narcissist, you need to seek professional help and spiritual counsel to help guide you on what to do in this abusive situation.

This outcome is why most narcissists are single; however, it does not consider how many relationships they are in and out of throughout their lifetime. The second largest percentage is divorced, and the smallest percentage is married. Longevity in relationships for those with NPD is bleak. The relationships that last are usually due to a spouse hanging in there despite the abusive situation, and they haven't been discarded yet (17).

You might think, "This is too bleak, and can't God change the person?" And, the answer is, YES, of course! God can change anyone, just as He did my dad before he died, and we should never give up praying for someone. But God doesn't infringe on free will. And as we talked about in the addiction section, the first step to getting well is admitting you have a problem and then surrendering yourself and your situation to God. The problem with NPD is that most will never acknowledge they are the problem. They will only see themself as the victim and, therefore, will never get the help they need to get better.

However, if someone is praying for them, I know that God will never stop wooing them. As we've talked about before, His wooing often involves uncomfortable situations that He uses to bring them to the end of themselves, in the hope that they will finally realize He is what they need. Yet, if the condition is intolerable and dangerous, you may need to pray from a distance.

As stated earlier, if you are married to a narcissist, encourage them to get help. If they won't, get counseling yourself, and spiritual guidance from a trusted priest or therapist that is experienced in dealing with NPD. Pray as never before for God to show you His will in this situation. Only you and God can determine the course of action you need to take. And, if you are discarded, remember that that too may be God's way of forcing you to leave a situation you never would on your own. Without God's help or being forced, you cannot leave due to trauma bonding, your faith, your vows, your commitment, you are too broken, your children, or many other reasons. So, you will never go unless God moves in the situation and forces you, as was the case in my marriage.

Making It Real

Again, throughout my life, I heard the term narcissist from time to time, but I had no real idea what it was and had never heard of NPD. It wasn't until a few years ago, when I got myself entangled in a very toxic online relationship I mentioned earlier, that I began to realize how this disorder had been a thread throughout my entire life. And unfortunately, it took almost losing myself and damaging essential relationships in my life before I finally had my eyes open to what it is. By the Grace of God and lifesaving help from one of my best friends, an expert on NPD, I began to learn about narcissism and what it entails. This new understanding was the key to allowing me to start healing from the narcissistic abuse I had encountered since childhood.

As I began learning about NPD, it was vital for me to remember what Katherine Allen stated about them: that narcissists "were at one time victims and are crippled and injured people who, because of this, go on to perpetuate this pathology, repeating the cycle" (18).

This quote aligns with the timeless adage that hurting people often hurt others. Sadly, my dad was an injured person. And it was a travesty that he did not invite the Holy Spirit into his life to heal him from the abuse he suffered as a child until his deathbed conversion. So, just like alcoholism can be genetic, NPD or strong narcissist traits often are as well, especially in situations like my dad's.

My dad was never diagnosed, but as with not attending A.A., he would have never gone to see a counselor about this or anything. It just wasn't part of his makeup. However, with all that I have learned about narcissism over the last few years, I am confident that, at a minimum, he had high traits for this disorder and was more than likely a covert narcissist.

My childhood made me one of the most vulnerable empaths I discussed earlier. I grew up in a home where I learned how to play the game. I learned how to read the room and act accordingly. As a result, from a very early age, I took on the false sense of responsibility of needing to be the peacemaker. I mainly took on this responsibility when my mom started working nights to deescalate my dad's verbal abuse towards my oldest brother. And, like the traits of most vulnerable empaths discussed earlier, I also wanted more than anything to please my dad, yet I always felt that I fell short.

My dad wasn't mean to me like he was to my brother, but he was a man of few words and didn't show affection to us kids, so in my little mind, I took it to mean he wasn't proud of me. It wasn't until I was around 14 that I finally had my dad verbalize something about me that made him proud. He told me that people who had met me told him how pretty I was, and I could see him beam with pride when he said this to me. Of course, I felt anything but pretty, but these words went straight to my soul. In one way, it made me feel so happy because I was desperate to please him. Yet, I also know it was then that I subconsciously began to believe that if I wasn't pretty, I had no value and was unlovable. When I shared what my dad had told me with my mom years later, she told me that he had done the same thing with her when they were in college. Other guys had said to him that they thought my mom was pretty, and it had similarly affected her.

I know my brothers struggled with this, too; yet, I always thought my second-oldest brother was the apple of my dad's eye. I have learned that with a narcissistic parent, there is always a "Golden Child" amongst the siblings. My dad was very open about his displeasure with my oldest brother. Still, my second-oldest brother always made my dad laugh, and he seemed to hold him in high regard.

However, I didn't realize that being the "Golden Child" comes with other significant problems. That child will only remain "golden" as long as they perform or behave in the way the parent expects or drives accolades from them. The pressure on this child is intense, as they know the admiration is conditional. My brother has suffered a great deal because of this, and I was shocked when he told me he never felt "golden" in my dad's eyes.

As I say this, I'm sure there were many things my dad was proud of about each of us. Still, the wall he had erected around himself made it impossible for him to open up and share what was happening inside him with anyone. Perhaps that is one of the reasons he drank, to try to chip at that wall and find some relief from it, but instead, it had the opposite effect. It kept him enslaved. I also believe that the abuse he suffered as a child made him stoic, with little empathy and deep-seated insecurities. If he didn't feel, he couldn't get hurt. So, he had learned to use people, such as my mom, me, and my brother, to try to bolster his ego and make up for these deep-seated wounds. Sadly, this overshadowed the exceptional qualities in my dad, such as his brilliance in math, unparalleled work ethic, and his incredible sportsmanship in fishing and hunting.

Toxic Attractions

Entering the dating scene as a teen, I had no idea that my childhood had made me vulnerable to attracting people who could have NPD or high narcissistic traits. I also didn't know what an empath was, let alone that I was one and a vulnerable one at that. Looking back, I realize that the worst thing I could have done at this time was to enter any relationship. Even if I had been in a relationship with a healthier person, I was in no shape to be in one at all.

You will often hear me say throughout this book that a relationship can only be as healthy as the least healthy partner, and I was not a healthy person. As previously mentioned, I was a severely bulimic, binge drinking, self-loathing mess, and not following our Lord. It was so dangerous for me to even think about being in a relationship in this vulnerable state. But this was when I met my now ex-husband, and once I gave my heart to him in the state I was in, I couldn't find my way out.

As I've mentioned in previous chapters, I knew deep in my heart that things weren't right. Still, I didn't have the strength, tools, or mental capacity to question whether my actions in moving ahead in a relationship with him were best for me. Additionally, at this time in my life, I didn't think about praying for God's will regarding a spouse or whether I should marry my now ex-husband. We won't make good decisions when we are not in God's will. And we should never make the most crucial decision of our life, after our salvation in Christ, without intense prayer. However, I wasn't following Christ at the time. So, at 19, I blindly said "I do," not realizing that a large part of me was trying to find love and acceptance through my ex-husband that I was ultimately still seeking from my dad. And I had not yet recognized how many things my dad and ex-husband had in common.

Repeating Patterns

In the chapter "The Broken Promise," I discuss how neglect was the most challenging aspect of my marriage. Looking back, I realize that pattern was there even while dating, yet I was sure marriage would magically fix it. As I mentioned in a previous chapter, but it is worth repeating, if you are unhappy about a significant issue before getting married, be assured that it will most likely only worsen once you tie the knot. This is especially true if NPD or narcissism is on board.

Regardless, though, and as I've mentioned also in previous chapters, you should never marry someone as a project to change. No one is perfect, certainly not me, and no one likes not feeling accepted for who they are. So, you need to be really happy with who you marry when you take your vows and acknowledge that they won't change. And, if you notice any red flags, don't ignore them. Instead, be sure to recognize each one thoroughly. Write down the pros and cons of the person and be realistic about who you are marrying (19). Make sure you can live with their flaws as well.

However, suppose, while doing this, you decide you cannot tolerate a significant issue about your future spouse. In that case, it's best to determine this before the wedding. Then, you should either postpone or walk away. It is a million times better than after. Yet, sadly, if you were like me then, I was not in a healthy mental or emotional state, and I didn't have the tools or the self-worth needed to walk away.

So, I walked down the aisle, pushing the red flags deep down, and I lived with the neglect and other issues. My ex-husband liked having a family and the whole image, but he always remained a single man in his heart. And his absence confirmed to me each day that, like my dad, I wasn't pleasing to him. So, I spent my entire marriage trying desperately to finally be so.

Yet fast forward 18 years, and my chances for doing so ended, and the discard finally came from my ex-husband. And although there were many unpleasant words between us during the divorce, one thing stuck out perhaps more than any other. It was when he told me, "You are a very beautiful woman, but that's not enough anymore." My ex-husband, like my dad, had a difficult time giving compliments. And now, at the end of my marriage, he was telling me he thought I was beautiful? And that was the only reason he had stayed with me all these years? The beautiful part meant nothing. All I heard from his words was that the only thing he had found of value in me was my looks, and now even that wasn't enough to make me lovable and worth keeping his vows for. These words reiterated the same message I had received from my dad.

The Narcissist Playbook

After the divorce, I was too busy raising my children, pursuing my teaching degree, working, and trying to make ends meet financially, even to consider dating. Over the next 11 years, I worked hard with Jesus to try to heal from a lot of the emotional trauma I had experienced throughout my life, including starting the annulment process. I thought I had made significant progress, but I had not entered the dating arena. And, to this point, I still had no real knowledge of NPD or my vulnerabilities to someone with this disorder.

Because I did not know about NPD, I didn't realize that most narcissists have a playbook they follow to capture their prey (20). I don't know if they do it consciously or not, but when you become aware of the patterns, it is uncanny how similar they all operate, despite which mask of narcissism they wear. Ignorance of this makes us even more vulnerable to being lured in, as we are unaware of their schemes. And as an uneducated empath, it was natural for me to fall into this trap again and again. And it was in hindsight, and the incredible expertise from Katherine Allen's determination of the stages in the "Play Book", that I was able to clearly see how it played out in my own experience.

Stage 1
The Patient Pursuit (21)

At this same time, my oldest son convinced me that I needed to get a Facebook account. I had resisted up to this point because I was afraid it would take up too much time and any extra was sacred. Despite my resistance, he helped me get started. I quickly began enjoying Facebook and spent too much time on it. I justified the time by interacting with many other Catholics and immensely enjoyed their fellowship. From the start, I was vocal about my beliefs and interests. I didn't state my relationship status, but someone could have figured it out, as there were a lot of pictures of the kids and me, but no husband to be found. And at this point, I was very naïve about the dangers that lurk on social media. I pretty much accepted any friend request as long as the person listed 'Christian' or 'Catholic Christian' on their profile.

I stayed away from Private Messenger as much as possible, as I knew that it could start to occupy my time. And I was horrified at how forward men were there, and it was a huge turn-off. One man, however, had sent me a couple of messages that I also noticed liking a few of my posts. So, out of curiosity, I decided to open his message. I knew that if it were the typical offensive and forward pick-up attempt, I would unfriend him like I did the rest.

I was pleasantly surprised to see he had shared a beautiful prayer with me. I sent a quick thank you response, but it intrigued me enough to go on his profile and check him out further. I have to be honest, and I don't mean to sound shallow, but I didn't find him attractive, and I also didn't like that all of his pictures, and there were hundreds, were of himself. So, I dismissed him and went about my day. A few hours later, he responded to my thank you by sending a cute emoji. After that, I didn't hear from him again for a while.

About a month later, I started back to school and had to take the yearly staff photo. I decided to post it as my profile picture on Facebook, asking for prayers for a good school year. He was one of the first to like my picture, commented that he would be praying for me, and told me he admired my faith. I did appreciate his comment as it was respectful, and I thought it was sweet that he said he would pray for me, but, again, I just wasn't interested.

Over the next six months, he continued to like most of my posts and would send me a direct message every now and then. I made an exception for him and opened them because they were generally about God. I would send a quick thank you, which was always followed by a cute gif or emoji.

Stage 2
The "Secret" Drop (22)

I don't know when I started to have feelings for him. But it was almost as if he knew when I did, as the tone of his comments started to change subtly as well, and he would every now and then comment about my appearance. I must admit that I was pretty flattered. It was also around this time that I began to have more extended conversations with him on Messenger, beyond a quick 'thank you' in response to what he had shared. The extended messages led him to ask if we could talk on the phone. I was afraid to give him my phone number, so I suggested we chat on Messenger instead. He didn't mind at all and was very polite, scheduling a time to do so.

I was terribly nervous about talking, but I was excited at the same time. I wondered what we would talk about. I had no idea what to say and wasn't even sure this was safe. Still, I eased my worries by thinking about what an outstanding Catholic he appeared to be. I also thought about the beautiful prayers he had sent me and how he had never stopped pursuing me. And what could it hurt? It was just one phone call. If it didn't go well, I could end it right there. I only wish I had remembered that I told myself the same thing when I accepted an invitation for my first date with my ex-husband. Instead of a phone call, though, I told myself, *It's only one date. What can that hurt?*

I remember my hand trembling as I clicked to answer the phone. I was thankful that we didn't include video, as it was hard enough just talking. As soon as I heard his voice, I felt very drawn to him. And I was delighted that he spoke most of the time, so I didn't have to. We ended up talking for hours. And, in one phone call, he shared so many secret things about himself, things he said he rarely shared with anyone.

I couldn't believe how much I learned about him in just a few hours. He told me about his abusive childhood in California due to both of his parents' alcoholism and their divorce and remarriages. I also learned he had a crazy ex-wife who kept him from seeing his son because she was a pathological liar and had lied about him. He told me about his years in sales and what his current sales job entailed. And how his own battle with alcoholism had led him to become a convert to the Catholic faith. And it was his faith that helped him to stop drinking.

I was flattered that he felt so comfortable sharing so many personal details about his life right from the start. He also told me that as soon as he saw my picture on Facebook, he began praying he would have a chance to meet me. I was blown away, and by the end of the phone call, I felt like I had known him for years. I went from being somewhat attracted to feeling entirely smitten in one phone call. I began asking God to show me if He had sent him to me. And sadly,

I was not aware that he was laying the groundwork to hook me. The "secret dropping," unbeknownst to me, is a manipulation tactic to develop an immediate connection and trust with their prey. It drops your guard and makes you feel comfortable sharing intimate details about your life with them (23). After all, they were willing to open up to you, so it must be "safe" to share with them, right?

Stage Three
Love Bombing (23)

In our following conversation, he began asking me about myself. I was a bit more cautious than he was about sharing, but I felt so comfortable with him. And he had shared so much with me. It made me feel safe. I shared with him things about my childhood and a few things about my marriage. Still, I didn't want to talk about my ex-husband, so I only mentioned that he didn't like spending time with me and the comment about only seeing value in my looks. He listened so intently and was so compassionate and encouraging. I couldn't believe how well he seemed to understand me. It was as if I had known him for years. Of course, it didn't hurt that something about his voice was so attractive. I know that might sound strange, but I realize now that a voice in itself can lure you in.

We began talking every night, and I felt myself falling for him more with every phone call. Early on, he began expressing how much he wanted to take me out to a beautiful dinner, even asking for suggestions on where I would like to go. He had started telling me the most beautiful things. He told me how much he loved my faith and my devotion to my children. He laughed at my jokes and told me how funny I was. He complimented me on the things I had accomplished and told me how attractive my voice and appearance, as seen in my pictures, were to him. But perhaps one of the sweetest things was when he would tell me how much he wished he had known and been with me his whole life, and wished I were the only one he would have ever been married to. He even said he knew I was the "one" and that we would grow old together.

I had never been treated so incredibly wonderfully in my entire life. I was literally floating on cloud nine. Although I didn't find him to be attractive from his pictures when he first started pursuing me, I now found him to be very handsome. His voice made my heart skip a beat. It was no wonder why he was such a successful salesman. It meant the world to me that he seemed to genuinely enjoy my company, so much so that he wanted to spend time on the phone every night into the wee hours of the morning. Of course, I wasn't getting any sleep, but I was on a love "high," so it didn't seem to affect me at first. He convinced me that we should wait to "see" each other until we met in person and assured me he would come visit me as soon as his work schedule was less demanding, so I agreed it was best to wait for this moment, too.

Most importantly, we shared an intense love for Jesus and were passionate about our Catholic faith. I was thrilled that staying pure before marriage was a must for us both. I was delighted to hear that he had always been faithful to his ex-wife and was entirely against cheating. We even started praying together; something he said would bring us closer together, and he was right. I had certainly hit the jackpot, and I knew he must have been sent straight from God. He seemed too good to be true, yet I was convinced he was the real deal.

Sadly, I had no idea how meticulously he was following the narcissist's "playbook," that Katherine Allen told me about (24). Even keeping me up half the night is a manipulation tactic to make you weak and vulnerable. His love bombing was another manipulation tactic narcissists use to seal the deal with their prey. And he was a professional at it. They shower their victim with compliments, time, gifts, and promises about the future. The effects of love bombing are even likened to the high of cocaine and are just as addictive (25). And I was addicted, all right. My head was in the clouds, and I had no idea of the danger that I was in. And that soon, this relationship would take me as low as it had made me high.

Stage Four
Ghosting (25)

Over the next few weeks, however, I began to notice that his calls weren't coming in as regularly. I had grown used to a call every night at 8:00 or 8:30 pm, yet I saw that they were coming a bit later, more often than not, or not coming at all. On the weekends, it was even worse. We had always talked every Saturday morning, yet suddenly, it was often Sunday before I could get a hold of him. Years ago, I read in a dating book that a girl should never call a guy. Still, I started to experience actual panic and such extreme anxiety when I didn't hear from him that it made me feel almost crazy. I would call 20 times and would still get no answer. And with every unanswered call, my anxiety only grew. I had never experienced panic attacks before, but I was having full-blown ones now when this would happen. I felt embarrassed that I was allowing this extreme panic to set in because he wasn't calling like he had so regularly for several months. Still, I couldn't seem to stop them and didn't understand what was happening to me.

When I finally got a hold of him, I was furious and tried to stay quiet, but he would prod me to tell him what was wrong. Then, finally, when I would give in, I would blow up at him and say to him that he didn't seem interested in me anymore. Yet, he would reassure me with his soothing voice that everything was okay and that he was just working extra hours to save money so he could move by me as soon as possible so we could get married. Unfortunately, I chose to blindly believe him because, after all, he was such a Godly man; he surely wouldn't lie. And I was hopelessly hooked on this man I had never met in person. I wanted more than anything to marry him, and I had never felt this attracted and in love with anyone in my entire life, so I desperately wanted to believe him. When I was talking to him, everything felt right, and I felt at peace. But that became the only time I felt normal. When I wasn't talking with him or messaging with him, I felt like I was continually being scratched from the inside out.

Sadly, I didn't realize that his new inconsistency and more extended periods between talking to me were another manipulation tactic of a narcissist. He was purposefully ghosting me to see just how far he could push and how willing I would be to forgive him (26). He knew how hooked I had become in the love bombing stage, and now he was putting it to the test.

Stage Five
Gaslighting (26)

As the weeks passed, the inconsistency persisted. I was dropping weight, losing a great deal of hair, could barely function at work, and was a nervous wreck every minute of the day, unless I was talking to him. It was as if the sound of his voice was a drug, and I only felt normal when I was partaking. My kids and family were getting on me, telling me that I wasn't acting like myself at all, and encouraging me to break up with him. Yet, I was so caught up, I couldn't see how far gone I had become, or wouldn't let myself. I would tell myself, it would all be okay, after all, we prayed together, right?

Another thing I started to notice was his comments on other single women's Facebook posts, one woman in particular. Noticing this made me feel even worse, so I began spying on them by paying attention to when he was active at the same time as her. I began to notice that this was happening all day long, and even into the evening. My spying got so bad that I started to check even when I was talking to him. And I noticed it was happening even then.

I finally gathered the nerve to ask him about it. He vehemently denied it, saying he only liked her posts because he felt sorry for her as she was going through a difficult time, but that he had never Private Messaged her. I knew this was a lie because she had told me what a nice man he was on one occasion saying she had messaged him for advice on how to deal with a recent breakup, and he really helped her. When I confronted him about this, he began telling me I was insane. He asked if I had ever been diagnosed with bipolar or borderline personality disorder. And this questioning of my mental health began to be a regular occurrence with him almost every time we talked, especially if I had caught him in a lie, which started to happen regularly. I didn't realize it then, but he was gaslighting me, making me question my own sanity and concrete evidence that was right before me.

Stage Six
The Narcissist Web (27)

As I write about this, I recall feeling crazy at the time. The longer I talked with him, the crazier I felt. I began questioning my sanity, thinking maybe I did have a personality disorder that had never been diagnosed. Perhaps I was imagining things I was seeing. I had never felt so terrible in all my life. As I mentioned above, I constantly felt like I was being continually scratched from the inside out.

Besides questioning my sanity, I had lost all confidence in myself in every way; in my teaching ability, in being a mother, in simply being able to get through the day. I have no idea how I managed to keep my job during this time, as I was unable to function well. My relationships with my children and family were not good, and this had never been the case before. They continued to tell me that my relationship with this man was toxic, that I was not myself, and that they wanted nothing more than for me to end the relationship. Still, I am ashamed to this day of admitting that no one could get through to me.

I have often heard people say that they lost themselves in a relationship, and I couldn't understand how that could happen, but this is exactly what had happened to me. It's difficult to describe, but I began to feel as though I was "out of body." I could literally feel myself disappearing with each passing day. Just a year and a half earlier, I was confident and grounded in who I was, with beautiful relationships with my kids and family. But now, I had literally lost myself – and I couldn't find my way back. I was caught in a narcissist's web, and despite how horrific I felt, I couldn't get out, and I couldn't see how to escape. And as crazy as it sounds, despite all of this, the thought of living without him, the drug he had become, filled me with actual terror.

Stage Seven
The Discard (28)

I continued with this toxic relationship, as I was in so deep, I had no idea how or the mental capacity to get out. I continued to be compelled to spy on his social media activity even though I knew it was not healthy and made me feel even worse, as I usually found he had been quite busy talking to other women. One night, while spying, I noticed he had commented on a beautiful young girl's Facebook page saying how attractive she was, and I became hysterical. I called him in my hysterical state and confronted him. As always, he denied doing this even though I had sent him a screenshot. We got in a terrible fight that ended with him breaking up with me, saying I was insanely jealous and was making things up. He couldn't deal with my jealousy anymore.

The next day, I received a call from two of his roommates, who said they felt compelled to call me to warn me never to get back with him. His roommates started telling me all the things I feared most. They told me that he had laughed about stringing me along and never had any intention of meeting me. His roommates proceeded to tell me that he was a frequent visitor, not to Sunday Mass, but to the local strip club, and that he was especially interested in much younger women. They said he claimed to be a devout Catholic to them, too, but that his lifestyle showed otherwise. My head was spinning, but I knew they were telling the truth. They said that if I met him in person, I would never have agreed to even talk with him.

I was incredibly grateful for their warning, but despite all that they had told me, I felt like I was dying, and I feel embarrassed even admitting this. After he broke up with me, I experienced the most horrendous emotional pain knowing that our relationship was over. I didn't understand how I could feel so horrible, even after learning all that his roommates had told me. My family was elated that this nightmare was finally over. Still, I didn't know how I would ever get past the pain I was experiencing.

By the Grace of God, I mustered up the strength to reach out to a dear friend who is an expert on narcissism, and cried to her, telling her how bad I was hurting. What I hadn't realized was that she had been worried about me all along, knowing I was caught and blinded in a narcissist's web, and knew she would need to be there to help me navigate through the pain when the discard finally came.

In her wisdom, she gave me permission to continue in this relationship. Still, she prefaced it by saying, "You get to go back to him.

That is your right, but you must know that it will be at the expense of your children, your career, and possibly your life . . . but you get to" (29). For the first time since I had become entrenched in this terrible relationship, I felt the gravity of what she was saying. Her words pierced through the insanity I was living in, and I knew she was right.

About a week later, he called me, begging for forgiveness, and told me how much he loved me and couldn't live without me. He was crying and begging me to take him back, promising that he would take the first flight he could get to meet me in person. The only reason I took the call was to tell him never to call me again, that I wanted nothing more to do with him, but hearing his voice was literally like a drug. With his every word, I could feel myself being sucked into the black hole of delusion again. Before we hung up, he convinced me we would live happily ever after. All the warnings and all that I knew to be true about him were drowned in delusion.

My daughter overheard the conversation, and I tried to tell her that things would be better now, that he was really coming out this time. Yet instead of being convinced, she looked at me in horror and started screaming and crying hysterically, thrashing on the bed, screaming, "NO, NO, NO!" Seeing her so incredibly upset over my actions was one of the lowest, most shameful moments of my life. In that moment, God opened my eyes to see how badly I had hurt my beautiful daughter, my family, and all those who truly loved me. The blinders fell off, and I could finally see how sick and wrong this whole relationship had been, how horribly I had behaved, and that I had to end it now and for good. The profound words of my dear friend were right, and in this web, I almost lost my very life, and everything that is so dear to me, and no one is worth that.

After spending time in prayer for strength, I called him and told him not to come, and explained that we were truly over. He became furious, but by the Grace of God, I was able to hang up and never accept a call from him again. I blocked him in every way I possibly could, but I eventually had to call the police to get him to stop calling and leaving messages, as he started using different phone numbers to contact me. Once he realized the police were involved, the nightmare finally came to an end.

Soon after, the fire department visited my school to give a seminar to all the staff about the dangers of online predators. As I listened, I had chills running down my spine as I realized that even as an adult, I had become prey to a real predator, and it had almost cost me everything. Only by the Grace of God, the support of my family and friends, and especially the help and wisdom of my dear friend, who is an expert on narcissism, was I able to finally escape this nightmare.

One of the greatest gifts that God gave me in this relationship was never meeting him in person. Many people who become the prey of online or otherwise predators aren't so fortunate. It is how people get assaulted, trafficked, and even murdered. If you are in an online relationship or physical relationship and these signs are present, please seek help. Investigate the situation. Do your research, and do not be trusting, but rather be very cautious. Just as I was, you can get caught up in a dangerous situation before you even realize what has happened, and your very life could be at stake!

Healing

It took a lot of time, support from my dear friend, prayer and counseling from my priest, and educating myself on narcissism to finally begin to heal from all the years of narcissistic abuse I had suffered. I still consider myself "a work in progress." In this latest incident, I can see how much Jesus protected me by not allowing me to meet this man in person. Now that I am on the other side of this, I can thank Jesus for letting me go through this, as it caused me to dive in and read and listen to everything I could get my hands on about dealing with a narcissist. I learned about being an empath and why I have attracted and been attracted to narcissists my whole life.

If you are suffering from narcissistic abuse, I cannot encourage you enough to seek professional help. As stated throughout this book, I am in no way an expert on this subject, and this chapter sheds light on just a small portion of the horrors of narcissistic abuse. In addition to seeking professional help, I found it extremely helpful to watch educational videos, read relevant books, and educate myself as thoroughly as possible. As I stated earlier in the chapter, "A narcissist's worst nightmare is an educated empath" (30).

Learning about narcissism will validate the abuse you suffered or are suffering and help you to understand it. It will help you identify a narcissist before letting them into your inner circle, teach you how to live or work with a narcissist if you have no choice in being around them, show you any patterns you have had in your life in dealing with this, and provide you with a path to healing.

With all of this said, it is essential to remember that God always promises us, saying, "And we know that to them that love God, all things work together unto good, to such as, according to his purpose, are called to be saints" (31). I can attest that He has done this with anything and everything I have gone through in my life, and this has been no exception. I read a beautiful example of this in the book *You Can Be Happy Now*, by one of my favorite authors, the late Pastor Merlin Carothers. He wrote that "our lives can be likened to a motion picture film containing a large number of single pictures" (32). If one picture were to be cut, the film would not run smoothly or make sense. He further explains that "our moments here on earth are choreographed by God, our Savior Director, to progress picture-by-picture toward their final end-our destiny in Heaven" (3). So, it is crucial that when painful, even traumatizing things happen to us, "each event, each frame, is necessary if our life (film) is to reach its final conclusion" (3).

It was through my experiences (pictures) with this current man online that God was able to shed light on my past traumas and show me how narcissism has been a common thread. I know one night while attending Adoration of the Holy Eucharist, I heard God's still small voice teach me the importance of this "picture" by saying to me:

> You were never properly loved by your father because he was a damaged man, and you have worked so hard trying to finally receive this love and approval all your life. You have picked men just like your dad, trying to win over his love, finally. Transfer this over to Me and let Me love you properly, showing you what true love and acceptance are. If you don't, you will keep seeking this from men until you learn to surrender it to Me. That is why you stay in bad situations - starving, fighting, and hoping to finally "win" their love and acceptance. You won't let go until you have it, but you will never get it because your dad is no longer alive, and only God can heal the damage and fill the

> void of a father's love. You have thought all your life that if you just do this or that a little more, a little better, they will finally love you, and you will finally gain the love you are desperately seeking from your father, but it is only I Who can do this for you. Let me do this for you, and you will finally begin to heal.

Since this experience, I have heard that we often marry the parent with whom we have unfinished business, and God has clearly shown me how true this has been in my life. Married or single, you can surrender this striving for love and acceptance over to God, and let Him love you and fill the voids you are ultimately seeking from a parent. I assure you, He will do this, as once He made me aware of why I kept going back to similar narcissistic situations, and let Him fill this void and properly love me, I was finally able to begin to heal from this striving, and all that I had experienced previously, and all the "pictures," despite how painful they were, suddenly began to make sense.

Chapter Twelve

"The Only Way Out Is Through."

It's a They Problem.

Abuse of any kind is not acceptable. If you are a victim of abuse of any form, I urge you to step out and get the help you need. Don't suffer in silence, and don't be afraid to report issues that put you in harm's way. Remember, the courts will only validate issues reported to the authorities. Most of all, remember that abusers will allow you to assume a false sense of responsibility. Still, it is their problem, not yours. Encourage yourself in the Word of God, meditate on who He says you are, and focus on this, not on ugly, untrue things people might be telling you that contradict the Word of God. You can make it, and even your marriage can survive, but only if you can live in safety and peace.

The Only Way Out Is Through.

Whether you can safely salvage your marriage, or it ends in divorce, it is crucial that you work on healing from any abuse you have experienced. As our dear family priest has said, to truly heal, you have to start at the root. And, for me and for the majority of people I know, this root cause of trauma began in early childhood. All of our life experiences are interconnected, so if you skip one major event or circumstance, you may not be able to fully heal from a later situation because the earlier event shapes our reaction and the level of trauma we experience in a more recent circumstance. Healing comes in layers, like the layers of an onion. You have to keep peeling one layer at a time to heal fully.

Moreover, I once heard it said that the only way to heal is to go through. With that in mind, I have spent years in prayer asking Jesus to show me wounds that need healing and words spoken over me in my childhood and adult life that have caused trauma. Our dear priest has been God-sent, as he has prayed over traumatic events in my life and situations of abuse and counseled me through them as well. I cannot recommend this enough. Although there are good secular counselors, they don't pray with you or work on the trauma's spiritual aspect. I honestly don't believe I would have ever experienced the healing I have without addressing the spiritual component as well.

Healing takes a lot of work, patience, and time. Only Jesus knows when we are ready to heal from each traumatic experience of our lives. I've found that I will make great strides in healing, and then He will show me something else I had forgotten, and I must take that issue to Him to heal me of it as well.

One of the most important things Jesus has shown me is that I must first forgive the abuser and any person who hurt me before healing can take place. It is equally important that we forgive ourselves. I have found that forgiving myself is often the hardest thing to do. I can forgive others much more readily than I can forgive myself, but unforgiveness towards ourselves shuts us off from God, just as unforgiveness towards others does.

As I've mentioned throughout this book and will still address in future chapters because it is so key, without forgiveness, recovery of myself or others cannot take place. It is crucial to remember that forgiving doesn't necessarily mean inviting that person back into your life; there are many situations where it would be dangerous or unwise to do so. You can forgive without doing so.

Again, it is essential to remember that forgiveness is a choice of will. It is a gift to us, and those whom we need to forgive, hence why it is called for – give. Once we choose to forgive ourselves and our abusers, sometimes a hundred times a day, the feeling will eventually follow. It is important to remember this and let Jesus' Grace come in and heal the deep wounds caused by abuse, whether physical, emotional, spiritual, or verbal, or all of them.

It has been equally important to ask Jesus to show me the pain and hurt I have caused others, and the words I have spoken to people that have been damaging. When I have the opportunity, I try to apologize directly to the person I have hurt. Still, when this isn't possible, I pray for Jesus to heal them from my words spoken over them. As said above, we must also forgive ourselves if we are to find true healing, and a big step in this is facing the hurts we have caused others.

Jesus Will Walk Through With You.

Healing is a painful process, but again, the only way to achieve it is to go through it. So, first, I envision Jesus walking into the traumatic memory with me. Then, while our priest is praying over me, I imagine Jesus healing me from this experience or situation. Finally, once Father has finished praying, I envision Jesus walking back through the door with me, closing it, locking it forever behind me, and sealing it with His Precious Blood.

It is important to remember that this process unfolds in layers, and each layer peeled back and brought before the Lord will be painful. We may not feel any different at first, so it may take faith and time to experience our healings fully - sometimes it can even be a lifelong process. Still, every step we take toward victory is well worth the effort and will keep us motivated and encouraged to keep moving forward with Jesus! As the words in my favorite journal say, "Jesus wants our life, character, and personality to be as beautiful and lovely as he visualized us to be when he created us" (1).

Receiving the Love of God

I understand well that it is often difficult, especially for those who have suffered abuse, to receive the love of God and believe that He loves and accepts you. That said, the Christian rock band MercyMe wrote a beautiful song called "You're Beautiful," which I highly recommend setting aside time to listen to, as it might help you with this (2). Besides being a beautiful song, God used it several years ago to illustrate His love and acceptance for me when I was going through pretty desperate times, feeling like a complete failure, and struggling to believe He could love me.

One morning, while listening to the words, I remember thinking, *You cannot believe this about me, God. I mess up too much. How could You ever see me this way?*

Right after thinking this, I know in all my heart that I heard God say, "Look at your daughter."

She was sitting right by me, coloring. I immediately glanced over at her and answered God in my thoughts, *Yes, God, I see her.*

I felt the impression continue, which I know was God, go on to say, "Pick her up in your arms. Hold her tight while you sing this song to her."

I quickly picked her up in my arms and rocked her as I sang along with the lyrics.

While singing and holding her, I heard God continue speaking, saying,

"Is she perfect? Does she ever disappoint you?"

I thought back, *Yes, God, she does, but she and her brothers are the most unbelievably beautiful people to me. There is no possible way I could love them more.*

God went on, "Now you know. This is how I see you, and this is how I love you."

I continued singing the rest of the song to my daughter, crying so deeply, never feeling more loved by God.

Even today, this makes me cry so much. People, myself included, so often struggle to believe that such a perfect God could ever love us/me, such a flawed and imperfect person. Suffering from abuse can make this even harder to accept because it can make you feel so unlovable, unworthy, tarnished, and ashamed. I continued singing the rest of the song to my daughter, crying so deeply, never feeling more loved by God.

Yet as a parent, I completely get it! If I, a very flawed parent, can love my children with such intensity despite their imperfections, imagine how much a perfect God can love us - despite us! I encourage you to take a minute to meditate on the lyrics of this song (available on Google), written as a love letter from God the Father to us, and through the words, let God love you and begin to heal you as you receive His love and accept that you are His.

YOU, yes you, are a CHILD OF THE MOST HIGH GOD, and you do not have to live in fear and shame any longer. You do have a right to be treated with respect and honor. You are lovable, worthy, and, again, you are HIS! Don't make the mistakes I did of becoming the "frog in boiling water," and don't accept mistreatment from others. And, while you are working towards change, don't waste your suffering. Offer it up to Jesus for the salvation of souls, for others suffering abuse, and ask Him to use it for good.

The Aggrandizement of Jesus Glory!

One of the most beautiful ways He will use our suffering for good is through the aggrandizement of His Glory! A beautiful devotion in the Catholic Church is the Adoration of the Blessed Sacrament. I highly recommend going to Eucharistic Adoration to become closer to Jesus, and also as an integral part of your healing process. Where better to be healed than basking in the literal Presence of Almighty God! Spending time in Adoration has been a crucial aspect of my continued healing and walk with Jesus.

One night in Adoration, I was in deep worship, praising Jesus for my life and all my messes, and during this time of praise, Jesus showed me how He uses even our deepest wounds for His glory. He first showed me an image of myself as ugly, full of holes, with blood all over my body, as if I had been blown up all over with grenades. Then I saw God's Glory Light begin to fill all of my wounds, and instead of my body being bloodied and severely wounded, God's light was emitting through the holes, and because there were so many, all I could then see was His light, shining brightly, illuminating me in His dazzling, healing light. I was so overwhelmed as in His mercy, He was showing me how He uses our wounds and suffering to shine forth His glory in our lives when we will give them to Him, offer Him the sacrifice of praise, even for the worst suffering, and then trust Him to use them for His glory!

Tough Love

Finally, practice tough love for your sake and those who misuse and abuse you. Learn to set boundaries and don't feel guilty for keeping them. Trust God to work miracles in your life, heart, emotions, and marriage. Fight for your marriage, but also be willing to remove yourself, either temporarily or permanently, from the situation if it is necessary. You can continue to work on restoring your marriage, even if it must be done from a distance for a time, if you are fortunate enough to have a partner who is willing to work on change and take the necessary steps to ensure that you and your children can live safely.

Clearly, all forms of abuse are most definitely weapons satan uses against us in this final battle. Still, with Jesus, despite satan's best efforts to destroy us, we can overcome and find victory for ourselves and society.

Chapter Thirteen

"Help . . . Is Anybody Out There?"

In the last chapters about various types of abuse, we discussed very heavy, serious, and glaring issues, but what about those we are unaware of? What is our line of defense for problems that are hidden from our sight? And how can we avoid being blindsided by sudden news that our spouse wants out of the marriage, like what happened to me on my 18th anniversary? Unfortunately, our commitment to our marriage often makes it easy for a straying, disgruntled spouse to plan our demise behind the scenes without us being aware.

I will never forget one night towards the end of my marriage. It was about 9:30 p.m. I had just gotten the kids to bed and was downstairs doing laundry. While I was folding clothes, I saw my ex-husband sitting on the couch watching television, and I felt a deep sense of contentment. As I've discussed, we had been through so much in our marriage. Still, now, at almost eighteen years, I was finally in a place where I had made peace with his absences. Our marriage, at this point, seemed better than ever before; God had given me the ability to trust him again, and we could finally relax and settle into our lives and routine.

For me, this routine was what I'd always wanted, and I remembered smiling, thinking that if a marriage lasted eighteen years, it had definitely passed any possible danger zones and would last forever. I wanted to believe this so badly for my children's sake that I truly did.

I marvel, however, how amazing it is that two people can live in the same home, yet view life from entirely different perspectives. I was thrilled with the routine, completely happy and content in my life and with my family and felt more blessed than I could express. I had no idea that while I thought my marriage was finally in a "good place," my ex-husband had been secretly planning his "get-away" for over a year.

When he told me he wanted a divorce about a month later, this particular night was one of the first things I thought of. I couldn't believe that I had been so blind that I didn't see it coming. Here I was celebrating the fact that we had endured the test of time, when all along he was miserable and wanted out.

Too Content Can Breed Trouble.

As I think back on this, I caution everyone to be aware of feeling too content in a marriage. This wasn't what I was doing consciously, but my ex-husband wasn't home very often in the evenings. I should have put the laundry aside that night and focused on spending time with him exclusively instead. I don't think it would have made a difference, as he was already well-entrenched in a new relationship at this point, unbeknownst to me. Still, it never hurts to give our spouse our full attention, even if we are the only one making it a priority. After years of marriage, children, and life, it's very easy to settle into a routine and become too complacent.

Even the strongest marriages need to stay fresh, and every day we should find a way to let our spouse know we love them and that they are special to us. To the men reading this, women never tire of hearing that they look beautiful, and to the women, men desire to be respected and honored. Anytime we can show our spouse how special they are to us, we must do it, especially when we don't want to.

One way we can do this is to take the time to find out what makes your spouse happy, if we don't already know. Author Gary Smalley has an excellent book entitled The *Five Love Languages (1).* This book is fantastic at taking the guesswork out of discovering how you and your spouse need to be loved. The tape and book series *Light His Fire* (2) and

Light Her Fire (3) have also achieved phenomenal success in turning marriages on the brink of divorce into thriving, strong marriages.

The most important thing we can do with our spouse that can keep our marriage fresh and alive is to pray together. Whenever I come across a couple that has been married for years, I always ask them what their secret is, and, including my grandparents, the answer I have received most often is a God-centered marriage and the power of prayer! I have heard praying together described as being the single most intimate act you can do with your spouse, and one that will unite you as nothing else can, even above sexual intimacy.

Do whatever it takes to have the best marriage you can possibly have. If your spouse won't follow along, start out doing things on your own first. The movie *Fireproof (4)*, starring Kirk Cameron, is one of the best examples of the payoff that will often come in a marriage, even if only one partner is willing to work on it to start.

I remember saying to my ex-husband, "If we are going to be in a marriage, let's not settle for mediocre, let's have the best possible marriage we can have!" In my case, it didn't work out, but I know that in many cases, just as in the movie *Fireproof*, if even one spouse starts out trying, the other will eventually come on board. You may say, "I don't want to do nice acts for them; they don't deserve it," and they very well may not, so at first do them for God until He changes your heart, and you can do them for your spouse. I know from experience that God will bless you with peace, contentment, and joy, even if you are the only one trying.

My mom learned that if she wanted change in her and my dad's marriage, she would pray and ask God to change her first. She has said that time and time again, she would see God bring healing into their marriage when she would humble herself and do this.

You Can't Make Someone Love You.

Unfortunately, there are cases where no matter how many attempts are made to make a person feel loved and special, it will not be enough to deter them from getting a divorce if they want one. You cannot make someone love you or be committed to you or your marriage, nor do you want to have to make someone do this. It shows me why God gives us free will. He wants us to love and commit to Him freely, because we want to, not because we are forced to, and this same thing applies in a marriage.

And although it is not healthy to live in a marriage, afraid of divorce at every turn, it does help to have some signs to look for if your spouse may be secretly contemplating one. I have often heard that hindsight is a great teacher, and once I knew my ex-husband wanted a divorce, all of the signs I didn't, or wouldn't let myself acknowledge, began flooding my mind.

At first, I felt foolish and mad at myself for not having seen or let myself acknowledge the signs, but God helped me realize that He had given me the ability to fall in love with my ex-husband again after the incident when our third son was born. When God provides us with this love, it enables us to bear up under anything and everything that comes. We are ever ready to believe the best of every person; our hopes are unfading under all circumstances, and we endure everything without weakening (5).

I knew this love had come from God because, before this, I had not generally thought the best of my ex-husband and didn't trust him. Believe me, thinking the best of someone is a much healthier way to live. Even if they are up to no good, you will live in peace, and eventually, the truth will come out anyway.

The Ten Sure Tell Signs

One thing I have noticed is that when you go through something, especially if it is traumatic or life-changing, God will begin to put other people experiencing the same thing in your path. Before my divorce, I only knew a few people personally who had gone through a similar experience. As time went on, I was suddenly inundated with other women going through the same situation. As we were all talking, we began to notice that our situations seemed remarkably similar, and when we discussed our husbands' steps in the process, they were all a bit too similar for comfort.

Another lady and I began comparing notes, and from them we established a list of the ten things a spouse should be most concerned about if they start seeing these things happen in succession. Below is a list of what we witnessed, and someone else might not agree with these or have others that are entirely different. Still, the majority of these signs were the same, if not very similar, to those of each of the ladies I know who have recently gone through a divorce. Our list is as follows:

1. Encouraging a spouse who has been staying home with the children to "suddenly" work on getting a job, regardless of day care costs, the commute, or any other logical factors.
2. Wanting to refinance the home to obtain a home equity loan in the event money "suddenly" becomes exceptionally "tight." (This is particularly geared for self-employed people.)
3. Your spouse becomes absent from the home more frequently.
4. Even when they are home, they have become detached from the family and/or have become increasingly short-tempered, agitated, or even cruel.
5. They are spending a great deal more time on their phones and become nervous or angry if you glance at what they are texting or posting.
6. You notice new "friends" on social media, and they are giving a significant amount of attention in "likes" and comments.
7. They are either disinterested in sex when they usually are interested, or they suddenly are asking to do new and different techniques.
8. The cell phone bills are suddenly rerouted to the office, and they become very secretive about their cell phones.
9. Suddenly, income is frozen, or there is a significant pay cut with no reasonable explanation.
10. They are hiding that they have a new credit card or cards, and you have no access to the statements.

Take It to Prayer.

The first thing to do if you notice these signs or other similar ones in succession is to take it to prayer and ask God to lead and direct you on what you should do. Talk to a trusted friend who won't tell anyone, but with whom you trust for advice and prayer. Spend time with the Lord, building up your spirit, because you will need it if divorce becomes inevitable. Without letting them know you are aware of the specific signs (See further details below), confront your husband or wife and ask for their honesty. If they admit they are contemplating a divorce, see if they are willing to try and work it out and go to counseling. Remember, if you have been married in a church, you are in a covenant with God, and unless there are unquestionable reasons for a divorce, staying in your marriage should be your first and foremost goal if you are to be obedient to your vows.

Seeking Help Before You Need It

With all that said, confronting your husband or wife is advisable, but you don't necessarily need to let them know you are aware of the signs, especially regarding money. If they are hiding money rather than bringing it home, this could backfire on you, with them lashing out. Besides, it is very doubtful they will ever admit it, which will only alert them to hide it further.

One thing to keep in mind is that if your spouse is contemplating a divorce, they may have been planning their "get-away" for months, so persuading them to stay in the marriage could be an uphill battle. You can be in prayer, doing what you can to try to convince your spouse to stay, while at the same time checking in on what is needed to protect yourself. If your spouse has been contemplating this for some time, they are already miles ahead of you in terms of how to protect themselves during the process, and, sadly, how to ensure your demise.

Offense is often better than defense, but if you are not the one planning for a divorce, you will need to play catch-up. Ask reliable sources of competent attorneys in your area. Most of them will offer a free consultation, which is essential. If you cannot afford any of the divorce attorneys in your area, check with your county on avenues for financial assistance. The county I am in would only provide financial aid for the initial divorce decree, but I was unaware at the time I was going through my divorce that such a service was even available.

Universities are another avenue you can try to help save costs. They may sometimes allow a law student to represent you for a significantly reduced fee, and occasionally they will even handle the matter for free.

I can't urge you enough to be proactive, take charge, and ensure that you, your children, your rights, your possessions, and property are protected. Unfortunately, there are even websites out there giving out information on "How to screw your wife!" and are directing women as well, so you cannot afford not to pursue options, even before you are sure you will need it, if all of the signs point to your spouse actively seeking a divorce, yet won't admit it. Again, staying in constant prayer and seeking support is crucial to help you navigate in a Godly, yet wise way, following the advice from Matthew 10:16 which says, "Behold I send you as sheep in the midst of wolves. Be ye therefore wise as serpents and simple *(That is, harmless, plain, sincere, and without guile.)* as doves" (6).

Is It Worth Saving?

By the time my ex-husband asked me for a divorce, he had already entirely made up his mind, and there was no convincing him of anything different. He agreed to counseling once; however, after the session, he said he went, so I couldn't say he didn't try. Two of my friends experienced the same situation. When their husbands let them know they wanted a divorce, it was a done deal, and nothing they could have said or done would have changed their ex-husbands' minds.

I have seen this be the situation, especially when infidelity is the cause of the divorce, and it generally is, as people aren't usually willing to leave a 20-year marriage unless someone is waiting in the wings. The spouse leaving is already vested in their new partner, and their only goal is to get free from their marriage and move on to what they consider "bigger and better things."

When this is the case, you have to make peace with the fact that you can't make someone stay with you, and, as we talked about earlier, you can't make someone love you, and you have to let go. Because of my children, I tried at first to say I wouldn't give my ex-husband a divorce, but I was told by my attorney that he could sue me for one if I wouldn't consent, so either way, he would get what he wanted.

Suppose a believer is married to a non-believer. In that case, Jesus tells you to do just this: "But if the unbelieving partner [actually] leaves, let him do so; in such [cases the remaining] brother or sister is not morally bound. But God has called us to peace" (7).

Every Situation Is Different.

One of my good friends just found out her husband had been cheating on her and had taken a great deal of money from the family to help set him up to leave her. When the girlfriend found out he was married (apparently, she didn't know before), she dumped him! My friend, who is a Christian, wanted to divorce him at first, but after a period of time, he began going to church, counseling with a priest, begging for forgiveness, and reaching out to her.

The fact that he wanted to stay in the marriage caused her great confusion. Part of her desperately wants to trust her husband, but because of the betrayal, she doesn't feel she ever can again. She is attending counseling with him, and they are talking a fair amount, but she is being very wise not to let him back into their home right away, until she is entirely sure of what she wants to do. She realizes that he needs to have consequences for his actions, or he will feel he can get away with it again.

Every situation is different; no two situations are the same, and only you and God can decide if your marriage is worth fighting for. In most situations I am familiar with, as well as my own, the decision was made for us. The marriage was over, and reconciliation was not an option.

Again, I believe we have a duty to pray for restoration for a time, yet we also have to pray for the Grace to accept when it is over and then begin the long and painful journey with God to what the dissolution of a marriage is soon to bring. It is excruciating and will cause great suffering, but with God, there is always light at the end, and He will eventually make all things work for good (8), even our suffering, if we trust Him.

CHAPTER FOURTEEN

"IT'S OVER, NOW WHAT?"

After surviving the initial shock that my ex-husband wanted out of our marriage, I went into a denial stage, holding out hope that we would somehow reconcile and refusing to accept the reality that he was actually going to divorce me. We had been through so many troubled times in our marriage before, yet we always managed to keep on going. I had convinced myself this was another phase, and we would get through it.

For about a month and a half after he revealed his intentions, he appeared to vacillate, placing me on an emotional roller coaster that kept my false hopes afloat. One day, he would act as though he wanted to reconcile, tearing up and showing tenderness towards me, and the next day, his entire demeanor would change entirely. It was as if he felt guilty for showing me kindness the day before.

Up to this point, the kids had no idea that their stable world was about to completely unravel. I had let my ex-husband know from the very beginning that I would never tell our children, and that if he wanted a divorce, he would have to be the one to break the news to them. I could not imagine ever looking my precious children in the eye and telling them life as they knew it would never be the same. As far as I was concerned, they never needed to know. I put on a "happy face" for their sake, hoping the whole mess would blow over without them ever knowing anything about it.

Your Secret Is "Safe" With Me.

Every August, the kids and I took a week-long vacation to the western part of our state to visit family. I especially looked forward to the trip that summer, wanting to remove my children and me from the situation at home. I needed a place to escape and get alone with the Lord, and I needed to surround myself with the support of my family. I was also hoping this would give my ex-husband time to "come to his senses" before we returned home.

I find humor in this now, but while I was away, I contacted a private investigator who lived near my home to ask what would be involved if I were to hire her. Although my ex-husband completely denied that there was someone else, I believed otherwise. I knew his history and that there was a "force" behind him, pushing him to continue when he began to vacillate, yet I couldn't prove it, and I felt I had to know. I explained my situation to the investigator, and she assured me she was the best and would have a definitive answer for me in no time.

A few days after I contacted her, I received a call from my ex-husband. Apparently, while we had been away, this "top-notch" private investigator left a message on our home answering service, saying she needed additional information before she could continue her investigation. My ex-husband was livid that I was having him investigated, and informed me that because I had done this, he had filed the divorce papers, and I would be receiving them when I returned home from my trip.

I was thankful I had not given this lady any money. She obviously needed some practice in working "undercover." I understand why my ex-husband was upset over this, yet I have never accepted that my seeking out a private investigator was responsible for him taking the final step in filing the papers. He was looking for any reason to proceed, and I had just sped up the process.

You Have Been Served.

I could have stayed on vacation forever; in fact, I never wanted to come home. I was terrified, literally gripped with fear about what I was coming home to. I was thankful my ex was away on business when we returned home, but true to his word, I received a knock on my door the day after we returned home, and a man I had never seen before, verified my name. And at my acknowledgement, thrust a stack of papers into my hand, told me to have a good day, and left before I had a chance to say another word.

I remember feeling like the world had shifted into slow motion as I turned around to come back in the house, holding the evidence that forced me to accept the fact that my marriage was over. After eighteen tumultuous and well-fought years, I was being thrown away, discarded, abandoned, and basically widowed. I could no longer hold out hope that it was a phase, and whatever "work" God was going to do in my ex-husband as mentioned in the chapter, "The Broken Promise," I now realized, was going to be completed without us as a married couple. Soon, my children would know the truth, and our lives as we knew them would change forever.

Seeking Wisdom

Once served with papers and divorce appears inevitable, the first place we should always seek wisdom is from God and His Word. God promises that "if any of you is deficient in wisdom, let him ask of the giving God [Who Gives] to everyone liberally and ungrudgingly, without reproaching or faultfinding, and it will be given him" (1). It is more important than ever to spend time alone with God during this time to allow Him to build us up in spirit as He promises us in His word that "the strong spirit of a man sustains him in bodily pain or trouble, but a weak and broken spirit who can raise up or bear?" (2).

One of the most unfortunate aspects about going through a divorce is that potentially life-altering decisions have to be made at a time when we are the most weak, vulnerable, and emotionally wounded. I know, for me, my mind was not clear, and I was not in any state to make the types of decisions I was forced to make. Just the thought of having to select an attorney created a tremendous amount of fear and anxiety.

I had no idea how to proceed or select one. Because I was not the petitioner, my ex-husband was already miles ahead of me, had already secured a real "shark" attorney, and seemed very familiar with the entire process. Spending time alone with God to be renewed and built up in spirit was literally a matter of whether I would be able to continue successfully or would shrivel under the weight of adversity and be unable to keep fighting.

As I immersed myself in the Word of God, I found great comfort and strength; spiritually, physically, emotionally, and mentally meditating on Scriptures like:

Lamentations 3:58-66 - "Lord, you are my lawyer! Plead my case! For you have redeemed my life. You have seen the wrong they have done to me, Lord. Be my judge, and prove me right. You have seen the plots my enemies have laid against me" (3). Because I had never had to retain an attorney before, this gave me great comfort knowing that no matter who I chose to represent me, ultimately, it was Jesus who would plead my case through them.

Hebrews 13:5 - ". . . For He [God] Himself has said, I will not in any way fail you nor give you up nor leave you without support. [I will not, I will not, I will not in any degree leave you helpless, nor forsake nor let {you} down (relax my hold on you)! [Assuredly not!]" (4). During this time of great trials, it is easy to feel alone. Yet, it is precisely at this time that we must lean into Jesus as never before, taking Him at His Word that He is our support, our help, and that He will never fail us or leave our side. He is literally with us every minute of every day and night. Although I couldn't always see or feel it at the time, hindsight has shown me that He literally carried me through it all.

Ephesians 3:20 - "Now to Him Who, by (in consequence of) the [action of His] power that is at work within us, is able to [carry out His purpose and] do superabundantly], far over and above all that we [dare] ask or think [infinitely beyond our highest prayers, desires, thoughts, hopes, or dreams]" (5). One good thing about this incredible trial is that it gives us ample opportunity to truly surrender all things to Jesus. As I surrendered each hardship to Jesus, I witnessed this scripture played out over and over again. There is no prayer too difficult for Jesus. We honor Him by asking much of Him, and in our suffering, He will prove Himself faithful, even exceeding our needs and expectations.

Philippians 4:19 - "And my God will liberally supply (fill to the full) your every need according to His riches in glory in Christ Jesus" (6). Like with the last Scripture, Jesus will truly take care of our every need, if we surrender our worries, trials, and hardships to Him. I would often lay in fear, worrying how I would cover the grocery bill, the mortgage, an attorney bill, and through prayer and surrender, I would just happen to get a check in the mail that was just enough to cover my immediate need. It was in this crisis that I learned more than ever how faithful Jesus is to us.

Philippians 4:13 - "I have strength for all things in Christ Who empowers me [I am ready for anything and equal to anything through Him Who infuses His inner strength into me: I am self-sufficient in Christ's sufficiency]" (7). There were many days when I didn't know how I could even get out of bed, let alone continue fighting a court battle, all while trying as hard as I could to keep my children's lives as normal as possible. Again, without Jesus and His strength carrying me, I would never have made it. When I was too weak, I would pray, sometimes a prayer as simple as saying Jesus over and over again, and He never failed to fill me with His strength, allowing me to carry on.

> Isaiah 41: 10 - Fear not [there is nothing to fear], for I am with you; do not look around you in terror and be dismayed, for I am your God, I will strengthen and harden you to difficulties, yes, I will help you: yes, I will hold you up and retain you with My [victorious] right hand of rightness and justice (8).

I already knew that fear is satan's greatest tool, but he wastes no opportunity to inundate you with fear during this time. The battle over fear will be intense and ongoing. The only way to overcome this is to cast it out in Jesus' Name and cling to Scriptures, such as this one, that address Jesus' promises that we have nothing to fear. I also visually imagined Him holding my right hand when I would become so paralyzed with fear that I was shaking. Eventually, satan would back down if I continued in deep prayer, casting him out in Jesus' Name, and speaking this over and over and over, until I would finally be filled with Jesus' peace instead.

Help Is on the Way.

I am also very blessed to have an incredible family that supported, guided, advised, directed, and prayed for me every step of the way, each equally in their own ways. I never had to make legal decisions without first bringing them before my whole team of supporters. I realize how blessed I am and understand, especially after watching many others go through divorces after me, that not everyone is this fortunate.

Many people have to face this crisis completely on their own, and I can't even imagine how difficult this must be. Divorce has the potential to bring utter destruction to people's lives. With this destruction, it becomes very easy to see why people end up on the street, completely bankrupt, living in impoverished conditions, or laden with insurmountable debt. It is difficult enough in this world to provide for our families. When incomes are slashed or terminated overnight, the results are, more often than not, completely devastating.

One example of this happened to a dear friend. Her husband literally locked her entire family out of their home. She didn't have family nearby, and until she could get a court order to move back in, she and her boys had to take up residence in a friend's home, sleeping on their basement floor for over a month. Granted, her friend was very gracious to allow them to stay there and was very kind to take them into her home, but it is difficult to understand how a father could do this to his own children, yet stories like this, and much worse, happen every day because of divorce.

Even though I have gone through a divorce and now years of litigation petitioned by my ex-husband and his wife, I still in no way feel qualified, nor am I qualified to provide legal advice. That said, I have learned some things along the way that may help someone facing this situation that, like me, had no idea where or how to seek help, and found themselves forever on the defensive, always trying to play catch up to what my ex-husband was already initiating.

As I mentioned in the last chapter, if your spouse is contemplating a divorce or you strongly suspect they are, don't wait until they serve you papers to take steps to protect yourself. The fact that you are checking into things does not mean you advocate a divorce or will end up getting one; it is just providing you with a safety net in the event you need one. Remember that most divorces are not amicable (I have yet to see one that is.), and unfortunately, you most likely will need to prepare for high conflict.

If you don't know of any attorneys in your area, call the county you live in and ask them if they can recommend any names to you. While on the phone with them, it is also a great time to ask about legal assistance, as many counties provide financial aid for the initial decree. If the county doesn't help with recommended attorneys, search the internet for names in your area who specialize in domestic law, or ask around at your church or among people you know who have been through it.

Many attorneys will provide a free initial consultation. If possible, visit with several, compare notes and prices, and try to research references. Once you have met with them, your spouse can no longer be represented by them. Choosing an attorney is one of the most important decisions you will ever make, and it is crucial to research this and not just assume that all of them will be successful or helpful.

Once you have been served with papers, you should proceed immediately with retaining an attorney. The first step an attorney should work on is to file for temporary orders as soon as possible. Temporary orders will ensure that your spouse continues to pay for expenses until the final decree is established, and it is essential for stay-at-home moms or dads, or if you have been completely reliant financially on your spouse.

I know of a supposed "well-known" attorney who did not do this for her client, and she ended up having to spend her entire savings and accrue an enormous amount of credit card debt, even before the divorce was final, just to survive. Many others don't have a savings account or any other source of funds to fall back on. Without the temporary orders in place, her ex-husband refused to pay for any of her expenses while they were going through the divorce proceedings. He had already moved out of the house and didn't seem to care how her, and their children's needs were met.

The private investigator I spoke with may have entirely failed in her ability to work "under cover"; however, she did offer me some invaluable advice. If you have been solely dependent on your spouse's income, now is NOT the time to get a job, especially if you have been a stay-at-home mom or dad. As mentioned in the previous chapter, one sign to be concerned about is if a spouse suddenly becomes adamant that you seek immediate employment, especially if it is not a reasonable request given your situation or if it comes out of the blue. Their purpose in doing so is to reduce the amount of maintenance and child support they will be required to pay once the final divorce decree is determined.

Tread Carefully and With Wisdom.

I married at nineteen and had worked as a travel agent for the first eight years of my marriage, which allowed my ex-husband to attend college and build his business. When he decided to divorce me, I had never attended college, had not worked outside the home for over 10 years, and the travel business had changed drastically and was no longer a viable option for me to return to.

My original attorney provided excellent advice, telling me to enroll in school full-time immediately. Quickly enrolling in college full-time served two purposes: 1) The courts will not impute income on a spouse who is enrolled in college full-time, provided they do not have a previous degree or training enabling them to support themselves. (This only applies to obtaining a bachelor's; graduate education is not considered a viable reason not to impute income.) 2) This provides a window of time and opportunity to obtain training and education while having the financial support to make it possible to pursue this.

I am incredibly grateful that, six years later, I was able to obtain my bachelor's and master's degrees. God opened doors to make this possible for me and provided me with the grace to succeed every step of the way. I encourage anyone in a similar situation to pursue this avenue. Online programs enabled me to complete these degrees while still being available to my children. It was not an easy task; however, it provided me with an invaluable opportunity to become self-sufficient and support my children, and it served as an excellent outlet for positive growth and progress in my life, despite the extremely adverse circumstances I faced.

Make sure to cancel any joint credit cards (you may not be aware of all credit cards opened in your name), safeguard your joint banking accounts as much as possible, and make a record of all marital property. These steps can be recorded either on paper or filmed. Your spouse has no legal right to remove anything from the marital home until it is jointly decided how they are to be allocated.

If you haven't already, begin journaling everything and keeping explicit records and correspondence, such as emails, especially regarding issues related to the children's well-being. Any type of substantial evidence you can gather is invaluable. Explicit record-keeping and the gathering of evidence will be essential if a Child Family Investigator (CFI) becomes involved and if a hearing is held. I always think I will remember key events and situations, but if I haven't written them down, they slip from my memory and become less valuable to me.

If at any time you feel you are in danger during this process, don't hesitate to contact the authorities. A restraining order can be issued, and police surveillance is also possible. One lady I know who recently went through a very high-conflict divorce advised the police that her husband had verbally threatened her. She couldn't prove his threats, but the police did take her claims seriously enough to patrol her neighborhood and home in the evenings for a period of time. Don't take threats lightly; someone should know if you have been, or are feeling threatened, especially if there is a history of domestic violence in your marriage.

Your Children's Fate Is at Stake.

Try to meet with your spouse to devise a parenting plan that you can both agree on, but be prepared that you may have to request a Child Family Investigator (CFI) to investigate if you and your spouse are not able to reach an agreement. Involving this type of representative is a process that your attorney should be able to advise you of if this should become an issue.

Never accept any CFI unless you have interviewed them and checked their credentials and references, if possible. If you and your spouse cannot reach an agreement on a CFI, the courts will determine this for you. The courts generally rule in favor of whatever recommendations the CFI makes and are rarely overturned. Your children's fate can literally rest in their findings.

Two Minds Are Safer Than One.

Most counties require the parties to attend mediation to reach an agreement before bringing the matters to court. My first experience was one of the most frightening encounters of my life. Unfortunately, my first attorney was terrible and did not advise me that my entire life could be determined in one afternoon during mediation.

I went into mediation with just my attorney, and I don't recommend this, especially while you are in the vulnerable emotional state the divorce process creates. Two heads (plus your attorney's) are always better than one, and it is a much safer route to go. If I could do it over again, I would have had one of my brothers attend with me.

I had no idea what I was getting into that day or how long we would be there. I suffer from hypoglycemia and had not brought any food with me, and we were there for over seven hours. My blood sugar was terribly low which makes it almost impossible to think rationally, and I was heavily pressured by both my attorney and the mediator (He wanted to get to a soccer game!) to make decisions I wasn't sure if I wanted or should agree to. And not to be dramatic, but I felt like I was under interrogation at a prison camp. I had no idea what I should or should not agree to, nor was I advised that I didn't have to agree to anything.

Being both emotionally and physically exhausted and not fully understanding what I had just done, I literally "signed my life away." Up to that point, I had been in a separate room from my ex-husband, but we all had to come together for the final signing. I will never forget walking into that room and seeing my ex-husband sitting there with his attorney. Everyone in that room seemed gleeful, and completely unaware and unaffected that a tragedy had just taken place; my eighteen-year marriage had just ended, and four children's lives had been permanently altered because of one person's decision. . . their own father's.

It was more than I could take, and I began sobbing, quite uncontrollably, right in that room in front of everyone! My ex-husband's attorney looked across the room at me with the most sinister expression; it was as if he were saying, "Ha, you just got yours." I wasn't sure what I was supposed to "get", but I was certain he did not have one ounce of sadness for what had just taken place. In my mind, I could picture him, my ex-husband, and his undisclosed mistress tinkling champagne glasses to celebrate my demise.

"Under Duress" Is a Real Issue.

After this horrible night was over, I was, thankfully, able to claim duress legitimately, and my brother helped me put together a new proposal, hire a new attorney, and have it all amended and signed by my ex-husband without having to attend court. I finally felt that after seven months of living hell, we had reached a final decree that would allow for the nightmare to be behind me, and I could begin going forward, making a new life for my children and me. Little did I know at the time, however, that it was just the beginning of what would be eight more long and painful years of court motions, legal battles, and two horrible child investigations, all petitioned by my ex-husband and his new wife before the nightmare finally ended.

Knowledge Is Power.

There are many websites, books, and legal information available that can provide you with much more detailed, professional, and qualified advice. I have provided just basic information, and I can't encourage you enough to study, research, and use all possible reputable resources. It is such a tragedy that divorce is more often than not such an ugly, hostile form of literal terrorism. It should stop with the final decree; however, when children are involved, and money is a factor, it unfortunately can drag on for years, and can be used as a form of continued abuse, manipulation, and control.

Unfortunately, some attorneys insist on providing fuel and fodder to those who have a difficult time accepting the outcome of divorce and will perpetuate litigation to ensure job security. As I say this, there are also plenty of attorneys who don't fall into this category; however, don't always take what your attorney suggests at face value, particularly if they encourage you to continue litigation well past the initial decree. Attorney fees in any divorce case can, and often do, cost staggering amounts of money.

Single moms or dads can be struggling just to put food on the table for their children, and at the same time, are expected or are forced to continue with litigation. Imagine how this money spent on attorney fees could be better used: to provide for their children's needs, support extracurricular activities, and build family savings and college funds. What a tragedy it is that the laws protect continued litigation and that plenty of parents and attorneys willingly continue this without considering the devastating effects it can and often does have on their children's well-being.

After the third court motion, and realizing I was writing my attorney's motions for them and paying them to do so, I signed up with a company called Pre-Paid Legal (an independent company that hires attorneys to give advice) and began representing myself. After the first disastrous time representing myself, I learned what to do the next time, and it actually went very smoothly, and, thanks to Jesus, I came out well enough in court to finally put a stop to the eight long and terrorizing years of continuous court motions petitioned by my ex, and definitely saved thousands of dollars that would have been spent on additional attorney fees.

Bleeding Heart Syndrome

A beloved priest whom I have considered to be one of my spiritual advisers made a powerful comment to me when he learned that my marriage had ended in divorce. He stated rather matter-of-fact, "I am so sorry, my dear, it would have been better if your husband had died." Realizing what he had just let slip out, he added a chuckle, "Please know, I'm not wishing him dead . . . but with divorce the wounds are often almost impossible to heal, and it is the start of often life-long adversity. The spouse that wants out and to be done with you, will never be free of you as long as children are involved."

His comment was very sobering, but came from someone who had seen all too many people continuing to be bloodied and bleeding because of the ongoing tragedy that divorce more often than not brings upon countless people's lives.

In my opinion, divorce is, without a shadow of a doubt, a form of death. As I have said before, however, there are times when it is absolutely necessary, but in far too many cases, it is the result of selfishness at its finest. According to *Dictionary.com*, some definitions of death are "extinction; destruction; lethal; spiritual death, loss or absence of spiritual life; to put to death, kill, to execute; to repeat too often" (9). These definitions can be identified within the context of divorce.

It is the extinction and destruction of a family, even affecting the fates and destinies of future generations. It is a death of dreams, visions, hopes, and aspirations. Termination of a former way of life, and termination and destruction of God's ideal plan for a marriage and for the children. And like with sin of any kind, it often results in the worst kind of death, death of a conscience or spiritual life.

A friend of mine asked me while she was in the deepest depths of despair due to her own divorce, if she would ever be able to live again without feeling like a sword was continually piercing her heart. Another friend called me crying, apologizing that she had not been there for me when I was going through my divorce, stating that she could have never imagined what pain and horror divorce creates until she was now faced with it. "The pain, the rejection,' she cried. 'I believe it is going to kill me, I don't want to live, how will I ever go on?"

I would never want to undermine the pain that one experiences with the actual death of a spouse or loved one, and it shouldn't be compared with divorce because they are two different situations. Yet, divorce is its own entity, but what the priest meant is that with divorce, not only does a death take place, but then so often this person who was once supposed to love and cherish you all the days of your life, sadly, becomes your worst enemy. Where once there was, hopefully, unity, especially regarding the children, there is now discord, strife, and ongoing animosity.

Children are tragically too often placed in the crossfire. As soon as wounds begin to heal, the scabs are frequently torn off by new and ongoing attacks. Holidays become occasions for battlegrounds, loneliness, and the reminder that your life is altered forever. An empty nest becomes a situation you must deal with regularly, far earlier than should ever be expected. Children's sports events, extracurricular activities, graduations, and future marriages often become highly complex and stressful, especially for the children who are once again placed in the middle, trying to appease both parents.

Suddenly, step-parents and step-siblings are in the picture, creating even more complexity to an already difficult situation. Your reputation is often viciously attacked, through lies and slander, particularly in your children's schools, and amongst mutual acquaintances and friends. Your life becomes consumed, and I believe stolen by continued litigation, trying to function under extremely adverse situations and under constant scrutiny. Divorce too often makes those who were once lovers become arch enemies, with no one winning, people's lives being forever altered, and children becoming the innocent victims.

The Ultimate Test of Selflessness

One thing I have learned through all of this is that how you react to all of these extremely difficult situations is the most significant test of selflessness you will ever face. Once again, you cannot control how your ex behaves, and if they are married again, how their new spouse will treat you and react, but you can, only through the Grace of God, control your reactions. I have heard of divorces where everyone gets along reasonably well, and if this is your situation, consider yourself blessed! Although this should always be your goal, particularly if children are involved, unfortunately, it is not always possible, especially if there is ongoing litigation.

Our human instinct is to lash out, especially to our children, about how rotten the other parent is. As I have mentioned before, I have fallen prey to this type of inexcusable behavior on more occasions than I would like to admit, and I have wept and had to deal with terrible guilt and remorse for my actions because I then had to face the pain I was responsible for causing my children. I have had to realize that, regardless of the situation, children still love both parents, and when

I have given in to "bashing," it is as if my words are being directly aimed not at my ex-husband but at them. I have literally witnessed them "shrinking" in response to my words.

At the same time, I don't ever want them to think that divorce, except for specific situations, is acceptable. Not seeing divorce as an easy out is a message that we can instill, but it cannot be done by bashing the other parent. We must be able to release our emotions and express our anger and hurt, but save it for a close and trusted friend, a parent, a sibling, or seek professional help. When we fall in this manner, which more than likely we will from time to time, it is crucial to repent to God and to our children and seek their forgiveness.

As Christians, we also have the responsibility to God to do the right thing even when the right thing is not being done to us. That said, it doesn't mean becoming a doormat, but don't go around spreading lies and slander. You must conduct yourself appropriately at mutual events and remember that your actions must be considered in light of their effect on your children.

Less Is More.

I have learned the best thing for me to do is to limit communication as much as possible with my ex-husband and his wife, and I have seen this work best for those around me who are divorced as well. Limit as much as possible all avenues of communication that the other party may use as opportunities for abuse, manipulation, and control. If email becomes abusive, don't hesitate to block any offenders (collect sufficient evidence, however) or have it routed through a third party. Child support and maintenance payments can be sent through a third party, limiting their use as tools of manipulation and control. There are many services out there to help reduce conflict and improve communication. Contact your county's social services department; they can provide websites and contacts for how to access these services, which are offered at very minimal fees.

Get your mind set that your relationship is a business agreement, and treat it accordingly. Do your best to stay in touch only about issues related to the children, such as schedules, medical appointments, and extracurricular events. The sooner you can establish yourself as a separate entity, the sooner you can truly begin to move forward, creating a new future for yourself and your children.

Cast Your Cares.

There were many times through the divorce and post-divorce process when I literally didn't know how I could go on or how to even cope with situations that were coming at me. I never, in my wildest dreams, believed I would encounter the conditions I have had to face, and the majority of them exceed my human ability to handle them. "Cast your cares on the Lord . . ." (10) has taken on a whole new meaning and has literally become a way to survive life.

God isn't kidding when He says, ". . . Apart from Me ye can do nothing" (11). I have learned this the hard way as mentioned above, often living months plagued with great fear and anxiety, and had to learn little by little to abandon myself entirely into the Hands of the Lord.

Through adversity, God has taught me that we are not capable of solving our problems on our own, and that it is in this abandonment to His love and care that true humility can begin to rule in our hearts.

Casting your care on the Lord is admitting that there is nothing that we can do in our situation, that we are powerless. The sooner we learn to do this, the sooner we can truly begin to experience the joy and contentment that Paul talks about, regardless of our circumstances, and experience the peace that surpasses all understanding.

Part of casting our cares is praising God for exactly where He has placed us, and believing Romans 8:28 that says, "We are assured *and* know that [[a]God being a partner in their labor] all things work together *and* are [fitting into a plan] for good to *and* for those who love God and are called according to [His] design *and* purpose" (12). So often, I will truly cast my cares onto the Lord, releasing my burdens, and then the next hour, I have picked them back up again. I know when I have done this because I begin to be consumed by fear again. I realize that for me, this will be a life-long process.

God promises "He did not give us a spirit of timidity (of cowardice, of craven and cringing and fawning fear), but [He has given us a spirit] of power and of love and of calm and well-balanced mind and discipline and self-control" (13). Again, and as mentioned above, this is satan's greatest tool. Anytime we feel fear, worry, or anxiety, we have to recognize that it is not from God, is generally sent to torment us, and is a root of unbelief, which is sin. As aforementioned, address it immediately, speaking directly to it saying:

> In the Name of Jesus, I rebuke you, spirit of fear, doubt, and unbelief, and demand that you leave now. You have no right to torment me, and you go now in the Name of Jesus. I pray for the Precious Blood of Jesus to surround my mind, my home, and my children, and to protect us from all attacks of the evil one. Jesus promises that if I "commit my way to the Lord [roll and repose each care of my load on Him]; trust (lean on, rely on, and be confident) also in Him, He will bring it to pass" (14). I claim instead, in Jesus Name, ". . . the peace that surpasses all understanding, {keeping my heart and mind}in Christ Jesus" (15). (Brackets are my paraphrasing.)

Don't believe even for one minute that God is not aware of every single issue you are facing. He sees what others are doing to you, He bottles your every tear, and nothing can separate you from His love. Trust your life; every care, every thought, every action, every offense, every hurt, every fear to Him. Show our love back to Him by trusting Him, His care for you, His mercy, and His Grace. Most of all, ". . . take comfort and be encouraged and confidently and boldly say, The Lord is my Helper; I will not be seized with alarm [I will not fear or dread or be terrified]. What can man do to me?" (16). It won't be easy, even tormenting at times, you will suffer greatly, but you are never alone, and through Jesus, you and your children will make it.

Chapter Fifteen

"It's in the Children's Best Interest?"

Ever since I was a little girl and learned to write, journaling has been a large part of my life. I was never taught to journal; it was just an innate desire I had to record the events of my life. When I die, there will be many diaries and stacks and stacks of notebooks containing, within their pages, my most intimate thoughts, experiences, joys, spiritual journeys, and tragedies for my family members to read, if they can decipher my rather deplorable penmanship.

Because of the rather intimate nature of this book, I have relied in part on the pages of my journal to accurately portray my life, heart, and soul to my audience. As I was thinking about the title of this chapter, I came across the part in my journal where I had written about the day my ex-husband told my children he and I were getting a divorce. The events are initially recorded as they began to unfold and were finished later that evening. I share this very personal part of my journal to illustrate the reality of the tragedy that occurs when this decision is revealed to a family.

Before I begin, I should tell you again that I had informed my ex-husband that I wouldn't take part in telling our children we were getting divorced. I explained to him that I would accept some responsibility for his wanting a divorce, but I would not accept responsibility for getting a divorce. I was willing to do whatever it would take to restore our marriage for our children's sake, but I could not restore our marriage alone. I was very clear in telling him that I wouldn't place blame on him to the children. Still, they would know I didn't want the divorce, as it was against everything I had taught them and believed about the sanctity of marriage and the importance of laying down wants and desires, if necessary, to ensure the well-being of others.

This day was the blackest in the history of my life, and I can still barely read this section of my journal without crying, not just for my children, but for all of the children whose lives this very scene has become a reality in. From my journal I wrote:

> *I see them on the swings in the back yard, and time is beginning to stand still. Our beautiful children, our precious babies, so innocent and trusting, without a care in the world, completely unaware that their perfect world is about to be shattered. I want to scream . . . to stop him. My heart is beginning to race as he is calling them in the house. I realize he is actually going to go through with telling them. His entire demeanor has appeared to change, whether real or imagined; he seems to me as an enemy who is stalking his own children with a loaded gun and is about to blow their world to pieces.*
>
> *He is having them all sit on the couch. It makes me think of the order of a firing squad, and he will soon be executing them with his words. I can't bring myself to join them; I watch from the kitchen as the horror of the moment begins to unfold. He has started telling them he doesn't love me anymore . . . here it comes, their screams and sobbing. My anger is growing with every word. How can anyone do this to their children? We are called to lay down our lives for others; our happiness is secondary! I feel like attacking him. How will I ever forgive this? My tears are smearing the words on the paper. I feel like I'm going to die . . . this can't be happening. Our youngest son is now glaring at me, shouting, "YOU PROMISED MOMMY! How could you do this, MOMMY?"*
>
> *I rushed towards him to embrace him, but he pushed me away, covering his head with a pillow in an effort to shut out the world around him. I couldn't stop sobbing and desperately tried to comfort each of them. The crying didn't stop for what seemed*

like hours. Our eleven-year-old's cries could be heard above the rest as he continually began shouting, "No, No, No," covering his ears as though his protests could change the situation.

My ex-husband was trying hard to explain to them why he had to do this, failing to remember he was talking to children whose only concerns were that their family stayed together. He was seeking pity! This decision was HIS CHOICE! His tear-filled eyes were desperately begging for my help in explaining to our children why he had to do this, yet I could not and would not become an accomplice to his broken promise; all I could do was console and hug them. After what seemed like hours, their sobs gradually diminished, and we all lay there, no one having the strength or desire to speak. Our lives as we knew them had changed forever. My ex husband finally broke the silence and told them he was leaving me, not them, and that he would always be there for them. I felt such anger . . . hatred towards him.

I eventually got up; too exhausted to cook, I ordered pizza. The kids seemed happy, at least about this. This meal was the last we would ever eat as a family. All my hopes, dreams, and prayers for us to be a happy family together and forever had just ended. My children would have to live life now in a broken family.

After dinner, my ex-husband spent some more time with the kids. He explained that starting that night, he would be staying at his office. After he left, the kids and I just lay there on the living room floor, exhausted from crying and embracing one another for what seemed like an eternity. No one seemed able to speak, and the silence was welcome.

It was in the midst of the silence that I finally heard God's still small voice whisper that He would get us through, and for the first time that day, I felt a semblance of peace rush through my aching body. Father, I place our future in Your Hands. Help me to remember You alone will sustain my children and me. Don't let my children's lives be shattered beyond repair; place a shield around them and protect them. Let them look to You for their comfort . . . and please, God, don't ever let them blame themselves or You. I thank You now that you have never let me down before, and I know you will somehow make a way for us now in the future.

After reading this section in my journal, and after everything that my children and I have now experienced, I feel even more angered than ever that so many people justify divorce by trying to convince themselves and the world that it is "in the children's best interest." Author Barbara Dafoe Whitehead in her book, *The Divorce Culture: Rethinking our commitment to marriage and family,* exposes this lie for what it is when she writes that divorce has become a means of "self-expression" and is masked under the false pretenses that it is for "the children's sake" which has resulted in creating a culture of impoverished and neglected children who are often raised by an emotionally damaged parent or parents (1).

The atrocities that divorce has had on children is what initially prompted me to write this book from the very beginning. My passion for this cause in particular only increases the more I learn, witness as a parent and a teacher, and become better informed. The *Appalachian Journal of Law,* 2008 article entitled, "On Mutual Consent to Divorce: A debate with two sides to the story," reminds us that "despite the frequency of divorce, research and mental health practice both indicate that divorce has long-term detrimental impacts on children, often representing the single most traumatic experience of their childhoods" (2).

The bottom line is, people know this, but not enough are actually listening or caring enough to put aside their own interests and desires. Often, the mind is a dangerous place, and you can rationalize poor, damaging choices by convincing yourself that your children will be better off if you indulge your desires, which research shows is not usually the case.

That said, without any question, the acceptability of divorce has greatly benefited families and children where physical, sexual, or substance abuse was present. These families must receive and continue to receive liberation, support, and protection from these intolerable situations. Still, according to the article, "Divorce American Style," by William Galston in the *Public Interest* academic publication, tells how several leading researchers have subjected large amounts of data to stringent analysis since 1990. Their findings prove that the majority of divorces do not fall into this category, and this research still holds true today (3).

Their findings noted that "there is a critical distinction between divorces involving physical abuse or extreme emotional cruelty and those that do not. Minor children in the former category are better off than those whose parents remained married" (3). That said, it is not likely that these grave situations are applicable to most families that break apart. In the majority of families, it was one or both of the parents that were unsatisfied with the marriage, yet there was little conflict in front of the children. Several generations ago, the majority of husbands and wives would have stayed in the marriage, as it was seen as a moral and social obligation. Now that marriage today is so often entered into to bring personal fulfillment and is centered on self instead of the family and children, divorce is rampant (3). Perhaps one or both of the spouses are happier, but their happiness is very often at the expense of the children's psychological well-being (4).

What Do the Children Say?

One of the biggest comments my children made when they learned my ex-husband and I were divorcing was that they rarely heard or saw us fight, and they wondered if it was because they "ate their dad's ice-cream" that we were getting a divorce. As far as they knew, their parents had a good marriage. Sadly, kids often blame themselves, especially when they can't see any apparent reason for their parents' separation.

In situations where there at least appears to be a lower level of conflict, I will not accept that children are better off in divorce. My youngest son's comments completely convinced me of this scenario. He told me about eight months after the divorce that "I used to think I had the best life in the world. My parents were married, they love me, we live in a nice house, and I go to a private Christian school, but then I came to the end of the road . . . the divorce happened and ruined my perfect life."

Talk about "ripping your heart out." Here was my precious, thoughtful son, and at age seven, the experience of divorce had led him to believe he had "come to the end of the road." The effects of divorce literally dimmed the light in my once very cheerful, happy-go-lucky boy, and it was a continual struggle to try to heal and restore the damage it had on his young and tender spirit. The light did eventually come back, but divorce leaves a permanent wound in a person, whether realized or not, which often manifests itself in a myriad of ways.

My thoughts are supported by author William Galston, in his interview with researcher Gary Sandefur. This was mentioned above, but is well worth repeating. Sandefur explains that the majority of divorces occur because of a conflict between the parents, but this conflict doesn't often have a significant effect on the kids. That said, the parents might not like being together all that much, but the kids wouldn't be the wiser if the parents put their differences aside and focused on raising the kids (5).

Love and Commitment Are a Decision, Not a Feeling.

Given my children's thoughts, this statement is entirely accurate. Even with the high conflict and alcohol abuse I experienced growing up, I believe I am still better off than if my parents had gotten a divorce. I saw my grandparents' and my parents' marriage eventually turn around. I firmly believe that most marriages could become good, even terrific, if both parties contributed the effort and desire to do so.

The problem is, people don't value marriage as a life-long commitment where divorce is not an option. True love, Godly love, is a decision, not a feeling. You said your vows, brought children into the equation, and it is your responsibility to make it work. This approach, however, often requires denying ourselves of instant gratification, denying our flesh, and putting the well-being of others above our own selfish desires. Sadly, not many people are willing to do this today, and our children have become victims of this me-first mentality, with devastating fallout in society.

If getting married to someone else is going to finally make you happy, the divorce stats discussed in chapter two for second and third marriages, would show a different picture. My comments may not be popular, but as a parent, you are obligated to your children to do everything possible to make it work. The best thing you can ever do for your children is to love and commit to your spouse, and do everything possible to have a strong marriage where your children can thrive.

As talked about in a previous chapter, and a central theme for this book, is to illustrate just how true the grim prophecy has played out that Sr. Lucia, one of the visionaries from Fatima, spoke about when she told Cardinal Carlo Caffarra that a "decisive battle between the kingdom of Christ and Satan will be over marriage and the family" (6). It is undeniable that we are in a spiritual war as never before against marriage and the family. What better way for satan to attack our children than to cause the utter destruction of the marriage. If he can succeed at tearing marriages apart, our children are then fractured and much easier prey for him to attack and work to corrupt them.

Actions Driven by Self-Gratification Often Have Life-Long Consequences.

Divorce and especially the conflicts and results that follow are not in the "children's best interest" and often have life-long effects. When my dad died, my mom remarried a lovely man who had two sons from a previous marriage. He had experienced a very high-conflict divorce, and although his wife was guilty of infidelity and was the one who wanted the divorce, his sons have never forgiven him for leaving. They are now in their early forties, showing the life-altering effects their parent's divorce had on them.

In the *American Journal of Family Law,* Dr. Sanford Portnoy writes an article entitled, "The Psychology of Divorce: A lawyer's primer, Part 2: The effects of divorce on children," that includes the results of a 25-year longitudinal study, conducted by leading divorce researchers Judith Wallerstein and Julia Lewis, that shows that the effects of divorce continue into adulthood (7). They concluded that "the lives of children experiencing divorce changed radically almost overnight; that 25 years after the divorce the now-adult children still recalled the shock, unhappiness, loneliness, bewilderment, and anger," (8) providing substantial evidence that children are the greatest victims of divorce, and the effects are far-reaching and life-altering.

I have personally witnessed this in my now grown children, students, and others who experienced divorce in their childhood. It often skews their views on marriage, makes them distrustful and wary of marriage all together, and can be the root cause of a plethora of mental health issues, addictions, and issues in their own relationships. Oftentimes, they are not even aware that this is the root cause, and a great deal of these issues don't begin to surface until adulthood. The bottomline is that children are not resilient, and the long-term effects of divorce are far reaching, can be life-long, and even eternal.

Our Youth Are Resilient?

All of that being said, the key phrase adults use to justify their often selfish life choices is "kids are resilient." If I had a quarter for every time I hear this phrase, especially regarding children whose parents are going through divorce, I would be a rich woman. As an educator working with children and youth, I hear this term more than the average person.

From a superficial view, it may appear that kids are resilient. Yet, I believe "resiliency" is often mistaken for the idea that children are forced to accept circumstances over which they have little or no control.

Author Caitlin Flanagan's article, "Why Marriage Matters," published in *Time* magazine, reports that certain factors do affect the level of resilience children experience. Her article stated that the more-affluent kids of divorce tend to suffer fewer consequences than children facing poverty. Yet children who fall under the middle-class divorced category do not perform as well in school, including college, as children from two-parent households who are considered underprivileged (9).

Of course, there are always outliers, but the bottom line is consistent with what I see every day in the classroom, the children living with both parents score substantially better than the others, regardless of the parents' educational background or race (10).

Overall, I find this to be true with my students. One young man went from being a straight A student to a straight F student the year his parents were divorced, and I have seen this time and time again with many other students as well. It often causes kids to lose their drive and motivation to perform well.

Other issues discussed in Caitlin Flanagan's *Time* magazine article that prove children are not resilient to the effects of divorce and provide evidence for what we talked about above, show, when children experience divorce, it causes them to have a difficult time trusting, limiting their capacity to establish lasting relationships in adulthood. The study also showed significant differences between boys and girls. The effects of resentment and abandonment on boys tend to be acted out early. Girls, on the other hand, tend to turn inward and become depressed, yet often do not exhibit this until adulthood (10).

Devastating Outcomes

As I stated previously, as an educator and as a single mother, I personally witness a child or children hurt and wounded by divorce every day. A student confided in me the other day that ever since his parents' divorce, his mother has had her boyfriend living with them. His father had taken off, and he hadn't seen him. He admitted feeling so rejected by his parents, particularly his mother, because of her new love, that he didn't feel he had any reason to care about life anymore and wanted to drop out of high school.

I tried to convince him that with hard work and effort, he could still have a bright future ahead of him, but this fourteen-year-old boy looked me in the eye with a stone-cold, expressionless face and said that "his future was behind him!"

Another high school boy who was a good friend with one of my friend's sons had been an honor student, captain of the football team, and was truly liked and admired by the majority of the student body, not to mention the son of a reasonably affluent family. During his senior year of high school, his parents' marriage ended suddenly in divorce. His father lost his job and was not helping to support their family, and his mother found herself applying for food stamps literally overnight.

The stress of the divorce, coupled with the extreme change in this boy's financial situation, was more than he could bear. He began partying fairly heavily for the first time, and his friends could sense that, in addition, he was becoming increasingly depressed. His depression was greater than anyone realized, and just months after this boy's parents divorced, he decided that he could no longer handle his situation, and he took his life.

Another very bright female student composed a poem saying that since her parents' divorce she sees the world in dark colors. And, quoted a line from Langston Hughes famous poem, *Mother to Son,* which said that now that her parents are divorced "Life for me ain't been no crystal stair . . . Bare" (11).

Stories like this make me want to scream, "Wake up, America, and realize that our children are NOT resilient . . . what are we doing to them?" The fact that my own kids are part of this crisis is sometimes more than I can bear. Divorce has become so prevalent in our society that I have heard first-grade students discussing with one another that "they are divorced too." Their identities are such that they see themselves as divorced. I kindly correct them by saying, "You're not divorced silly's, you've never been married, so you can't be divorced."

The Grim Reality

Also, in her *Time* magazine article, "Why Marriage Matters," author Caitlin Flanagan interviews David Blankenhorn, president of the Institute for American Values, to ask what he has determined from years of studying the long-term effects of divorce on children. Mr. Blankenhorn's findings expose the grim realities that are distressing to acknowledge. They are as follows:

- Unfortunately, a phenomenon called the sleeper effect caused by divorce is just beginning to surface and be understood. Despite parents easing their conscience by convincing themselves that children are resilient and will be fine, the truth is, kids suffer extraordinarily from divorce, more than we will probably ever understand. Within a child's core, they have an instinctive desire to love and be loved by both parents. Divorce shatters this identity and leaves a wound that no amount of money, a fancy home, or an elite school can ever heal (12).

- The documented facts from the Assembly Committee on Judiciary for the State of California, regarding the effects of divorce on children, as well as children raised by one rather than two parents, confirm Mr. Blankenhorn's conclusions. A few of these facts are as follows:

- Children of divorce are twice as likely to drop out of school and are 70 percent more likely to be suspended or to have been expelled from school.
- Three out of four teen suicides are committed by children from divorced families.
- The Capitol Resource Institute reports that children from divorced families are two to three times more likely to have behavior or emotional problems than those who live with both parents present.
- Seventy percent of juveniles and young adults serving time in long-term correctional facilities come from broken homes.
- Children living with single mothers have a five times-higher rate of child poverty than those living with intact families.
- Children living in single-parent homes score lower academically, have lower attendance records, and show less cooperation and effort in school than children who are living in two-parent homes (13).

Many so-called experts (especially those in favor of the no-fault divorce law) refuse to see divorce as the main cause for these statistics and choose rather to blame economic hardship and post-divorce issues not divorce itself, as being the lead contributing factors behind many of these issues, but it is a proven fact that divorce often causes poverty and whether it is pre or post-divorce issues causing such hardship, is insignificant. Divorce is, undeniably, a major root cause.

According to author William Galston's article for *Public Interest,* "Divorce American Style," (14) it is well documented that divorce is a leading, if not the leading factor for the statistics provided by the Assembly Committee on Judiciary for the State of California with three principals being key contributors: (15)

- plummeting income – an approximately 30 percent drop for the custodial parent and the children (15)

This radical drop in income was entirely accurate in my case. I look back and am not sure how we made it. Miraculously, we were able to remain in the same home (something that usually doesn't happen). Still, I had to be very creative in paying the mortgage, covering all other bills, and putting food on the table. I did receive maintenance for five years, which enabled me to obtain my degree, but it did not come close to matching our income before the divorce. The child support I was receiving barely covered the grocery bill with four growing kids and teens.

After I finished school, I began teaching full-time and always had a second job to supplement our income, first a paper route that all the kids helped me with, and then a second teaching job a few nights a week at the local community college. This drastic drop in income immediately put me into survival mode and fight-or-flight for years. Jesus, in His mercy, always came through, but it was a constant process of surrendering each bill and need to Jesus, learning to trust Him as never before, and leaning on family to help us. I look back and honestly wonder how we survived as well as we did, and can clearly see how Jesus carried us and supplied our needs, showing Himself faithful.

- "Diminished parenting time from the non-custodial parent (usually the father) who detaches himself from his children and from the custodial parent (usually the mother) who has to combine work inside and outside the home" (15)

One advantage my kids had was that my ex-husband was absent a great deal during our marriage, so at least they were used to him being gone a lot. But they always had the security of our marriage, knowing that Dad would eventually be home. After the divorce, this obviously shifted, with them seeing him only during his parenting time and having to adjust to sharing that time with a stepmom and her children.

During the marriage, however, I was a full-time stay-at-home mom. After the divorce, I tried as hard as possible to keep my children's lives as similar as before. Still, I now had to add a lot more responsibilities, going to school full-time first, and then working two jobs, so my time could no longer be exclusively dedicated to them, and this was a big adjustment.

Also, something important to note, my daughter once said, "Parenting time means you are always missing one parent." It broke my heart knowing how painful this must be for each of my children. I also see how difficult this is for my students, who are shifting back and forth between their parents' homes. Homework gets left, the changing between parents often causes high anxiety, and the kids, like mine, have very different environments in each house. It is so sad, but true that pets are frequently treated far better than kids, who are shuffled like a commodity from home to home.

- "Disruption of established ties-to friends, neighborhoods and communities, and educational institutions" (15)

This issue greatly affected my children and me. During my marriage, my kids, except for my daughter, who was only four, were attending a private Christian school that they loved. Once the divorce was finalized, my ex-husband was no longer willing to pay the tuition, and I certainly couldn't, so my children had to change schools, which was very difficult for each of them. Children having to switch schools due to divorce is a very typical situation, and often causes a great deal of hardship for kids. Not only are their families ripped apart, but frequently their friends and community change overnight as well.

All of my boys were heavily into sports, and this continued for several years after the divorce, but it brought with it new problems, and often does. It was at the practices and games that I had to encounter my ex-husband, who was one of the coaches, and his new wife, and they wasted no time in using this as an opportunity to try to poison the other players' parents against me. Needless to say, it made attending the games often unbearable for me, and it forced me to become an outsider during this time in my children's lives. I refused to stop going and support my kids, and I was almost always their ride, but it was a time of great suffering that my children took note of as well, which was difficult for them.

I have heard this is a pretty common occurrence, and sporting events and schools can, and often are, as was in my case, opportunities for the other parent and their new spouse to try to shine in the community, while slandering the other parent to teachers, parents, and anyone who will give them their ear. As in my case, I would have to explain to the teachers that I was actually the mother of my own children because their step-mom claimed that she was their mother, which caused a lot of confusion to the teachers and staff.

One good thing about this was that Jesus used it to free me from caring what others thought of me. As long as I was doing my best to honor Jesus and do right in His eyes, what other people thought of me could no longer control me. That said, it was tough on my children witnessing this happening to their mom and not being able to do anything about it. I got to the point where I didn't care what they said about me, but it was much more challenging to move past what it did to my children. As a teacher, I witness this happening often, and it has made me realize my situation is, unfortunately, very common in divorce situations.

I decided to share these personal examples, not to paint my ex-husband and his wife poorly, but to validate those of you who have experienced these same situations. You are not alone nor imagining your suffering. The pain is real for both you and your children. We can find solace and healing, however, knowing and truly realizing that Jesus in His mercy, will make all things work for our good, if we offer our pain to Him and unite our suffering and our children's suffering with His redemptive work on the cross. In Genesis 50:20, we can say as Joseph did to his brothers that had terribly wronged him, "You thought evil against me: but God turned it into good, that he might exalt me, as at present you see, and might save many people" (16).

And, St. Theresa of Lisieux once said, "Never pray for suffering, but when it comes, don't waste it."

Let the Children Be Heard!

A common theme I have heard amongst my own children, as well as other children who are from divorced homes, is, "Why don't we have a say in the matter?" Children in this situation are expected to:

- Accept a divorce that they did not want to happen
- Be okay with the fact that they will never live in the same house with both of their parents again

- Be genuinely pleased that their parents are now "happy"
- Accept the fact that their mother will now have to work outside the home instead of devoting her full energy to caring for them
- Do not feel sad they are separated from one of their parents all the time
- Immediately love and respect a parent's new spouse
- Become instant siblings with kids who are strangers and expect to "share" their parents and often grandparents with them
- Immediately forgive their parents for ripping their lives apart
- Accept the fact that they will now have to live in two houses instead of one, at least four days every other weekend, and be shuttled back and forth like a piece of property
- Possibly quit their sports and activities because their parents can no longer afford to pay for them
- Maybe change schools
- Most likely move out of the "family" home
- Accept the fact that their parents hate each other and cannot get along, while they insist you get along with everyone
- Endure child and family investigations in which they are expected to disclose which parent they want to live with most of the time, knowing their parents will know what they said
- Completely change family traditions and holidays
- Do not talk about their past because it might offend the step-parent; instead, focus on making new memories.

I fully support that parents should be in charge of making decisions for their children. Still, when expectations become abusive and truly outlandish, I have to agree that their opinion should be heard and that they should have a voice in their lives and futures. How many adults actually want to listen to what their children think of them getting a divorce? Adults instead rationalize it in their minds that their children will be much better off if they are "happy." They convince themselves that they are acting in the "best interest" of their child or children by creating this new "happy" life for them, and even if they don't like it at first, they'll get used to it because after all, "children are resilient."

It is no wonder that the statistics are as grim as they are and that America's children are turning to drugs, alcohol, self-harm, eating disorders, crime, suicide, sex, gender dysphoria, and immorality in general to numb the pain created in their lives by those who are supposed to love them and put their needs before their own. The hideous tentacles of divorce are so far-reaching that it would be impossible to identify all of the utter destruction it has caused our children, which in turn has caused great devastation on society, affecting generations to come.

What would the divorce statistics and laws look like if children were able to decide and contribute to these decisions that are made? I have personally found that they often have more common sense and wisdom than most adults who are in positions of power. Jesus understood this concept completely. He went so far as to say ". . . Truly I say to you, unless you repent (change, turn about) and become like little children [trusting, lowly, loving, forgiving], you can never enter the kingdom of heaven [at all]. Whoever will humble himself therefore and become like this little child . . . is greatest in the kingdom of heaven" (17).

For the sake and well-being of our nation's children and our future generations, I echo their call to let their voices be heard and pray for our country that the cancer of selfishness that has taken over so many lives will be broken, so that the institution and sanctity of marriage can be restored. I plead for God's mercy and forgiveness for what we have done to our children. God help us all!

What Should I Do?

When I first went through my divorce, I was fortunate to be enrolled in classes that talked about the harsh consequences of divorce on children. Because there are so many, I had to focus on the three that stuck in the forefront of my mind, which were having to move from the family home, leaving behind friends and neighbors, having to switch schools as a result of this move, and the custodial parent (which is me) no longer being available for their children out of necessity to work to support the family.

The statistics I read put absolute terror in my heart and made me literally agonize in pain over the situation my children now faced and cry over the opportunities I feel had been stolen from my children's lives through divorce. I was determined to create a good life for my kids, despite the odds now against us.

I spent many hours in prayer, crying to God not to let my children suffer because of decisions that had been made, and begged Him to direct and guide me on what I should do that would truly promote their well-being. I announced to my children from the very beginning that through God, we would not become part of the statistics I had read about, and that with Him, they (we) would beat the odds.

Every decision I made became about preventing those three circumstances that continued to plague me with fear. As mentioned above, God was faithful and blessed me above and beyond by allowing me and the children to stay in the family home. I couldn't keep them in the same schools, so I tried to find the best possible alternatives, which meant driving a great distance every day to ensure they could attend. I relied heavily on support from my wonderful family, who without their help and support, I could not have made it. I was also extremely determined not to abandon my children and to remain available to them as much as possible, so I enrolled in as many online classes as I could.

Along with trying as hard as a I could to keep my children's life as much the same as possible, I soon realized that I had to be their advocate, and I had to be willing to do whatever it took to insure this, even if this meant confronting my ex-husband about certain issues they would bring to me.

The hardest part was in not flying off the handle in anger when they would vent to me about certain things that took place in their father's home. I failed miserably with this plenty of times, and still find it difficult to just sit and listen and remain calm, letting them express themselves without jumping in.

The most important thing you can do with and for your children is pray. Pray without ceasing; teach them to lean on God through all adversities. Reinforce to them that they are a child of the Most High God and remind them often that He has a good plan for their lives. Teach them Scripture and how to speak it out of their mouths and over their lives, and encourage them to remember that Jesus loves them unconditionally and is always with them.

On a larger scale, we need to do what we can to overturn the no-fault laws in our state. Author William Galston, who wrote the article discussed previously in the chapter entitled *"Divorce American Style,"* offers excellent suggestions we should present to those who have the power to change the existing laws (18). He explains that we may not be able to prevent divorce, but there are things we can do to lessen its consequences. Some of these things we can do include "adopt a child's first principle" (18). He goes on to explain that securing the children's economic needs should take precedence over any discussion of property division. And, also, much stricter laws need to be put in place to enforce child support. And most importantly, he believes that if it is even remotely possible, children must be allowed to stay in their pre-divorce neighborhoods, schools, and communities. That again, this must be provided above the equal distribution of property (18).

What I Shouldn't Do

As I mentioned earlier in the chapter, the worst possible thing you can do for your children is to bash your ex in front of them continually. Boys, in particular, have their identities wrapped up in their fathers until they are late teens. When you bash their father in front of them, it is as if you are actually doing it to them, and it is entirely unacceptable, as I have mentioned before. Once the words are out there, you cannot take them back. I regret this more than I can express..

In addition, try as hard as you can not to discuss legal issues in front of or with them. Everyone I know, including me, has fallen into this temptation, and I have had to repent of this as well. Children should not be burdened with these adults' decisions. It is hard enough to handle them myself, let alone expect a child to talk about them. It is just too much stress for them to handle.

Don't begin to "flake" out and lose it. I have known plenty of people who immediately rush out and jump back into the dating pool before they have even had time to heal. The odds of meeting up with Mr. or Mrs. Wrong is almost guaranteed.

My aunt, a counselor in New Mexico, told me that most parents are already dating just a few months, and sometimes a few weeks, after the divorce. Within a week, she says, they move in together, and within a month or two, they have already broken up! Imagine the effects this has on children who are already suffering from the divorce itself.

A CFI once told me that if one parent remains the stabilizing force in their children's lives and holds it together, the kids generally turn out okay. He explained, however, that all too often, both parents "flake," and the kids don't have a chance.

Kid's Aren't Stupid.

A lady I had do my taxes told me that the thing she appreciated most about her mom was that, even though her parents got a divorce when she was little, and her dad was not good to her mother, her mother never said anything negative about him. As she told me this, I felt guilty, because while I don't do it regularly, there have been too many times when my children have heard more than they should have about their father.

She explained that, even though her mom never said anything, she and her brother could see the situation clearly and understood all that their mother had gone through to provide a good life for them. Kids are smart, and they ultimately know what's going on, so you don't have to worry about defending yourself with them.

Raising Up a Standard

I heard the other day that four out of 10 people, especially those of college age, believe that marriage is now obsolete (19). This truly saddened me, yet given what this generation has seen modeled by their parents in regards to marriage, I cannot blame them. For our nation to return to a culture of marriage that honors and treats it as the covenant God created it to be, our youth must be educated about God's views and commandments on the subject and learn to have the utmost respect for its sanctity. It is our job as their parents to instill this within them. Let your children know, that except for in abusive and extreme cases, divorce is not a viable choice especially if children are in the picture. Teach them that the greatest gift they can give to their future children is to love their spouse and do everything they can to have a strong and Godly marriage in which to raise their children.

They must know that marriage and love are commitments, not feelings. They need to know they will go through difficult times, but if they hang in there and work through them, they will overcome them and have a thriving marriage. Teach them that marriage is literally "until death do us part" and that, aside from accepting Jesus as their savior, there is no greater decision to be made than who they marry.

Educate your children on current laws, and assist and encourage them to become world changers for Christ and for the sanctity of marriage. As stated in Fatima, we are in the battle of battles, and it is for marriage and the family, and, ultimately, for the souls of our children and grandchildren. We can never stop fighting in this war until marriage in our world is returned to all of the beauty God intended it to be. Our children deserve this!

Chapter Sixteen

"Suddenly Single"

In the last chapter, we discussed the horrors that happen to our children due to divorce, and our children must always be our priority. That said, this does not mean we can overlook the devastating effects that happen to the parent who didn't want a divorce and finds themself suddenly single. I know that for me, transitioning from being married to single was a very difficult and painful process.

At the age of nineteen, I had put away my childhood identity, left my father and mother, and gone from being a Miss to a Mrs., a now-married, spoken-for woman. At twenty, I renewed my vows as a Christian, and in addition to being a wife, I also became a renewed daughter of the Most High God. When I was twenty-five, I gave birth to my first child, and with great honor, I added "mother" to my identity, reinforcing this role by adding a new child to my repertoire over the next eight years, until I was finally finished with four. My roles as a Christian, wife, and mother completely defined who I was and gave clear direction and purpose to my life.

The night my ex-husband had informed me he wanted a divorce, he had left our house, and it was the first step in his leaving my life forever. I remembered waking up the next morning, in my sleepy state, and turning over to embrace his warm body, as I had so many times over the last eighteen years, when I felt the cold and empty spot next to me, my peaceful state was abruptly ended, and I was once again reminded of what had taken place in our room just the night before.

Instead of getting up, I had pulled the covers over my head to block out the cheerful sunshine that had insisted on lighting up my room and was completely oblivious to my pain. I remember closing my eyes as tightly as I could, wanting to believe it had all been a bad dream and that I would soon awaken to life as I knew it. I remember gently caressing my wedding ring, as I had so many times, wanting to grasp onto something familiar. I could feel the smooth contours of the gold that, over the years, had become like a part of my body, and that morning it represented a symbol of hope, reminding me of my purpose and identity.

Although I knew for sure shortly after that morning that my marriage was truly over, I couldn't take my ring off until the actual decree was final. It had been with me through every experience, joy, and tragedy. It was on my finger as I first held each of my newborn babies, it was there when I comforted each of them, held them, and was always there when I folded my hands in prayer. That ring represented much more than a pretty piece of gold and a diamond; it held all the experiences of my life, and told the world who I was.

After the decree was final, I took the ring off for the first time, and my hand felt incredibly strange, as if part of it were missing. I remember walking around feeling like everyone could tell something was different about me. For eighteen years, that ring had made a statement, and now it was removed. I was no longer a spoken for married woman, and for the first time since I was nineteen, I was suddenly single. I remember experiencing an identity crisis for quite a stretch of time. Everything I had thought was solid and could be counted on was suddenly shifting sand. I was still completely clear that I was a Christian and a mother, but it was very strange not to have the married component, and I didn't know how I was to be as a single woman.

Because I had struggled at times throughout my marriage with having fleeting fantasies about other men, I had made a commitment during my marriage to work with the Lord to become very faithful and chaste not only physically (I never physically cheated on my ex-husband.), but in my thought life as well, as I knew these thoughts were wrong. To overcome this, I did not permit myself to look at other men, and I had learned to be oblivious and not pay any attention to those who made it obvious they found me attractive. I knew these fleeting fantasies weren't respectful to my ex-husband, and I wanted more than anything to obey God's laws.

Suddenly, I found myself as a single woman, yet I still felt very uncomfortable at the thought of noticing other men, and still felt very much married. Yet, at the local health food store I frequented, there was a salesclerk who began to take considerable notice of me, and I must admit that, given the fact that my ex-husband had just left me for another woman and divorced me, I was flattered by the attention I was receiving from this much younger man.

Who Am I?

When my kids were around, however, and he would still show obvious interest, it made me feel almost sick to my stomach. I was their mother, and, to me, being single did not fit with that role. I was not the only one who struggled with the fact that I was now a single woman. A police officer had pulled me over as a reminder of the "move over law." I told my sister-in-law about the incident, mentioning that the cop was really cute. She yelled back at me, saying, "Watch what you say, Missy, you are a mother." I still laugh about it, but I realized that it was a difficult transition for everyone close to me.

It took me several years to settle into my new identity. I was so busy earning my degree, preparing for litigation petitioned by my ex-husband, and taking care of my kids that I didn't have time to really think about dating at this point post- divorce. I remember listening to Dr. Laura on one occasion when a newly single mom called in for dating advice. Dr. Laura very matter-of-factly told this woman that she had no business dating until her kids were out of the house and that it was her obligation to her kids to remain single until then. Her words made a great impression on me, and I took them to heart.

Besides these words of wisdom from Dr. Laura, I am thankful that I did not meet anyone early on because my kids needed me, my marriage was not annulled, and I needed time to heal from my marriage. I also took to heart the words of the first CFI, when he told me that he saw kids turn out well in divorce situations if they have at least one parent who remains stable and consistently there for them.

I desperately wanted them to have one place where there was as little change as possible. I knew that if my identity had been shaken, how much more my children must have felt this as well.

I did not want to be married to my ex-husband soon after he told me he wanted a divorce because I knew in my heart there was someone else, and the pain was so intense it blunted my love for him. Still, I realized I loved the security of being married, and being single made me feel very vulnerable and unprotected. I am now completely comfortable being a Christian, a mom, and a single woman, and being married seems like a faded memory, but the ease and comfort of this acceptance did not come easily.

Cutting the Umbilical Cord

Before my separation, I had literally never left my children, except for an occasional evening outing or if my older boys went to a friend's house for a sleepover. So, the first time they went to spend the weekend with their dad, I am not sure how I survived. If I could communicate the feeling of a sword repeatedly stabbing me, this is how I would describe the way my body and emotions felt the first night they left. I sobbed and wailed literally for the entire weekend. I'm sure it affected me much worse because I knew this was going to happen now every other weekend, and I couldn't imagine spending that much time without my children.

Having them leave home to go to their dad's, and any other issues that have come up that threaten to shorten the time I have appointed to spend with them, are, without question, the most horrendous aspects of divorce. I have likened it to being forced into an empty nest years before I should have had to be, and I realized that time with my children was stolen from me.

I have also struggled significantly with the fact that, when we were married, and he had unreserved access, he showed little interest in spending time with our children unless he was coaching one of their sporting events. And now that the divorce was final, he continually petitioned for more time with them, which has been a huge, painful issue. One of my friends has complained about the same situation. During their marriage, her husband was gone frequently, and even when he was home, he spent his time in the garage but did not interact with his children. Once he filed for divorce, he fought her tooth and nail to try to receive 50/50 custody, even though he didn't spend time with them during the parenting arrangement that he currently had.

I realized soon on, that, sadly, the battles with parenting time often have little to do with actually wanting more time with the children, and much more to do with finances, malice, and control.

Jesus Heals All Wounds.

Over time, I finally got used to my children being gone essentially every other weekend. For the longest time, I believed I should be sad and depressed when they were gone, and I felt guilty when I wasn't. One Saturday morning, I was enjoying my coffee and fellowship with the Lord, and it was as if Jesus asked me if I could control the fact that they were gone. I answered Him saying, "No, I could not," and I felt in my spirit that, because I couldn't control it, I had no reason to feel guilty. After that moment, I permitted myself to be happy and even joyful when my children were not with me, and I knew Jesus had given me the Grace to do so.

The time they were away from me proved invaluable for my education and for catching up on everything that fell behind during the week. It was also a special time I could enjoy fellowship with just the Lord and me, so that He could fill me with His Spirit and give me the strength and grace to pour into my children when they returned home.

It's Not About Me!

One phrase I have had to remind myself more times than I can imagine is that "it is not about me." Going through divorce and having to share my children with my ex-husband and his new wife has been one of the most challenging things I, as a mother, have had to go through, and if their marriage lasts, it will be an issue that will not go away, even with adult children.

However, because I wanted my children to be healthy, thriving people, then and as adults, I knew they must spend time with their father. In our modern society, many women with feminist views, believe that our "resilient" children do not need both a father and a mother, yet author, Maria Kefalas, feminist, sociologist and author of, *Promises I can Keep: Why Poor Women Put Motherhood Before Marriage,* has conducted studies that show "few things hamper a child as much as not having a father at home, and that growing up without a father has a deep psychological effect on a child" (1).

This is a very sobering thought, considering that the number of children living with single mothers is staggering. And of those children living with single mothers, only 40 percent have seen their fathers in the past year (2). This is a tragedy and has long lasting and staggering effects on children. The absence of the father in our society today, is a crisis that has to change, and I did not want this for my children.

That said, the allotted parenting time is not one-size-fits-all. Every situation is different, and, as we discussed in the last chapter, the parenting plan must be based on what is best for the children involved. This allocation should include time with both parents, if possible, but the amount of time spent with each will vary. Because my kids were old enough to have input, I asked them what arrangement they wanted. As painful as it would have been, if they had wished to have 50/50 (One week with mom, and the next week with dad), I would have conceded, but all four adamantly said they did not want that and instead wanted every other weekend with their dad, and the majority of the time with me.

Knowing this, I was willing to fight with everything in me to honor this request for my children. With the initial decree, this is what my ex-husband and I agreed on, but once his wife became involved, and as I've mentioned before, they started petitioning for 50/50 custody for eight long years. Each time they petitioned me, I would ask my children again, and each time, they remained adamant that they did not want a 50/50 arrangement.

Our children deserve to be heard, and it is they who are most affected by this decision. Parents get to stay in their homes and are not shuffled around from place to place. That said, if they want to stay with one parent more than another because there are no rules in one home, especially as teens, then we must use our wisdom to overstep their requests and fight for the safest environment and the one most conducive to their healthy formation.

With all of this considered, just about every decision I made as a single mother had to be weighed against the question, "How would it affect my children?" and I encourage everyone to keep this in mind as well. This perspective applies to their relationship with their father, their step-mother, and even their step-siblings. I mentioned earlier in this chapter that I am their advocate. If things weren't going well for them in some facet, I realized I had to be willing to address the issues and plead their case, even if it meant confronting their father.

Confronting their father and step-mother, especially being two against one, was never easy or pleasant, but there are issues where you must stand your ground. And, as difficult as it is, try to do so from the perspective that you are in a business relationship with them, as mentioned before, and make it as brief as possible. As a child of God and with respect to your children, try to remain as civil as possible, and the best way to do this is with the Grace of God, and remembering that it is not about you.

Heal, Heal, Heal

Although we must keep our children's needs in the forefront, one issue we must focus on, as a single person, is working with Jesus to help us heal as mentioned in previous chapters. Working on healing is one of the best gifts you will give to yourself, your children, and a future spouse if you decide to marry again. I highly recommend seeking professional help from a good Christian therapist, or, as I did, seek counseling and prayer from your local priest.

That said, one of the biggest deterrents to getting well and being able to completely move on with our lives, even if we are receiving professional help, is unforgiveness. Even secular doctors and studies recognize that any unresolved bitterness or unforgiveness can bring about life-threatening diseases, such as cancer. My grandpa always used to say that resentment was the acid that ate its own container, and I always thought this was such an excellent metaphor.

I also came across the following in my favorite daily journal, *Daily Moments in His Presence* which says, "I (Jesus) Am restricted when you hold negative thoughts about the actions of other people. Release them to Me, otherwise, you turn the action upon yourself to your own hurt" (3). This made me think of the saying that says, hanging onto unforgiveness is like drinking poison and expecting it to hurt those who hurt you. We hurt ourselves by allowing it to rule our lives.

Moreover, unforgiveness is such a major factor that it can steal your joy, prevent you from moving forward, hinder your intimacy with Jesus, block your spiritual growth, and even prevent prayers from being answered. Jesus says in His Word, "And when you shall stand to pray, forgive, if you have aught against any man; that your Father also, Who is in Heaven, may forgive you your sins But if you will not forgive, neither will your Father that is in heaven, forgive you your sins" (4).

Because of ongoing issues with my ex-husband and his wife, I have struggled tremendously in this area. I know that we are to pray for those who cause us pain in our lives, but it is an extremely hard thing to do. I make a conscious effort to pray for them by surrendering them to Jesus, but it seems as soon as I begin to heal, something else happens, and it is as if the scab is torn off and the healing process has to start all over again.

When I begged Jesus for an answer, all I got was Matthew 18:21-22, "Then Peter came up to Him and said, Lord, how many times may my brother sin against me, and I forgive him *and* [a]let it go? [As many as] up to seven times? **22** Jesus answered him, 'I tell you, not up to seven times, but seventy times seven!'" (5). This wasn't necessarily what I wanted to hear, but I knew it was what I was called to do.

Like love and commitment, forgiveness is a choice. We choose to forgive, making a conscious decision with our will, and then let Jesus bring the feelings to follow. It may be years before the feeling follows, you will most likely have to make this decision 70 times seven, but experiencing true forgiveness provides you with incredible freedom, peace, and joy.

We cannot expect to receive anything from those we are forgiving. Forgiveness is just that "for" + "give-ness". It is a gift we give to someone else from ourselves, and we profit greatly because holding on to it will only serve to poison ourselves and prevent God from moving us along the path to our destinies. It is the key to progress as a suddenly single person, will help you to be a much healthier parent, will help you enter into a new relationship in a much healthier state, and, most important of all, it will keep the lines of communication open with Jesus, Whose help we cannot live in a healthy state without.

Time Is Our Friend.

Time is also a gift from Jesus. It may not heal all wounds, as the old saying goes, but if we refuse bitterness, the longer we are removed from the situation, the less power traumatic situations will have over us. When we have regular interactions with our ex, this becomes more difficult to achieve, but as our children get older, these will become less and less frequent, and we will learn that time has become a great friend in helping us to find peace.

Jesus Is Our Everything.

Embrace this new chapter of your life, and use it as a time to let Jesus heal you and draw you closer to Him. You will need His strength and Grace more than ever before, as it will be an extremely challenging and often painful time.

I will never forget the occasion, soon after the divorce, when the reality set in that my life would never be the same. I remember no longer fitting in and relating to the other married moms on the baseball team as they talked about getting their nails done, going shopping with all the other moms, and their next time at the gym. I am in no way judging them, but I remember feeling so out of place as I was struggling so greatly with fear and feeling all alone at the time, with my only thoughts being on survival. Would I have enough money for food till the end of the week? How was I going to pay the new medical bill that just arrived? When would I possibly have time to finish my 10-page essay by midnight that night and still get the kids to bed at a decent hour? How was I going to fit in gathering all the documents my attorney needed for the next court hearing?

My life had overnight shifted from normal stay-at-home mom duties, which are massive in and of themselves, to complete survival mode, with the need to keep my nose to the grindstone at every hour. I was now solely responsible for my household and the care of my children, and my priorities had shifted, making many of the things I once stressed about seem frivolous. For several years after my divorce, the thought of being single for the long haul was horrifying to me, but the good thing is, it forced me to lean on Jesus as my Lifeline and my literal Everything.

Another issue that was a struggle at times is that I knew I had to honor Jesus and be celibate as long as I was single. Anyone called to this life understands how difficult it can be at times. I remember telling a priest in confession once that I felt it was unfair that I had to be celibate and that it wasn't what I had chosen for myself. He quickly answered me, saying, "You may not have chosen this, but God has now called you to this." His words pierced me, and I knew his simple, straightforward answer came straight from God, as it greatly blessed me and helped me realize that if I offered up this struggle to Him, He would fulfill me in other ways.

Throughout the years, Jesus used this time of being single to draw me closer and closer to Him. I have had to rely on Him, literally, for everything. And He has shown Himself faithful. I remember one time when I was struggling a great deal with finances, I felt envious of someone I worked with who never seemed to have any financial concerns. I don't like feeling this way, so I cried out to Jesus to please help me overcome this. Right after this prayer, I heard Him say to me, "Anna, who's your Daddy?" It made me laugh out loud, but I quickly understood the message He was trying to convey to me.

As believers, we have the richest daddy in the entire universe, and we have nothing to fear. Since then, he has shown me that He is everything to us. He is our Provider, our Supply, our Comforter, our Counselor, our Redeemer, our Vindicator, our Doctor, our Teacher, our Father, our Business Partner, our Friend, and, yes, even our Spouse if we ask Him to be. Receiving Jesus in this way doesn't mean you will never marry again, but in the time of waiting, He will be the most faithful Husband to you.

When I have a concern with one of my kids, I say, "Jesus, You are their Father. What are You going to do about it?" Or if an unexpected bill comes up, I say, "Jesus, how will You fix this?" I know how lonely and tiring it can be not to have an earthly person to share responsibilities and life with. But if you cry out to Jesus, He will fill the loneliness and fear and replace it with His presence, joy, and peace. He will show you without a shadow of a doubt, what the enemy meant for your harm and to try and destroy you, He will work for your greatest good.

CHAPTER SEVENTEEN

"HE HAS GREAT PLANS FOR YOU!"

> For I know the thoughts and plans I have for you, says the Lord, thoughts and plans for welfare and peace and not for evil, to give you hope in your final outcome. You will call upon Me. You will come and pray to Me, and I will hear and heed you. Then you will seek Me, inquire for, and require Me [as a vital necessity] and find Me when you search for Me with all your heart (1).

What an extraordinary promise this is! I have a plaque with this Scripture that hangs in my bedroom window, and I never tire of reading it and being encouraged by it every single time I walk by.

This Scripture encourages me not only for my own life, but it is a promise from our Lord to everyone who has been ravaged through a divorce, as well as those who are struggling to hang on to their marriages, and for our society. We can heal, we can move on, and we can be fully restored. We must keep believing that *with God, all things are possible,* and that through prayer, action, sacrifice, and education, we can also move beyond our own situation and work together to restore America to the culture of marriage it once held.

As we talked about in the Prologue and second chapter, Sr. Lucia of Fatima prophesied, "Whoever works for the sanctity of marriage and the family will always be fought against and opposed in every way, because this is the decisive issue," (2) but that we should not fear, as Mary has already crushed satan's ugly head (2).

Albert Einstein also had the same thinking when he said, "Great spirits have always encountered violent opposition from mediocre minds. The mediocre mind is incapable of understanding the man who refuses to bow blindly to conventional prejudices and chooses instead to express his opinions courageously and honestly" (3). This is precisely what anyone determined to fight this battle will encounter, but it will be worth it. Besides mediocre minds, all of the forces of hell will do whatever is in their power to prevent progress as they, too, know this is the critical issue, the final battle, for the survival of our society. satan hates traditional marriage because it is born from the very hand of God, and it is the ideal union to bring forth human life making the health of the family and marriage the key to a thriving society.

Like with the success of an individual marriage, it will take more than one party being willing to see marriage in America restored and to turn the tide. In author William Galston's article "Divorce American Style," he summarizes both the cause and solution of this growing crisis when he states:

> In the end, the future of marriage in America hinges on a handful of moral questions. Are we willing to put the well-being of children first, even when this conflicts with adult desires and restrains our current passion for unfettered autonomy? Are we willing to honor claims of justice and fairness in the case of those who have sacrificed personal advancement for the good of the family? And are we prepared to return to contentment that stems not from monetary impulse but from loyalty to commitments that endure? (4)
>
> Our goals must be to First, endeavor to reduce the number of divorces, especially those with minor children. Second, when divorces are inevitable, we should seek to mitigate the consequences for the children and Third, restore a level playing field with adequate protections for women and men who have chosen the role as full-time parents (4).

It is my sincere desire and prayer that this book served to educate and inform you on why Our Lady of Fatima said the final battle would be against marriage and family, the root causes for the breakdown of marriage and the family, the tragedy and devastation divorce is having on children and families in America, that it has better equipped you to select your God given mate and recognize warning signs before you say, "I do," to face domestic violence head on, to have a basic direction on how to protect yourself and your children better if a divorce is inevitable, and to have hope that regardless of your circumstances, God will be with you every step of the way, as Comforter, Healer, Provider, Defender, Protector, and Miracle Worker. Give your life, your children, your marriage, your divorce, and future into His hands today, and watch Him make something out of it all that *is super abundantly, far over and above all you could ever ask, think, or imagine . . . (5).*

Remember, He has good plans for you!

Works Cited by Chapter

First Page

Page v

(1) Editor, CNA. "Fatima Visionary Predicted 'Final Battle' Would Be over Marriage, Family." *Catholic News Agency*, Catholic News Agency, 13 Feb. 2020, www.catholicnewsagency.com/news/fatima-visionary-predicted-final-battle-would-be-over-marriage-family-17760.

Prologue

Page 7

(1) "First Apparition (May 13, 1917): EWTN." *EWTN Global Catholic Television Network*, EWTN Inc. , 2025, www.ewtn.com/catholicism/devotions/first-apparition-of-our-lady-23363.

Page 8

(2) Montagna, Deborah. "Letter #28: The Last Battle." *Inside The Vatican*, TygerOnline Website Design & Development, 4 June 2018, insidethevatican.com/news/newsflash/letter-28-last-battle/.

(3) "Bible Gateway Passage: 1 John 4:4 - Amplified Bible, Classic Edition." *Bible Gateway*, The Lockman Foundation , 1987, www.biblegateway.com/passage/?search=1+John+4%3A4+&version=AMPC.

Introduction - Chapter One - "Until Divorce Do Us Part"

Page 10

(1) "Bible Gateway Passage: Proverbs 16:18 - New International Version." *Bible Gateway*, www.biblegateway.com/passage/?search=Proverbs+16%3A18&version=NIV. Accessed 24 July 2025.

Page 12

(2) "Matthew 19:26." *Douay-Rheims Bible, Matthew Chapter 19*, DRBO.org, www.drbo.org/cgi-bin/d?b=drb&bk=47&ch=19&l=26-#x. Accessed 24 July 2025.

(3) "Bible Gateway Passage: Isaiah 61:3 - New International Version." *Bible Gateway*, www.biblegateway.com/passage/?search=Isaiah+61%3A3&version=NIV. Accessed 24 July 2025.

(4) "Bible Gateway Passage: Joel 2:25 - New International Version." *Bible Gateway*, www.biblegateway.com/passage/?search=Joel+2%3A25&version=NIV. Accessed 24 July 2025.

(5) "Bible Gateway Passage: Psalm 27:13-14 - Amplified Bible, Classic Edition." *Bible Gateway*, www.biblegateway.com/passage/?search=Psalm+27%3A13-14&version=AMPC. Accessed 24 July 2025.

Chapter Two - "America's Rising Crisis"

Page 14

(1) "CDC - NCHS - National Center for Health Statistics." *Centers for Disease Control and Prevention*, Centers for Disease Control and Prevention, 7 July 2021, www.cdc.gov/nchs/.

(2) Wang, Wendy, and Kim Parker. "Record Share of Americans Have Never Married." *Pew Research Center's Social & Demographic Trends Project*, Pew Research Center, 27 Aug. 2020, www.pewresearch.org/social-trends/2014/09/24/record-share-of-americans-have-never-married/#will-todays-never-married-adults-eventually-marry.

(3) Horowitz, Juliana Menasce, et al. "The State of Marriage and Cohabitation in the U.S." *Pew Research Center's Social & Demographic Trends Project*, Pew Research Center, 26 May 2020, www.pewresearch.org/social-trends/2019/11/06/the-landscape-of-marriage-and-cohabitation-in-the-u-s/.

(4) Barroso, Amanda. "More than Half of Americans Say Marriage Is Important but Not Essential to Leading a Fulfilling Life." *Pew Research Center*, Pew Research Center, 18 Aug. 2020, www.pewresearch.org/fact-tank/2020/02/14/more-than-half-of-americans-say-marriage-is-important-but-not-essential-to-leading-a-fulfilling-life/.

(5) Graf, Nikki. "Key Findings on Marriage and Cohabitation in the U.S." *Pew Research Center*, Pew Research Center, 30 May 2020, www.pewresearch.org/fact-tank/2019/11/06/key-findings-on-marriage-and-cohabitation-in-the-u-s/.

Page 15

(6) Horowitz, Juliana Menasce, et al. "The State of Marriage and Cohabitation in the U.S." *Pew Research Center's Social & Demographic Trends Project*, Pew Research Center, 26 May 2020, www.pewresearch.org/social-trends/2019/11/06/the-landscape-of-marriage-and-cohabitation-in-the-u-s/.

(7) Stanton, Glenn T. "Why Your Risk for Divorce Is Probably A Lot Lower Than You Think." *The Federalist*, The Federalist, 18 Jan. 2017, thefederalist.com/2017/01/18/why-your-risk-for-divorce-is-probably-lower-than-you-think/.

(8) Rousselle, Christine. "Survey Says: Most Catholics in US Reject Church Teaching on Cohabitation." *Catholic News Agency*, Catholic News Agency, 6 July 2021, www.catholicnewsagency.com/news/42751/survey-says-most-catholics-in-us-reject-church-teaching-on-cohabitation.

(9) *1 Corinthians 6:9 Do You Not Know That the Wicked Will Not Inherit the Kingdom of God? Do Not Be Deceived: Neither the Sexually Immoral, nor Idolaters, nor Adulterers, nor Men Who Submit to or Perform Homosexual Acts,* 2021, biblehub.com/1_corinthians/6-9.htm.

(10) *Catechism of the Catholic Church.* - "Paragraph 2370 - The Sixth Commandment", United States Conference of Catholic Bishops, 2026, p. 584. usccb.cld.bz/Catechism-of-the-Catholic-Church2/584/.

(11) "Saint Bridget Saw What Happens When Couples Live Together Without God's Blessing." (Source: Revelations of Saint Bridget of Sweden, Book 7). *YouTube*, Divine Mysteries of the Saints , 26 Dec. 2025, youtu.be/37z2OfiT6tE?si=UY82HcS9JxWVX9GA.

Page 16

(12) "Padre Pio Saw What Happens When You Live Together 'As If Married' Without God." *YouTube*, Awaken Revelations, 14 Dec. 2025, youtu.be/7Q6lnSlc6vc?si=85bOAgq9UviVe-53.

(13) "Bible Gateway Passage: 1 Corinthians 10:13 - Amplified Bible, Classic Edition." *Bible Gateway*, Lockman Foundation, 1987, www.biblegateway.com/passage/?search=1+Corinthians+10%3A13&version=AMPC.

Page 17

(14) "Saint Bridget Saw What Happens When Couples Live Together Without God's Blessing." (Source: Revelations of Saint Bridget of Sweden, Book 7). *YouTube*, Divine Mysteries of the Saints , 26 Dec. 2025, youtu.be/37z2OfiT6tE?si=UY82HcS9JxWVX9GA.

(15) Bennett, Jessica. "Millennial Marriage, Sex and the Search for Long-Term Relationships." *Time*, Time, 25 July 2014, time.com/3024606/millennials-marriage-sex-relationships-hook-ups/.

Page 18

(16) Coe, Jonathan B. "Our Lady Of Good Success: A Message For Our Time." *Catholic Exchange*, Sophia Institute Press, 17 May 2019, catholicexchange.com/our-lady-of-good-success-a-message-for-our-time.

Page 19

(17) "The 6 Apparitions of Fatima." *Get Your Daily Bread Together With The Catholic Faith Store*, 17 June 2018, www.catholicfaithstore.com/daily-bread/6-apparitions-fatima/#:~:text=On%20May%2013%2C%201917%2C%20Blessed%20Mary%20appears%20for,nine%2C%20and%20Jacinta%20Marto%2C%20age%20-seven%20were%20cousins.

(18) Churchpop. "Final Battle Will Be Over Marriage/ Family, Fatima Visionary Secretly Told Cardinal." *Catholic For Life*, 14 June 2017, www.catholicforlife.com/final-battle-will-marriage-family-fatima-visionary-secretly-told-cardinal/#:~:text=Final%20Battle%20Will%20Be%20Over%20Marriage%2F%20Family%2C%20-Fatima,Satan%20would%20be%20over%20marriage%20and%20the%20family.

(19) Zondervan. (1987). The Amplified Bible. Grand Rapids, MI: Zondervan Publishing House

Page 20

(20) Ripperger, Chad, director. *State of the Spiritual Battlefield ~ Fr. Ripperger*. *YouTube*, Sensus Fidelium, 1 Mar. 2021, youtu.be/kDjy_K9--Ls.

Page 21

(21) Twitter, Tara Culp-Ressler. "Birth Control Goes Against Catholicism's Teachings, But Most Catholics Use It Anyway." *ThinkProgress*, 4 Aug. 2015, archive.thinkprogress.org/birth-control-goes-against-catholicisms-teachings-but-most-catholics-use-it-anyway-d22f2da560a1/.

(22) "Bible Gateway Passage: Matthew 24:4 - Amplified Bible." *Bible Gateway*, Lockman Foundation , 2015, www.biblegateway.com/passage/?search=Matthew+24%3A4&version=AMP.

Page 23

(23) "A Timeline of Contraception." *PBS*, Public Broadcasting Service, www.pbs.org/wgbh/americanexperience/features/pill-timeline/.

(24) "FDA Approves 'the Pill.'" *History.com*, A&E Television Networks, 9 Feb. 2010, www.history.com/this-day-in-history/fda-approves-the-pill.

Page 25

(25) MD, Dominic Pedulla. "Contraception Increases Rates of Divorce, Suicide, and Sexual Dysfunction." *Catholic Stand*, 4 Apr. 2013, catholicstand.com/contraception-increases-rates-of-divorce-suicide-and-sexual-dysfunction/.

(26) Buckley, Paul. "Contraceptives Responsible for Increased Divorce, Abortion Rates." *The Daily Nebraskan*, The Daily Nebraskan, 13 Sept. 2007, www.dailynebraskan.com/contraceptives-responsible-for-increased-divorce-abortion-rates/article_a519dfa6-1c0f-54d3-9eba-82238f26e412.html.

Page 26

(27) Larry Peterson |, et al. "The Holy Trinity: the Mirror of Traditional Marriage." *Catholic365*, 29 July 2014, www.catholic365.com/article/42/the-holy-trinity-the-mirror-of-traditional-marriage.html.

(28) "Genesis Chapter 2." *Douay-Rheims Bible, Genesis Chapter 2:24*, DRBO.org www.drbo.org/chapter/01002.htm.

(29) "Contraception: The Bible and Early Fathers." *Catholic.net*, Gen. Gen 1:28, 9:1,7; 35:11catholic.net/op/articles/3841/cat/1240/contraception-the-bible-and-early-fathers.html.

(30) Catholic Answers. "Canon Law." *Catholic Answers*, Catholic Answers, 24 Mar. 2021, www.catholic.com/encyclopedia/canon-law.

(31) "Canon 1057 and the Object of Matrimonial Consent - 'Giving Oneself.'" *Www.cormacburke.or.ke*, 29 July 2010, www.cormacburke.or.ke/node/276#:~:text=Matrimonial%20consent%20under%20the%20old%20Code%20was%20described,the%20generation%20of%20children%22%20%28c.%201081%2C%20§%202%29.

(32) Cornell Law School. "Marriage." *Legal Information Institute*, Legal Information Institute, www.law.cornell.edu/wex/marriage.

Page 27

(33) "A Quote by Charles J. Chaput." *Goodreads*, Goodreads, 2026, www.goodreads.com/quotes/7456006-evil-preaches-tolerance-until-it-is-dominant-then-it-tries.

(34) Ripperger, Chad, director. *State of the Spiritual Battlefield ~ Fr. Ripperger. YouTube*, Sensus Fidelium, 1 Mar. 2021, youtu.be/kDjy_K9--Ls.

(35) "Bible Gateway Passage: Romans 6:23 - Douay-Rheims 1899 American Edition." *Bible Gateway*, Douay-Rheims 1899 American Edition (DRA), 1899, www.biblegateway.com/passage/?search=Romans+6%3A23&version=DRA.

(36) "Genesis Chapter 38:9,10." *Douay-Rheims Bible, Genesis Chapter 38*, www.drbo.org/chapter/01002.htm.

Page 29

(37) *Catechism of the Catholic Church* - "Paragraph 2370." United States Conference of Catholic Bishops, 2026, p. 590. usccb.cld.bz/Catechism-of-the-Catholic-Church2/584/

Page 30

(38) Burke , Cardinal. "'Marriage 'Marriage and Contraception." and Contraception." ." *L'Osservatore Romano - English Edition*, L'Osservatore Romano, 10 Oct. 1988, www.osservatoreromano.va/en/pages/archive.html.

Page 30

(39) "Contraception: The Bible and Early Fathers." *Catholic.net*, Gen. Gen 1:28, 9:1,7; 35:11 catholic.net/op/articles/3841/cat/1240/contraception-the-bible-and-early-fathers.html.

Page 32

(40) Gynecology, Raleigh. "How Does An IUD Work?" *Raleigh Gynecology & Wellness*, 21 July 2021, gynraleigh.com/how-does-an-iud-work/.

(41) "PubMed." *National Center for Biotechnology Information*, U.S. National Library of Medicine, pubmed.ncbi.nlm.nih.gov/.

(42) Center, Willow Womens. "When To Take the Morning-After Pill and When Not To." *Willow Women's Center*, Willow Women's Center, 28 Jan. 2021, willowwomenscenter.org/2021/01/28/when-to-take-the-morning-after-pill-and-when-not-to/#:~:text=According%20to%20Mayo%20Clinic%2C%20the%20morning-after%20pill%20works,a%20fertilized%20egg%20from%20implanting%20in%20the%20uterus.

Page 33

(43) American College of Pediatricians . "When Human Life Begins." *American College of Pediatricians*, Mar. 2017, acpeds.org/position-statements/when-human-life-begins.

(44) "Abortion Definition & Meaning." *Merriam-Webster*, Merriam-Webster, 2026, www.merriam-webster.com/dictionary/abortion#medicalDictionary.

(45) Timmons , Jessica. ""Can You Get Pregnant on the Pill?"." *Healthline*, Healthline Media , 18 Oct. 2016, www.healthline.com/health/birth-control/how-to-get-pregnant-while-on-the-pill.

(46) Timmons , Jessica. ""Can You Get Pregnant on the Pill?"." *Healthline*, Healthline Media , 18 Oct. 2016, www.healthline.com/health/birth-control/how-to-get-pregnant-while-on-the-pill.

Page 34

(47) Steven. "62,502,904 Babies Have Been Killed by Abortion Since Roe v. Wade in 1973." *LifeNews.com*, 26 Jan. 2021, 1018AM, www.lifenews.com/2021/01/22/62502904-babies-have-been-killed-by-abortion-since-roe-v-wade-in-1973/.

(48) "Soon We Will Have Great Happenings: Father Gabriele Amorth." *CATHOLICITYBLOG*, 11 Jan. 2016, www.catholicityblog.com/2016/07/soon-we-will-have-great-happenings.html.

(49) Aglialoro, Todd. "Contraception and Abortion: A Love Story." *Catholic Answers*, Catholic Answers, 24 Sept. 2020, www.catholic.com/magazine/online-edition/contraception-and-abortion-a-love-story.

Page 36

(50) "TOP 25 QUOTES BY ST. CATHERINE OF SIENA (of 106): A-Z Quotes." *A*, www.azquotes.com/author/17881-St_Catherine_of_Siena.

Page 36

(51) "NFP Effectiveness." *USCCB*, www.usccb.org/issues-and-action/marriage-and-family/natural-family-planning/what-is-nfp/effectiveness.

Page 37

(52) Timmons , Jessica. ""Can You Get Pregnant on the Pill?""" *Healthline*, Healthline Media , 18 Oct. 2016, www.healthline.com/health/birth-control/how-to-get-pregnant-while-on-the-pill.

(53) *Catechism of the Catholic Church* - "Paragraph # 2370", United States Conference of Catholic Bishops, 2026, p. 590. usccb.cld.bz/Catechism-of-the-Catholic-Church2/584/

(54) *1 Corinthians 7 Douay-Rheims Bible*, 1899, biblehub.com/drbc/1_corinthians/7.htm.

(55) Fehring, RJ, and MD Manhart . "Natural Family Planning and Marital Chastity: The Effects of Periodic Abstinence on Marital Relationships." *Europe PMC*, 12 June 2020, europepmc.org/article/MED/33487745.

Page 38

(56) "Bible Gateway Passage: Ephesians 5:11 - Douay-Rheims 1899 American Edition." *Bible Gateway*, Douay-Rheims 1899 American Edition (DRA), www.biblegateway.com/passage/?search=Ephesians+5%3A11&version=DRA. Accessed 31 Jan. 2026.

(57) St Mother Teresa. "A Quote by Mother Teresa." *Goodreads*, Goodreads, 2026, www.goodreads.com/quotes/112196-never-worry-about-numbers-help-one-person-at-a-time.

(58) "Deuteronomy Chapter 30:19." *Douay-Rheims Bible, Deuteronomy Chapter 30*, Copyright DRBO.ORG 2001-2023, drbo.org/chapter/05030.htm.

Chapter Three - "No Fault?"

Page 40

(1) Oh-Willeke, A. (2006, February 14). What Is No-Fault Divorce? *The Washing Park Prophet* from http://washparkprophet.blogspot.com/search?q=no-fault+divorce

(2) Heshkowitz, D. & Liebert, D. Assembly Committee on Judiciary. (1997) *Divorce Reform in California: From Fault to No-Fault and Back Again?* USA from http://www.library.ca.gov/crb/98/04/currentstate.pdf

Page 42

(3) Gallagher, M. (1997, August-September). End No-Fault Divorce? *First Things* from http://www.firstthings.com/article/2008/09/001-end-no-fault-divorce-4

Chapter Four - "It's All About Me."

Page 45

(1) "Bible Gateway Passage: John 10:10 - Amplified Bible." *Bible Gateway*, Lockman Foundation www.biblegateway.com/passage/?search=John+10%3A10&version=AMP. Accessed 25 July 2025.

(2) "Bible Gateway Passage: John 10:11 - Amplified Bible." *Bible Gateway*, Lockman Foundation www.biblegateway.com/passage/?search=John+10%3A11&version=AMP. Accessed 25 July 2025.

Page 46

(3) "John 5:13." *Douay-Rheims Bible, John Chapter 15*, DRBO.org www.drbo.org/cgi-bin/d?b=drb&bk=50&ch=15&l=13-#x. Accessed 25 July 2025.

Page 48

(4) Carothers, Merlin R. *You Can Be Happy Now*. M.R. Carothers, Foundation of Praise. 2001.

(5) "Bible Gateway Passage: Ephesians 5:33 - Amplified Bible, Classic Edition." *Bible Gateway*, Lockman Foundation www.biblegateway.com/passage/?search=Ephesians+5%3A33+&version=AMPC. Accessed 25 July 2025.

Page 51

(6) Filz, Gretchen. "St. Charbel: All the Forces of Evil Are Focused on Destroying the Family." *The Catholic Company*, The Catholic Company, 24 July 2017, www.catholiccompany.com/blogs/magazine/family-st-charbel-6104.

Chapter Five - "What Does God Have to Say About It?

Page 55

(1) "John 8:32." *Douay-Rheims Bible, John Chapter 8*, drbo.org/chapter/50008.htm.

Page 56

(2) "Genesis 2:18-25." *Genesis 2:18-25 Now the Lord God Said, It Is Not Good (Sufficient, Satisfactory) That the Man Should Be Alone; I Will Make Him a Helper Meet (Suitable, Adapted, Complementary)*

for Him. And out of the Ground the Lord | Amplified Bible, Classic Edition (AMPC) | Download The Bible App Now, www.bible.com/bible/8/GEN.2.18-25.ampc.

(3) "Genesis 1:28." *Douay-Rheims Bible, Genesis Chapter 1*, drbo.org/cgi-bin/d?b=drb&bk=1&ch=1&l=28#x.

(4) "Matthew 19:4-6." *Douay-Rheims Bible, Matthew Chapter 19*, drbo.org/cgi-bin/s?q=Matthew%2B19%3A4-6&b=drb&t=0.

(5) Ordained Catholic Priest. Personal Interview. 27 July 2021.

Page 57

(6) "Ephesians 5:22-30." *Douay-Rheims Bible, Ephesians Chapter 5*, drbo.org/cgi-bin/s?q=Ephesians%2B5%3A22-30&b=drb&t=0.

Page 58

(7)Ratzinger, J. (1994). Catechism of the Catholic Church. Vatican: Libereria Editrice Vaticana

(8)"Mark 10:9." *Douay-Rheims Bible, MARK Chapter 10*, drbo.org/chapter/48010.htm.

Page 59

(9) "THE CATECHISM OF THE CATHOLIC CHURCH AND THE SACRAMENT OF MARRIAGE." *Catechism of the Catholic Church and Marriage.*, Catholic Doors Ministry, www.catholicdoors.com/misc/marriage/matri.htm.

Page 61

(10) *Catechism of the Catholic Church* - "Paragraph # 2385", United States Conference of Catholic Bishops, 2026, p. 593. usccb.cld.bz/Catechism-of-the-Catholic-Church2/584/

(11) Zondervan. "Malachi 2:16," *The Amplified Bible*. Grand Rapids, MI: Zondervan Publishing House, 1987.

Page 62

(12) "More than 40% of Domestic Violence Victims Are Male, Report Reveals." *The Guardian*, Guardian News and Media, 4 Sept. 2010, www.theguardian.com/society/2010/sep/05/men-victims-domestic-violence

Page 63

(13) Zondervan. "Matthew 19:8," *The Amplified Bible*. Grand Rapids, MI: Zondervan PublishingHouse, 1987.

(14) "Mathew 19:19." *Douay-Rheims Bible, Matthew 19:19* drbo.org/chapter/05030.htm.

Page 64

(15) Shawn. "(2021 Divorce Rate in America) How Many Marriages End in Divorce Statistics." *The Hive Law*, The Hive Law, 1 May 2021, www.thehivelaw.com/blog/divorce-statistics-us-divorce-rate-in-america/.

(16) "Annulment." *USCCB*, United States Conference of Catholic Bishops, 2021, www.usccb.org/topics/marriage-and-family-life-ministries/annulment#:~:text=An%20annulment%20is%20a%20declaration%20by%20a%20Church,binding%20union.%20The%20annulment%20process%20is%20frequently%20misunderstood.

Page 65

(17) Ordained Catholic Priest. Personal Interview. 27 July 2021.

(18) Ordained Catholic Priest. Personal Interview. 27 July 2021.

Page 66

(19) Roach, Becky. "Why Can't I Have a Catholic OUTDOOR WEDDING? The 3 Requirements for Catholic Wedding Venues." *Catholic*, Catholic Link, 27 June 2021, catholic-link.org/catholic-outdoor-wedding-3-requirements/.

(20) Ordained Catholic Priest. Personal Interview. 27 July 2021.

Page 67

(21) "1 Corinthians 7:12 - 15." *Douay-Rheims Bible, 1 Corinthians 7:12-15.* drbo.org/chapter/05030.htm.

(22) Ordained Catholic Priest. Personal Interview. 27 July 2021.

(23) Grondin, Fr. Charles. "Is Marriage of Non-Baptized Persons Valid?" *Catholic Answers*, Catholic Answers, 23 Feb. 2019, www.catholic.com/qa/is-marriage-of-non-baptized-persons-valid.

Page 68

(24) "What Is the Pauline Privilege?" *Canon Law Made Easy*, 25 Aug. 2020, canonlawmadeeasy.com/2013/04/04/what-is-the-pauline-privilege/.

Page 69

(25) "'PETITION FOR FAVOR OF THE FAITH - PETRINE PRIVILEGE.'" *DIOCESE OF COVINGTON TRIBUNAL*, DIOCESE OF COVINGTON TRIBUNAL, www.covdio.org/wp-content/uploads/2016/01/Petrine_Privilege_Form.pdf.

Page 74

(26) "Matthew 7:14." *Douay-Rheims Bible, Matthew 7:14.* drbo.org/chapter/05030.htm.

(27) "Deuteronomy 30:19." *Douay-Rheims Bible, Deuteronomy 30:19.* http://drbo.org/cgi-bin/d?b=drb&bk=5&ch=30&l=19-19&q=1#x

(28) "Annulment." *USCCB*, United States Conference of Catholic Bishops, 2021, www.usccb.org/topics/marriage-and-family-life-ministries/annulment#:~:text=An%20annulment%20is%20a%20declaration%20by%20a%20Church,binding%20union.%20The%20annulment%20process%20is%20frequently%20misunderstood.

(29) Ordained Catholic Priest. Personal Interview. 27 July 2021.

Page 76

(30) "Matthew 19:19." *Douay-Rheims Bible, Matthew 19:19.* http://drbo.org/cgi-bin/s?q=Matthew+19%3A19&b=drb

(31) "1 Corinthians 7:5." *Douay-Rheims Bible. 1 Corinthians 7:5.DRBO.org,* http://drbo.org/chapter/53007.htm

Page 79

(32) Ordained Catholic Priest. Personal Interview. 27 July 2021.

(33) Ordained Catholic Priest. Personal Interview. 27 July 2021.

Page 80

(34) Ordained Catholic Priest. Personal Interview. 27 July 2021.

(35) Shawn. "(2021 Divorce Rate in America) How Many Marriages End in Divorce Statistics." *The Hive Law*, The Hive Law, 1 May 2021, www.thehivelaw.com/blog/divorce-statistics-us-divorce-rate-in-america/.

Page 81

(36) Ordained Catholic Priest. Personal Interview. 27 July 2021.

(37) Onearmsteve4192, director. *The Final Confrontation b/w the Lord & Satan Will Be Over Family & Marriage. Sensus Fidelium*, YouTube, 15 Oct. 2015, www.youtube.com/watch?v=50B9nXt_tG8.

(38) "Matthew 19:1-10." *Douay-Rheims Bible. Matthew 19:1-10. http://drbo.org/cgi-bin/s?q=Matthew+19%3A1-10&b=drb&t=0.*

Page 82

(39) Zondervan. "Hosea 4:6," *The Amplified Bible*. Grand Rapids, MI: Zondervan Publishing House, 1987.

Page 83

(40) Zondervan. "Romans 8:38 - 39," *The Amplified Bible.* Grand Rapids, MI: Zondervan Publishing House, 1987

(41) "1John 1:9." *Douay-Rheims. 1 John 1:9.* DRBO.org http://drbo.org/cgi-bin/s?q=1+John+1%3A9&b=drb&t=0

Page 84

(42) "Proverbs 28:13." *Douay-Rheims. Proverbs 28:13.DRBO.org,* http://drbo.org/cgi-bin/s?q=Proverbs+28%3A13&b=drb.

Page 85

(43) Zondervan. "Romans 8:28," *The Amplified Bible.* Grand Rapids, MI: Zondervan Publishing House, 1987

(44) "Bible Gateway Passage: Romans 8:39 - Amplified Bible, Classic Edition." *Bible Gateway,* The Lockman Foundation , 1987, www.biblegateway.com/passage/?search=Romans+8%3A39&version=AMPC.

(45) "Bible Gateway Passage: Hebrews 13:5 - Douay-Rheims 1899 American Edition." *Bible Gateway,* Douay-Rheims 1899 American Edition (DRA), www.biblegateway.com/passage/?search=Hebrews+13%3A5&version=DRA. Accessed 16 Jan. 2026.

Chapter Six - "Before You Say, 'I Do'"

Page 89

(1) "2 Corinthians 6:14." *Douay-Rheims Bible, 2 Corinthians Chapter 6,* drbo.org/cgi-bin/d?b=drb&bk=54&ch=6&l=14-#x. Accessed 25 July 2025.

Page 91

(2) "Romans 8:28 ." *Douay-Rheims Bible, Romans Chapter 8,* Douay-Rheims Bible, www.drbo.org/cgi-bin/d?b=drb&bk=52&ch=8&l=28-#x. Accessed 19 July 2025.

Page 97

(3) "1 Corinthians 6:13." *Douay-Rheims Bible, 1 Corinthians Chapter 6*, www.drbo.org/cgi-bin/d?b=drb&bk=53&ch=6&l=13-#x. Accessed 25 July 2025.

(4) "Romans 6:23." *Douay-Rheims Bible, Romans Chapter* 6, drbo.org/cgi-bin/d?b=drb&bk=52&ch=6&l=23-#x. Accessed 25 July 2025.

Page 99

(5) "New Reports Highlight Depression Prevalence and Medication Use in the U.S." *Centers for Disease Control and Prevention*, Centers for Disease Control and Prevention, 16 Apr. 2025, www.cdc.gov/nchs/pressroom/nchs_press_releases/2025/20250416.htm.

(6) Queen of Peace Media. "Joyful Mysteries Recorded Live: NATIONAL 54 DAY ROSARY NOVENA with the Blount Fathers." *YouTube*, YouTube, 21 Nov. 2021, www.youtube.com/watch?v=YUdlOF871Rg.

(7) Institution, Wheatley. "New Report Finds Link between Strong Marriages and Sexual Restraint during the Dating Years." *PR Newswire: Press Release Distribution, Targeting, Monitoring and Marketing*, Cision PR Newswire, 19 Apr. 2023, www.prnewswire.com/news-releases/new-report-finds-link-between-strong-marriages-and-sexual-restraint-during-the-dating-years-301802184.html.

Page 100

(8) Smith, Jesse, and Nicholas H Wolfinger. "Re-Examining the Link between Premarital Sex and Divorce." *Journal of Family Issues*, U.S. National Library of Medicine, Mar. 2024, pmc.ncbi.nlm.nih.gov/articles/PMC10989935/.

(9) Nash, Tom. "Why Is Masturbation Wrong?" *Catholic Answers*, Catholic Answers, 12 Feb. 2025, www.catholic.com/qa/why-masturbation-is-wrong.

(10) Nash, Tom. "Why Is Masturbation Wrong?" *Catholic Answers*, Catholic Answers, 12 Feb. 2025, www.catholic.com/qa/why-masturbation-is-wrong.

Page 103

(11) "Bible Gateway Passage: Psalm 119:9 - Amplified Bible." *Bible Gateway*, www.biblegateway.com/passage/?search=Psalm+119%3A9&version=AMP. Accessed 18 Aug. 2025.

Chapter Seven - "The Broken Promise"

Page 110

(1) "Romans 8:28." *# Search Romans+8:28*, DRBO.org , 2001, www.drbo.org/cgi-bin/s?q=romans%2B8%3A28&b=drb.

Page 120

(2) "Numbers 32:23". *Numbers 32:23 ESV - - Bible Gateway*, www.biblegateway.com/passage/?search=Numbers%2B32%3A23&version=ESV.

(3) "Mark 4:22." *Douay-Rheims Bible, Mark Chapter 4*, DRBO.org, 2001, drbo.org/chapter/48004.htm.

Chapter Eight - "Sleeping With the Enemy"

Page 121

(1) Arnold, Elliott. *Blood Brother*. Duell, Sloan and Pearce, 1947.

(2) "John 10:10." *Douay-Rheims Bible, John Chapter 10*, www.drbo.org/cgi-bin/d?b=drb&bk=50&ch=10&l=10#x.

Page 122

(3) "Abuse Definition & Meaning." *Dictionary.com*, Dictionary.com, www.dictionary.com/browse/abuse.

Page 123

(4) "Fast Facts: Preventing Intimate Partner Violence |Violence Prevention|injury Center|CDC." *Centers for Disease Control and Prevention*, Centers for Disease Control and Prevention, 2 Nov. 2021, www.cdc.gov/violenceprevention/intimatepartnerviolence/fastfact.html.

Page 126

(5) Author(s) Raquel Kennedy Bergen Elizabeth Barnhill. "Marital Rape: New Research and Directions." *VAWnet.org*, vawnet.org/material/marital-rape-new-research-and-directions.

Page 127

(6) "Vawnet.Org." *VAWnet*, National Resource Center on Domestic Violence, 2025, vawnet.org/.

(7) "1 Corinthians 7:3 -5." *Douay-Rheims Bible, 1 Corinthians Chapter 7*, www.drbo.org/chapter/53007.htm.

Page 129

(8) "Proverbs 8:21." *Douay-Rheims Bible, Proverbs Chapter 18*, www.drbo.org/cgi-bin/d?b=drb&bk=22&ch=18&l=21#x.

Page 131

(9) Marriage Builders, Inc. "Why Women Leave Men." *Marriage Builders, Inc.*, www.marriagebuilders.com/graphic/mbi8111_leave.html.

Page 132

(10) Marriage Builders, Inc. "Why Women Leave Men." *Marriage Builders, Inc.*, www.marriagebuilders.com/graphic/mbi8111_leave.html.

(11) "Stockholm Syndrome: What It Is, Symptoms & How to Treat." *Cleveland Clinic*, my.clevelandclinic.org/health/diseases/22387-stockholm-syndrome.

Page 133

(12) Aiken , Elijah. "Is Trauma Bonding the Same as Stockholm Syndrome?" *Search Marquis*, UnfiltereddLLC, 2022, www.searchmarquis.com/?aid=260251&data=aWlkPTQwJnVpZD0xMjE5MzU3OTY&tb=1&dt=17576435459.

(13) Jacobsen, Sheri. "What Is Trauma Bonding? Is It Keeping You In a Bad Relationship? ." *Harley Therapy Counseling Blog* , Harley Therapy Blog , 14 June 2018, www.harleytherapy.co.uk/counselling/what-is-trauma-bonding.htm.

(14) Jacobsen, Sheri. "What Is Trauma Bonding? Is It Keeping You In a Bad Relationship? ." *Harley Therapy Counseling Blog* , Harley Therapy Blog , 14 June 2018, www.harleytherapy.co.uk/counselling/what-is-trauma-bonding.htm.

Page 138

(15) "Isaiah 61:3,4, and 7." *Douay-Rheims Bible, Isaias (Isaiah) Chapter 61*, www.drbo.org/cgi-bin/d?b=drb&bk=27&ch=61&l=3#x.

(16) "Ephesians 5: 25-28." *Douay-Rheims Bible, Ephesians Chapter 5*, www.drbo.org/cgi-bin/d?b=drb&bk=56&ch=5&l=25#x.

Page 139

(17) "Colossians 3:8-10, 12-14 ." *Colossians 3:8-10, 12-14 AMPC - - Bible Gateway*, www.biblegateway.com/passage/?search=Colossians%2B3%3A8-10%2C%2B12-14&version=AMPC.

Page 140

(18) Powell, Kevin. "Ending Violence against Women and Girls." *Oprah.com*, Oprah.com, 19 Mar. 2009, www.oprah.com/relationships/how-men-can-fight-domestic-violence/1.

Chapter Nine - "The Cheater"

Page 143

(1) Author, TED Guest. "10 Facts about Infidelity." *Ideas.ted.com*, 23 Jan. 2014, ideas.ted.com/10-facts-about-infidelity-helen-fisher/#:~:text=Current%20studies%20of%20American%20couples%20indicate%20that%2020%20to%2040%25%20of%20heterosexual%20married%20men%20and%2020%20to%2025%25%20of%20heterosexual%20married%20women%20will%20also%20have%20an%20extramarital%20affair%20during%20their%20lifetime.

(2) "Cheating Spouse Survey Results." *Truth About Deception*, Truth About Deception , 2022, www.truthaboutdeception.com/community-features/online-quizzes/cheating-spouse-results.html.

Page 146

(3) "Matthew 5:28." *Douay-Rheims Bible, Matthew Chapter 5*, DRBO.org , 2001, drbo.org/cgi-bin/d?b=drb&bk=47&ch=5&l=28#x.

Page 147

(4) Ssemakula, Yozefu B. *The Healing of Families: How to Pray Effectively for Those Stubborn Personal and Familial Problems*. Fr Yozefu B Ssemakula, 2012.

(5) "Bible Gateway Passage: Mark 3:27 - Douay-Rheims 1899 American Edition." *Bible Gateway*, Douay-Rheims 1899 American edition, www.biblegateway.com/passage/?search=Mark+3%3A27&version=DRA. Accessed 1 Feb. 2026.

Page 148

(6) Rehill , Dan. "What God Has Done for You - And Why the World Is in Crisis ." *YouTube*, Uploaded by *Audio BỮA CƠM QUÊ*, 16 Jan. 2026, (6:03 to 6:30), youtu.be/Oc-l_e81_5U?si=xdNj6nyvig6ei1z8.

(7) "Matthew 5:29." *Douay-Rheims Bible, Matthew Chapter 5*, DRBO.org , 2001, drbo.org/chapter/47005.htm.

Page 149

(8) "Bible Gateway Passage: Proverbs 7:1-3, 5 - New International Version." *Bible Gateway*, www.biblegateway.com/passage/?search=Proverbs+7%3A1-5&version=NIV. Accessed 2 Aug. 2025.

(9) "Bible Gateway Passage: Proverbs 6:21-23 - New International Version." *Bible Gateway*, www.biblegateway.com/passage/?search=Proverbs+6%3A21-23&version=NIV. Accessed 2 Aug. 2025.

Page 150

(10) "Bible Gateway Passage: Proverbs 6:25-29 - New International Version." *Bible Gateway*, www.biblegateway.com/passage/?search=Proverbs+6%3A25-29&version=NIV. Accessed 2 Aug. 2025.

(11) "Bible Gateway Passage: 1 Corinthians 10:13 - New International Version." *Bible Gateway*, www.biblegateway.com/passage/?search=1+Corinthians+10%3A13&version=NIV. Accessed 2 Aug. 2025.

(12) Rueb, Jerry. "The Lure of Lust; the Danger of Divorce." *Cornerstone Church Long Beach*, Cornerstone Church Long Beach, 10 Mar. 2019, www.cclb.org/sermons/2019/sermon-on-the-mount-005.

Page 152

(13) Rueb, Jerry. "The Lure of Lust; the Danger of Divorce." *Cornerstone Church Long Beach*, Cornerstone Church Long Beach, 10 Mar. 2019, www.cclb.org/sermons/2019/sermon-on-the-mount-005.

(14) "Cheating Spouse Survey Results." *Truth About Deception*, Truth About Deception , 2022, www.truthaboutdeception.com/community-features/online-quizzes/cheating-spouse-results.html.

Page 153

(15) "Proverbs 6:23 and 5:23." *YouVersion*, Life.Church Amplified Bible Classic Addition, 2022, www.bible.com/bible/8/pro.6.23 and 5.23.

Page 154

(16) "Psalm 119:9 AMPC Bible: Youversion." *Psalm 119:9 | AMPC Bible | YouVersion*, Life.Church, 2022, www.bible.com/bible/8/PSA.119.AMPC.

Page 155

(17) "John 15:5 ." *Douay-Rheims Bible, John Chapter 15*, DRBO.org , 2001, drbo.org/cgi-bin/d?b=drb&bk=50&ch=15&l=5#x.

(18) Chapman, Gary D. *The Five Love Languages: How to Express Heartfelt Commitment to Your Mate.* Northfield Publishing, 1995.

Page 156

(19) Orthodox in the District, and Orthodox in the District. "Incredible Words of Wisdom from St John of Kronstadt." *Orthodox in the District*, Orthodox in the District , 26 Feb. 2013, ryanphunter.wordpress.com/2013/02/26/incredible-words-of-wisdom-from-st-john-of-kronstadt-2/.

Page 157

(20) "Matthew 19:26." *Douay-Rheims Bible, Matthew Chapter 19*, DRBO.org , 2001, drbo.org/cgi-bin/d?b=drb&bk=47&ch

Chapter Ten - "The Addict"

Page 163

(1) Liguori, Alfonso Maria de', and Eugene Grimm. "The Holy Eucharist: The Sacrifice, the Sacrament, and the Sacred Heart of Jesus Christ, Practice of Love of Jesus Christ, Novena to the Holy Ghost." *Amazon*, Redemptorist Fathers, 1983, https://www.amazon.com/Novena-Holy-Ghost/dp/0895552620/ref=sr_1_1?crid=2N1CRMG7N1IHK&keywords=novena%2Bto%2Bthe%2Bholy%2BGhost&qid=1658683827&sprefix=novena%2Bto%2Bthe%2Bholy%2Bghost%2Caps%2C173&sr=8-1.

Page 169

(2) "What Is a Dry Drunk? - Dry Drunk Syndrome." *Alcohol.Org*, 25 Oct. 2022, alcohol.org/alcoholism/dry-drunk/.

Page 174

(3) "2 Corinthians 4:16 - NIV Translation ." *2 Corinthians 4:16 Therefore We Do Not Lose Heart. Though Our Outer Self Is Wasting Away, Yet Our Inner Self Is Being Renewed Day by Day.*, Biblehub.com , 2004, https://biblehub.com/2_corinthians/4-16.htm.

Page 175

(4) "Have a Problem with Alcohol? There Is a Solution." *Alcoholics Anonymous*, General Service Office (G.S.O.) of Alcoholics Anonymous, 2022, https://www.aa.org/.

(5) "Narcotics Anonymous WORLD SERVICES ." *NAWS : Find A Meeting*, Narcotics Anonymous WORLD SERVICES , 2022, https://www.na.org/meetingsearch/.

(6) Amen, Daniel G. "'How I Help Patients Quit Drinking' - Instagram Reel ." *Mental Healthcare Clinic Focusing On Your Brain Health | Dr. Amen*, Amen Clinics, 21 July 2022, https://www.amenclinics.com/.

Page 177

(7) (1892-1971), reinhold niebuhr, and Reinhold Niebuhr (1892-1971). "Serenity Prayer." *Beliefnet*, Beliefnet Beliefnet Is a Lifestyle Website Providing Feature Editorial Content around the Topics of Inspiration, Spirituality, Health, Wellness, Love and Family, News and Entertainment., 20 Sept. 2018, https://www.beliefnet.com/prayers/protestant/addiction/serenity-prayer.aspx.

(8) ThoughtCo. "The Prayer of Saint Francis of Assisi." *Learn Religions*, Learn Religions, 8 Mar. 2017, https://www.learnreligions.com/prayer-of-saint-francis-of-assisi-542575.

(9) Ssemakula, Yozefu B. "Abebooks." *By Yozefu B. Ssemakula: Good (2011) | Goodwill*, Example Product Manufacturer, 1 Jan. 1970, https://www.abebooks.com/Healing-Families-Pray-Effectively-Stubborn-Personal/31246825481/bd?cm_mmc=msn-_-comus_shopp_used-_-naa-_-naa&msclkid=dfd841d29b99152c74fc230f1e878fa6.

Page 178

(10) "Anon Family Groups." *Al*, Al-Anon Family Group Headquarters, Inc., 18 Aug. 2021, al-anon.org/.

Chapter Eleven - "The Narcissist"

Page 180

(1) "⚘ Narcissus :: The Self-Lover." *Greek Mythology.Com* , 1995, www.greekmythology.com/Myths/Mortals/Narcissus/narcissus.html.

(2) Campbell , Josephine. "Narcissism (Psychology): EBSCO." *EBSCO Information Services, Inc. | Www.Ebsco.Com*, 2024, www.ebsco.com/research-starters/health-and-medicine/narcissism-psychology.

(3) "Turning Your Attention to Narcissistic Personality Disorder." *Cleveland Clinic*, 2 June 2025, my.clevelandclinic.org/health/diseases/9742-narcissistic-personality-disorder.

Page 181

(4) *Diagnostic and Statistical Manual of Mental Disorders, 5th Edition, Text Revision.* 2022 APA Publishing

(5) Katherine Allen, M.A., Psychotherapist. Expert in Narcissistic Personality Disorder and Trauma Recovery from Narcissistic Abuse. Personal Interview. 2025

Page 182

(6) Being, Grace. "Narcissistic Personality Disorder Statistics: 2022." *Grace Being*, Grace Being , 13 Aug. 2023, grace-being.com/narcissistic-abuse/narcissistic-personality-disorder-statistics/.

(7) Being, Grace. "Narcissistic Personality Disorder Statistics: 2022." *Grace Being*, Grace Being , 13 Aug. 2023, grace-being.com/narcissistic-abuse/narcissistic-personality-disorder-statistics/.

(8) "Turning Your Attention to Narcissistic Personality Disorder." *Cleveland Clinic*, 2 June 2025, my.clevelandclinic.org/health/diseases/9742-narcissistic-personality-disorder.

(9) "Turning Your Attention to Narcissistic Personality Disorder." *Cleveland Clinic*, 2 June 2025, my.clevelandclinic.org/health/diseases/9742-narcissistic-personality-disorder.

Page 183

(10) Katherine Allen, M.A., Psychotherapist. Expert in Narcissistic Personality Disorder and Trauma Recovery from Narcissistic Abuse. Personal Interview. 2025

Page 184

(11) Katherine Allen, M.A., Psychotherapist. Expert in Narcissistic Personality Disorder and Trauma Recovery from Narcissistic Abuse. Personal Interview. 2025

(12) Katherine Allen, M.A., Psychotherapist. Expert in Narcissistic Personality Disorder and Trauma Recovery from Narcissistic Abuse. Personal Interview. 2025

Page 185

(13) Katherine Allen, M.A., Psychotherapist. Expert in Narcissistic Personality Disorder and Trauma Recovery from Narcissistic Abuse. Personal Interview. 2025

Page 186

(14) Allison, Debi. "The Educated Empath Is a Narcissist's Worst Nightmare." *Awareness Act*, 28 Oct. 2020, awarenessact.com/the-educated-empath-is-a-narcissists-worst-nightmare/.

(15) Katherine Allen, M.A., Psychotherapist. Expert in Narcissistic Personality Disorder and Trauma Recovery from Narcissistic Abuse. Personal Interview. 2025

Page 187

(16) Katherine Allen, M.A., Psychotherapist. Expert in Narcissistic Personality Disorder and Trauma Recovery from Narcissistic Abuse. Personal Interview. 2025

Page 188

(17) Being, Grace. "Narcissistic Personality Disorder Statistics: 2022." *Grace Being*, Grace Being , 13 Aug. 2023, grace-being.com/narcissistic-abuse/narcissistic-personality-disorder-statistics/.

Page 189

(18) Katherine Allen, M.A., Psychotherapist. Expert in Narcissistic Personality Disorder and Trauma Recovery from Narcissistic Abuse. Personal Interview. 2025

Page 192

(19) Katherine Allen, M.A., Psychotherapist. Expert in Narcissistic Personality Disorder and Trauma Recovery from Narcissistic Abuse. Personal Interview. 2025

Page 193

(20) Katherine Allen, M.A., Psychotherapist. Expert in Narcissistic Personality Disorder and Trauma Recovery from Narcissistic Abuse. Personal Interview. 2025

(21) Katherine Allen, M.A., Psychotherapist. Expert in Narcissistic Personality Disorder and Trauma Recovery from Narcissistic Abuse. Personal Interview. 2025

Page 194

(22) Katherine Allen, M.A., Psychotherapist. Expert in Narcissistic Personality Disorder and Trauma Recovery from Narcissistic Abuse. Personal Interview. 2025

Page 196

(23) Katherine Allen, M.A., Psychotherapist. Expert in Narcissistic Personality Disorder and Trauma Recovery from Narcissistic Abuse. Personal Interview. 2025

Page 197

(24) Katherine Allen, M.A., Psychotherapist. Expert in Narcissistic Personality Disorder and Trauma Recovery from Narcissistic Abuse. Personal Interview. 2025

(25) Katherine Allen, M.A., Psychotherapist. Expert in Narcissistic Personality Disorder and Trauma Recovery from Narcissistic Abuse. Personal Interview. 2025

Page 199

(26) Katherine Allen, M.A., Psychotherapist. Expert in Narcissistic Personality Disorder and Trauma Recovery from Narcissistic Abuse. Personal Interview. 2025

Page 200

(27) Katherine Allen, M.A., Psychotherapist. Expert in Narcissistic Personality Disorder and Trauma Recovery from Narcissistic Abuse. Personal Interview. 2025

(28) Katherine Allen, M.A., Psychotherapist. Expert in Narcissistic Personality Disorder and Trauma Recovery from Narcissistic Abuse. Personal Interview. 2025

Page 202

(29) Katherine Allen, M.A., Psychotherapist. Expert in Narcissistic Personality Disorder and Trauma Recovery from Narcissistic Abuse. Personal Interview. 2025

Page 203

(30) Allison, Debi. "The Educated Empath Is a Narcissist's Worst Nightmare." *Awareness Act*, 28 Oct. 2020, awarenessact.com/the-educated-empath-is-a-narcissists-worst-nightmare/.

Page 204

(31) "Romas 8:28." *Douay-Rheims Bible, Romans Chapter 8*, Douay-Rheims Bible, www.drbo.org/cgi-bin/d?b=drb&bk=52&ch=8&l=28-#x. Accessed 19 July 2025.

(32) Carothers, Merlin. "Every Breath." *You Can Be Happy Now* , Foundation of Praise , Escondido, California , 2001, pp. 126–127.

Chapter Twelve - "The Only Way Out Is Through."

Page 209

(1) Roberts, Francis J. "January 5th." *Daily Moments in His Presence: 365-Day Devotional Journal*, Deluxe ed., Barbour Pub Inc, Accessed 4 Jan. 2026.

Page 210

(2) Mercy Me. "You're Beautiful." *The Generous Mr. Lovewell,* INO Records, 2010.

Chapter Thirteen - "Help . . . Is Anybody Out There?"

Page 214

(1) Chapman, Gary D. *The Five Love Languages*. Walker Large Print, 2010.

(2) Kreidman, Ellen. *Light His Fire: How to Keep Your Man Passionately and Hopelessly in Love with You*. Villard Books, 1989.

Page 215

(3) Kreidman, Ellen. *Light Her Fire: How to Ignite Passion, Joy, and Excitement in the Woman You Love.* Dell, 1993.

(4) Kendrick, Alex. *Fireproof.* Affirm Films, 2008.

Page 216

(5) "Bible Gateway Passage: 1 Corinthians 10:13 - New International Version." *Bible Gateway*, www.biblegateway.com/passage/?search=1+Corinthians+10%3A13&version=NIV. Accessed 2 Aug. 2025.

Page 219

(6) "Matthew 10:16 ." *Douay-Rheims Bible, Matthew Chapter 10*, DRBO.org, www.drbo.org/chapter/47010.htm. Accessed 26 Nov. 2025.

Page 220

(7) "Bible Gateway Passage: 1 Corinthians 7:15 - Amplified Bible, Classic Edition." *Bible Gateway*, The Lockman Foundation , 1987, www.biblegateway.com/passage/?search=1+Corinthians+7%3A15&version=AMPC.

(8)"Romans 8:28." *DRBO.ORG*, Douay-Rheims Bible Online, 2023, www.drbo.org/cgi-bin/s?q=romans%2B8%3A28&x=0&y=0&b=drb.

Chapter Fourteen - "It's Over, Now What?"

Page 223

(1) "Bible Gateway Passage: James 1:5 - Amplified Bible, Classic Edition." *Bible Gateway*, Biblegateway.com , www.biblegateway.com/passage/?search=James+1%3A5&version=AMPC. Accessed 29 Dec. 2025.

(2) "Bible Gateway Passage: Proverbs 18:14 - Amplified Bible, Classic Edition." *Bible Gateway*, Biblegateway.com, www.biblegateway.com/passage/?search=Proverbs+18%3A14&version=AMPC. Accessed 29 Dec. 2025.

Page 224

(3) "Bible Gateway Passage: Lamentations 3:58-60 - Living Bible." *Bible Gateway*, Biblegateway.com , www.biblegateway.com/passage/?search=Lamentations+3%3A58-60&version=TLB. Accessed 29 Dec. 2025.

(4) "Bible Gateway Passage: Hebrews 13:5 - Amplified Bible, Classic Edition." *Bible Gateway*, Biblegateway.com , www.biblegateway.com/passage/?search=Hebrews+13%3A5+&version=AMPC. Accessed 30 Dec. 2025.

(5) "Bible Gateway Passage: Ephesians 3:20 - Amplified Bible, Classic Edition." *Bible Gateway*, Biblegateway.com , www.biblegateway.com/passage/?search=Ephesians+3%3A20&version=AMPC. Accessed 31 Dec. 2025.

Page 225

(6) "Bible Gateway Passage: Philippians 4:19 - Amplified Bible, Classic Edition." *Bible Gateway*, Biblegateway.com , www.biblegateway.com/passage/?search=phillipians+4%3A19+&version=AMPC. Accessed 31 Dec. 2025.

(7) "Bible Gateway Passage: Philippians 4:13 - Amplified Bible, Classic Edition." *Bible Gateway*, Biblegateway.com , www.biblegateway.com/passage/?search=phillipians+4%3A13+&version=AMPC. Accessed 31 Dec. 2025.

(8) "Bible Gateway Passage: Isaiah 41:10 - Amplified Bible, Classic Edition." *Bible Gateway*, Biblegateway.com , Lockman Productions, www.biblegateway.com/passage/?search=Isaiah+41%3A+10&version=AMPC. Accessed 31 Dec. 2025.

Page 233

(9) "Death Definition & Meaning." *Dictionary.Com*, Dictionary.com, www.dictionary.com/browse/death. Accessed 31 Dec. 2025.

Page 236

(10) "Bible Gateway Passage: 1 Peter 5:7 - Revised Geneva Translation." *Bible Gateway*, Five Talents Audio, 2024, www.biblegateway.com/passage/?search=1+Peter+5%3A7&version=RGT.

(11) "Bible Gateway Passage: John 15:5 - Darby Translation." *Bible Gateway*, Biblegateway.com , www.biblegateway.com/passage/?search=John+15%3A5&version=DARBY. Accessed 31 Dec. 2025.

(12) "Bible Gateway Passage: Romans 8:28 - Amplified Bible, Classic Edition." *Bible Gateway*, Biblegateway.com , www.biblegateway.com/passage/?search=Romans+8%3A28+&version=AMPC. Accessed 31 Dec. 2025.

Page 237

(13) "Bible Gateway Passage: 2 Timothy 1:7 - Amplified Bible, Classic Edition." *Bible Gateway*, Biblegateway.com, www.biblegateway.com/passage/?search=+2+Timothy+1%3A7&version=AMPC. Accessed 31 Dec. 2025.

(14) "Bible Gateway Passage: Psalm 37:5 - Amplified Bible, Classic Edition." *Bible Gateway*, Biblegateway.com , www.biblegateway.com/passage/?search=psalm+37%3A5&version=AMPC. Accessed 31 Dec. 2025.

(15) "Bible Gateway Passage: Philippians 4:7 - Douay-Rheims 1899 American Edition." *Bible Gateway*, Biblegateway.com , www.biblegateway.com/passage/?search=phillipians+4%3A7&version=DRA. Accessed 31 Dec. 2025.

(16) "Bible Gateway Passage: Hebrews 13:6 - Amplified Bible, Classic Edition." *Bible Gateway*, Biblegateway.com , www.biblegateway.com/passage/?search=Hebrews+13%3A6+&version=AMPC. Accessed 31 Dec. 2025.

Chapter Fifteen - "It's in the Children's Best Interest?"

Page 242

(1) Whitehead, Barbara Dafoe. *The Divorce Culture: Rethinking Our Commitments to Marriage and Family*. Vintage Books, 1998.

(2) Kohm, Lynne Marie. "On Mutual Consent to Divorce: A debate with two sides to the story." *Appalachian Journal of Law*, vol. 8, no. 1, winter 2008, pp.8,35. *Gale Academic OneFile*, link.gale.com/apps/doc/A196017474/AONE?u=anon~ac5855c6&sid=googleScholar&xid=95e5fa5d. Accessed 2 Jan. 2026.

(3) Galston, W. "Divorce American Style". *New York Times,* 19 February, 2006. pp.L13.

Page 243

(4) Galston, W. "Divorce American Style." *Public Interest,* vol.124, 1996, pp. 12-26.

Page 244

(5) Galston, W. "Divorce American Style." *Public Interest,* vol.124, 1996, pp. 12-26.

Page 245

(6) Kosloski , Philip. "Fatima Visionary Said Final Battle Would Be Over Marriage and Family." *Aleteia*, 13 May 2022, aleteia.org/2022/05/13/fatima-visionary-said-final-battle-would-be-over-marriage-and-family/.

(7) Portnoy, S. "The Psychology of Divorce: A lawyer's primer, Part 2: The effects of divorce on children." *American Journal of Family Law.* vol. 21(4), 2008, pp.126-134.

(8) Portnoy, S. "The Psychology of Divorce: A lawyer's primer, Part 2: The effects of divorce on children." *American Journal of Family Law.* vol. 21(4), 2008, pp.126-134.

Page 246

(9) Flanagan, C. "Why Marriage Matters." *Time,* vol. 174, 2008, pp.45-49.

(10) Flanagan, C. "Why Marriage Matters." *Time,* vol. 174, 2008, pp.45-49.

Page 248

(11) Hughes , Langston. "Mother to Son | the Poetry Foundation." *Poetry Foundation* , poetry foundation.org , 2026, www.poetryfoundation.org/poems/47559/mother-to-son.

(12) Flanagan, C. "Why Marriage Matters." *Time,* vol. 174, 2008, pp.45-49.

Page 249

(13) Flanagan, C. "Why Marriage Matters." *Time,* vol. 174, 2008, pp.45-49.

(14) Galston, W. "Divorce American style." *New York Times,* February 19, 2006, .p. L13.

(15) Heshkowitz, D. & Liebert, D. "Divorce reform in California: From fault to no-fault and back again?" *Assembly Committee on Judiciary,* 1997, http://www.library.ca.gov/crb/98/04/currentstate.pdf

Page 252

(16) "BibleGatewayPassage: Genesis 50:20 - Douay-Rheims 1899 American Edition." *Bible Gateway*,douay-rheims1899Americanedition, www.biblegateway.com/passage/?search=Genesis+50%3A20&version=DRA. Accessed 3 Feb. 2026.

Page 254

(17) "Bible Gateway Passage: Matthew 18:2-5 - Amplified Bible, Classic Edition." *Bible Gateway*,Biblegateway.com , www.biblegateway.com/passage/?search=Matthew+18%3A+2+%E2%80%93+5&version=AMPC. Accessed 2 Jan. 2026.

Page 256

(18) Galston, W. "Divorce American Style". *New York Times,* 19 February, 2006. pp.L13.

Page 257

(19) Cohn, D'Vera. "Barely Half of U.S. Adults Are Married – a Record Low." *Pew Research Center*, Pew Research Center, 14 Dec. 2011, www.pewresearch.org/social-trends/2011/12/14/barely-half-of-u-s-adults-are-married-a-record-low/.

Chapter Sixteen - "Suddenly Single"

Page 264

(1) Edin, Kathryn, and Maria Kefalas. *Promises I Can Keep: Why Poor Women Put Motherhood before Marriage*. University of California Press, 2011.

(2) Flanagan, C. "Why Marriage Matters." *Time,* vol. 174, 2008, pp.45-49.

Page 265

(3) Roberts , Francis J. "January 5th ." *Daily Moments in His Presence: 365-Day Devotional Journal* , Deluxe ed., Barbour Pub Inc, Accessed 4 Jan. 2026.

Page 266

(4)"Bible Gateway Passage: Mark 11:25-26 - Douay-Rheims 1899 American Edition." *Bible Gateway*, Biblegateway.com , www.biblegateway.com/passage/?search=Mark+11%3A25-26&version=DRA. Accessed 4 Jan. 2026.

(5) "Bible Gateway Passage: Matthew 18:21-22 - Amplified Bible, Classic Edition." *Bible Gateway*, Biblegateway.com, https://www.biblegateway.com/passage/?search=Matthew%2018%3A21-22&version=AMPCwww.biblegateway.com/passage/?search=Matthew+18%3A21-22&version=AMPC. Accessed 4 Jan. 2026.

Chapter Seventeen - "He Has Great Plans for You!"

Page 269

(1) "Bible Gateway Passage: Jeremiah 29:11-13 - Amplified Bible, Classic Edition." *Bible Gateway*, Lockman Foundation , 1987, www.biblegateway.com/passage/?search=Jeremiah+29%3A+11-13&version=AMPC.

Page 270

(2) Editor, CNA. "Fatima Visionary Predicted 'Final Battle' Would Be over Marriage, Family." *Catholic News Agency*, Catholic News Agency, 13 Feb. 2020, www.catholicnewsagency.com/news/fatima-visionary-predicted-final-battle-would-be-over-marriage-family-17760.

(3) Einstein , Albert. "A Quote by Albert Einstein." *Goodreads*, Goodreads, 2026, www.goodreads.com/quotes/470750-great-spirits-have-always-encountered-violent-opposition-from-mediocre-minds.

(4) Galston, W. "Divorce American Style". *Public Interest,* 1996, pp. 124, 12-26.

Page 271

(5) "Bible Gateway Passage: Ephesians 3:20 - Amplified Bible, Classic Edition." *Bible Gateway*, Lockman Foundation , 1987, www.biblegateway.com/passage/?search=Ephesians+3%3A20&version=AMPC.

Front and Back Cover Design

ChaptGPT

About the Author

Anna M. Hughes is a writer, speaker, and college-level educator. She is the mother of four, grandmother of four, a beloved daughter of the Most High God, and a survivor of life, divorce, and all that it entails.

www.ingramcontent.com/pod-product-compliance
Lightning Source LLC
LaVergne TN
LVHW100515110826
845146LV00002B/654

* 9 7 9 8 9 9 4 9 0 2 2 0 2 *